NINETEENTH-CENTURY BRITISH LITERATURE THEN AND NOW

Envisioning today's readers as poised between an impossible attempt to read texts as their original readers experienced them and an awareness of our own temporal moment, Simon Dentith complicates traditional prejudices against hindsight to approach issues of interpretation and historicity in nineteenth-century literature. Suggesting that the characteristic aesthetic attitude encouraged by the backward look is one of irony rather than remorse or regret, he examines works by Charles Dickens, George Eliot, Anthony Trollope, William Morris and John Ruskin in terms of their participation in significant histories that extend to this day. Liberalism, class, gender, political representation and notions of progress, utopianism and ecological concern as currently understood can be traced back to the nineteenth century. Just as today's critics strive to respect the authenticity of nineteenth-century writers and readers who responded to these ideas within their historical world, so, too, do those nineteenth-century imaginings persist to challenge the assumptions of the present. It is therefore possible, Dentith argues, to conceive of the act of reading historical literature with an awareness of the historical context and of the difference between the past and the present while allowing that friction or difference to be part of how we think about a text and how it communicates. His book summons us to consider how words travel to the reality of the reader's own time and how engagement with nineteenth-century writers' anticipation of the judgements of future generations reveal hindsight's capacity to transform our understanding of the past in the light of subsequent knowledge.

T0300560

The Nineteenth Century Series
General Editors' Preface

The aim of the series is to reflect, develop and extend the great burgeoning of interest in the nineteenth century that has been an inevitable feature of recent years, as that former epoch has come more sharply into focus as a locus for our understanding not only of the past but of the contours of our modernity. It centres primarily upon major authors and subjects within Romantic and Victorian literature. It also includes studies of other British writers and issues, where these are matters of current debate: for example, biography and autobiography, journalism, periodical literature, travel writing, book production, gender, non-canonical writing. We are dedicated principally to publishing original monographs and symposia; our policy is to embrace a broad scope in chronology, approach and range of concern, and both to recognize and cut innovatively across such parameters as those suggested by the designations 'Romantic' and 'Victorian'. We welcome new ideas and theories, while valuing traditional scholarship. It is hoped that the world which predates yet so forcibly predicts and engages our own will emerge in parts, in the wider sweep, and in the lively streams of disputation and change that are so manifest an aspect of its intellectual, artistic and social landscape.

Vincent Newey
Joanne Shattock
University of Leicester

Nineteenth-Century
British Literature Then and Now
Reading with Hindsight

SIMON DENTITH
University of Reading, UK

Routledge
Taylor & Francis Group

LONDON AND NEW YORK

First published 2014 by Ashgate Publishing

Published 2016 by Routledge
2 Park Square, Milton Park, Abingdon, Oxfordshire OX14 4RN
711 Third Avenue, New York, NY 10017, USA

First issued in paperback 2016

Routledge is an imprint of the Taylor & Francis Group, an informa business

British Library Cataloguing in Publication Data
A catalogue record for this book is available from the British Library

The Library of Congress has cataloged the printed edition as follows:
Dentith, Simon.
  Nineteenth-Century British Literature Then and Now: Reading with Hindsight / by
    Simon Dentith.
    pages cm. — (The Nineteenth Century Series)
  Includes bibliographical references and index.
  ISBN 978-1-4724-1885-2 (hardcover: alk. paper)
  1. English literature—19th century—History and criticism. I. Title.
  PR461.D47 2014
  820.9'008—dc23

                                                                              2013033642

ISBN 13: 978-1-138-24873-1 (pbk)
ISBN 13: 978-1-4724-1885-2 (hbk)

Contents

Contents

Preface

The starting point of this book is the idea that it is possible to use the notion of hindsight, characteristically associated with some of the paradoxes of individual memory, as a way into comparable problems in the ways that we read and understand the past, especially the nineteenth-century past. The book's subtitle, *Reading with Hindsight*, thus points to its principal topic: the practices and possibilities for reading past texts when we inevitably do so, in the case of the nineteenth century, with a whole social and political history having unrolled since they were written, a history which has inevitably changed our sense of them. But in writing the book I have also been drawn into numerous discussions of texts – novels, poems, essays and so on – where hindsight is itself a topic, or perhaps even suffuses the whole way of telling a story or making a case. So while this is predominantly a book about how we read and how we might read, it is also a book about the presence of hindsight in texts from the nineteenth century.

Hindsight has been deliberately chosen because it is more than merely another word for memory, despite its suggestive etymology as 'backward look' or 'retrospect'. Hindsight has a meaning in English which distinguishes it from a simple act of memory, in that it suggests a transformed valuation of the events, actions or situations that are being recalled: the benefit of hindsight is precisely that more is known now, at the moment of recall, than could possibly have been known *at the time*. In that respect hindsight conveys a promise of greater enlightenment, a disenchanted capacity to make sense of the past, both personal and historical, in ways that were unavailable as that past was being lived. This presses both upon literary and historical scholarship (indeed widespread popular attitudes also), and the writing of historical novels set in the nineteenth century; I discuss the latter, and the way that such novels draw upon the benefit of hindsight, in a concluding chapter.

But the sense of greater subsequent enlightenment also suggests the threat that hindsight poses to the authenticity or adequacy of the knowledge or feelings that were available to the original actors. If we were to live our own lives in constant anticipation of the future judgement of hindsight, it would cripple our capacity to live fully. So there is also a widespread and justified suspicion of hindsight, and this too is part of the topic of the book. In relation especially to reading those texts which appear to be subject to disabling forms of hindsight, this means the capacity to attend to those original writings in the terms in which they first presented themselves, even if this is only a provisional act of attention, or, to use a vocabulary that I occasionally adopt in this book, a phase in the hermeneutic process. There is no suggestion here of attempting that kind of romantic historicism which imagines that it is possible to read with the mentality of the original readers. My contention in the book is in a way much simpler. It is possible to attend to what our interlocutors say to us, to hear the force of their utterances, without abandoning our sense of our own position: to hear the other's voice depends upon our capacity to hear it, but we can still recognise it as coming from elsewhere. By analogy – and the following book depends on the force of this analogy – it is possible to hear voices which come from the past, come marked, that is to say, as emerging from social and historical realities which are radically different from our own, and yet to recognise them as charged with an authenticity which is resistant to hindsight. Against a certain kind of humanism, I assert the radical historical alterity of those voices from the past. But against an equally disabling version of historicism, I claim that the very capacity to hear those historically marked voices suggests limits to the reign of the historically particular. The accounts of various nineteenth-century topics that follow are constructed out of these dual assertions.

Acknowledgements

It is a pleasure to acknowledge the help and support of my colleagues in the Department of English Literature at the University of Reading. Peter Robinson generously took over the role of Head of Department to allow me to complete this book, while Alison Donnell has been unfailingly helpful and supportive. I would also like to thank Stephen Thomson and Lucy Bending for their frequent and stimulating conversation on the matters discussed below. Diane Watts too has been enormously helpful; I am grateful to them all.

Over the years my intellectual and professional life has been greatly enriched by my involvement with the British Association for Victorian Studies; this book has profited from this association, and I would like to thank the many colleagues and friends from whom I have learnt so much about nineteenth-century literature, culture and society. I would especially like to thank Joanne Shattock, Martin Hewitt, Isobel Armstrong, Carolyn Burdett, John Plunkett, Regenia Gagnier, Angelique Richardson, Holly Furneaux and Helen Rogers. I also thank the organisers of the Conference on 'The Century of the Novel' at the University of Coimbra, Portugal, especially Maria João Simões, for inviting me to give the paper which formed the germ of Chapter 5, on Trollope.

Finally I am very grateful to my family, above all my wife Kath, for their love and support over the years that I have been writing this book.

Chapter 1
The Ambivalence of Hindsight

I: A Sketch of the Problematic of Hindsight

A powerful ambivalence attaches to hindsight. On the one hand it bears the promise of an improved knowledge, of a reconstructive backward look which allows one to make fuller sense of the past, to realize more adequately the conditions and determinants of one's being. On the other hand it threatens to rob that past of its authenticity, to sell short the legitimate beliefs, attitudes and actions that were taken or adopted in the light of the best knowledge then available. Hindsight can be accompanied by regret or remorse; but it can also lead to a particular pathos, that felt by an older and wiser person looking back on a younger self. It can be the look that leads to teleology, to the reconstruction of the past in the light of the one true line of development that has led to the present; but it can also suggest alternative possibilities in the past, paths not taken or unrealized potentialities that would have led to a different future.

These ambivalences all press with particular force on the individual life, where hindsight can impinge most powerfully. It is a special kind of knowledge that affects or even afflicts some memories: the hindsight, retrospect, or backward look that brings with it a greater knowledge of the past than that available at the time. It seems especially appropriate to invoke when seeking to explain, understand or even to exculpate a past mistake, the invocation of 'hindsight' underlining the impossibility of having a knowledge only revealed subsequently or by the course of events. But here the repudiation of hindsight, the insistence on the impossibility of having *at the time* a knowledge that only came available subsequently, can be an alibi for carelessness, shortsightedness, or, in legal phrase, lack of due diligence. Hindsight comes accompanied by irony: it marks an earlier self as acting, believing or feeling according to an insufficient light, thus giving those earlier actions, beliefs of feelings the doubleness that characterizes irony, since, with benefit of hindsight, they become both true and not true. The repudiation of hindsight is often an attempt to keep such ironies at bay, to defend that earlier self against the corrosion of the too knowledgeable backward glance.

If hindsight is a special kind of knowledge, it is also potentially another name for memory at its most active and diligent, engaged in what can seem like a ceaseless task: the effort to come to terms with, to make new sense of, one's own past. In this perspective hindsight is the work that memory, as an active power of mind, performs upon its memories, reconstructing them or placing them in new alignments as they are made to serve the needs of the present. In a benign account, this process can be therapeutic: indeed it is the promise of psychoanalytic therapy to bring one's past under the control of hindsight, so to rework those past memories that their potential to damage or impede is at least mitigated. This is the big promise that hindsight brings with it, to know the past better than it could know itself. For the individual this can mean the possibility of control, of seeing in a new light those otherwise overwhelming or too insistent memories of an earlier self, or of the looming presences that surrounded that self. This is the process of getting matters 'into perspective', a spatial metaphor which seeks to organize the visual world from the observer's viewpoint as hindsight organizes the interior landscape from the moment of the act of memory.

It is the contention of this book that these various and conflicting tensions and ambivalences, this problematic of hindsight, which is characteristically a domain of the individual life, apply also in relation to broader historical and literary knowledge. Hindsight is at once the condition of our knowledge of the past, and the viewpoint which we need to resist or abrogate if our knowledge is to make any claim to authenticity. The book sets out to explore this duality, or this necessary double perspective. On the one hand we recognize the inevitability of our present knowledge, which ceaselessly constructs and reconstructs the past according to its own best light. On the other hand we recognize, as we confront the multiple artifacts of the past – above all those texts which this book will especially consider – that they emerge from a historical space which is not our own, and that they are fully adequate products of, and responses to, the conditions of their own existence. The book tries to hold both of these recognitions simultaneously, or to find some way of balancing or ordering them so as to reconcile their apparent tendency to undermine or undo each other.

It is indeed to understate the case to describe our present knowledge as inevitable, as though it were merely the unavoidable condition we find ourselves in – though it is this. Hindsight is more than this; in some domains of knowledge it is an active principle which is the predicate for any kind of knowledge at all. The experimental method itself, with its oscillation between hypothesis and experiment, continually reconstructs both, as hypothesis is confirmed or denied and as phenomena are more thoroughly understood. Or consider the pioneering cartographic expeditions of the seventeenth, eighteenth and nineteenth centuries: only in the light of subsequent knowledge, which can only be completed at the conclusion of the initial efforts, can those initial doublings, new seas which turn out to be bays or estuaries, and false summits, be understood. The prior state of ignorance is the condition of subsequent knowledge; the subsequent knowledge explains the prior state of ignorance. Sometimes this benign hindsight is the privilege of successful explorers or mapmakers, who can explain their own earlier ignorance in the light of their now completed maps; but sometimes, as with the notorious and tragic case of the search for the North-West passage, it is left to subsequent generations to know how near or how far those earlier explorers were to reaching destinations which have now been thoroughly mapped. Cartography can be taken as an exemplary instance: retrospective knowledge is real, and can really explain, better than the knowledge available *at the time*, the real conditions of existence of historical protagonists.

But the opposing or complementary phase of the problematic of historical hindsight requires that the reality of this retrospective knowledge be put into abeyance, as we seek to re-enter the life-world, adequate to itself, of the inhabitants of the past. This too is an act of reconstruction, though of a different order than that of the reconstructive backward look which explains that previous world in explanatory terms imported into it and which can explain both its knowledge and its ignorance. This second type of reconstruction seeks rather to respect the self-understanding of the people of the past, to allow the meanings and actions of the past to work in their own terms. We cannot of course be those past actors or writers, whose multiple traces in the form of artifacts, institutions or writing we attempt to re-inhabit: that is the delusion of music on ancient instruments, an experience inevitably different from that of the first auditors, however accurate the reconstruction, simply because we now hear it as different from other musical possibilities when it was once heard simply as music. But we can enter into the life-world of the past in a way which puts to one side for the time being at least the potentially corrosive modern perspective which threatens to reduce the artifacts and texts of the past to error. Indeed we can see this putting into abeyance or warding off of the destructive ironies of hindsight to be a condition of authentic historical knowledge, which paradoxically requires, for the force of a past meaning to be recaptured, both the acquisition and the shucking off of all necessary contextual information. At all events to know the past requires, as one of the phases of understanding, an attention to past meanings protected from the too-ready imposition of hindsight.

These briefly sketched considerations on hindsight trespass, of course, on some of the most contested and difficult areas of historical method, literary scholarship, and hermeneutics. This introductory chapter will shortly continue with some further consideration on these matters, more explicitly addressed to debates within these different disciplines. Before doing so I should emphasise the nineteenth-century focus of this book; in it I discuss the transformative effects of hindsight on our understanding of some central nineteenth-century themes, as they come to us in some familiar texts. Hindsight presses on the nineteenth century in particular ways, as the multiple valencies of the word 'Victorian' suggest: invoked both positively and negatively, 'Victorian' is shorthand for a complex of cultural attitudes which are still live in our culture but which are presumed to have their definitive location in the century before last. That complex of attitudes includes those directed to class and the persistence or repudiation of its importance; to gender, sexuality, self-expression and self-repression; to the meanings of liberalism and the liberal state, reinvented in the late twentieth century as neoliberalism; to the whole legacy of the notion of 'progress', discussed in this book in its most extreme utopian form; and to a cluster of meanings that gather round the nineteenth-century empire. The liveliness and salience in our culture of the 'Victorian' is expressed among other things by the extraordinary proliferation of 'neo-Victorian' texts of one kind or another – texts which are suffused with hindsight but played out, nevertheless, with widely differing aesthetic effects. At all these instances hindsight operates, dependent, as we shall see, on the historical continuities and ruptures which connect and divide us from the nineteenth-century past.

II: Individual Hindsight

'Hindsight' in its etymology seems to indicate an activity that is indistinguishable from one phase at least of memory, insofar as it indicates the activity of looking back, literally 'retro-spect'. However, current usage in English – and the usage which will be followed in this book – indicates for 'hindsight' a particular kind of backward look, one that involves not only the act of recall (though this itself is complicated enough) but a reconstructive or repositioning act of recall that re-orders or re-evaluates memories in the light of a subsequent knowledge. Nevertheless it is helpful to consider briefly the phenomenology of memory to help understand more fully the nature of hindsight.

In the previous sketch I briefly defined hindsight as the work that 'memory, as an active power of mind, performs upon its memories'. There is of course a rich tradition of philosophical reflection upon memory, which this distinction between 'memory' and 'memories' invokes. I take as my guide through this tradition the work of Paul Ricoeur, whose *Memory, History, Forgetting* (2004) is at once a summation of, and an argument within, this tradition. Part 1, 'On Memory and Recollection', includes 'A phenomenological sketch of memory', in which the distinction between recall and the objects of recall – memories – is made:

> The first expression of the splintered nature of this phenomenology stems from the object-oriented character of memory: we remember something. In this sense a distinction must be made in language between memory (*la mémoire*) as intention and memory (*le souvenir*) as the thing intended. We say memory (*la mémoire*) and memories (*les souvenirs*). Fundamentally, what is at issue here is a phenomenology of memories. In this regard, Latin and Greek use the preterite forms (*genomenou, praeterita*). It is in this sense that I speak of past 'things'. Indeed once the past has been distinguished from the present in the memory of memories, then it is easy for reflection to distinguish at the heart of remembering the question 'What?' from 'How?' and from 'Who?...'[1]

This is just the beginning of a full and complex account, but it allows us to see a basic distinction, between the act of memory itself, placed on the side of the remembering subject, and the objects of that act of memory, the multiple memories which make up its contents. The act of memory is intentional; the contents of memory, memories, are 'objective' in the sense of being thing-like – though their objectivity in its other sense, their accuracy, has been in effect the predominant axis of debate in discussions of memory. Hindsight is to be placed firmly on the side of the remembering subject; it is not synonymous with memory (*la mémoire*) but consists of a particular kind of activity of memory which involves re-contextualizing or re-evaluating the contents of memory (*les souvenirs*).

---

[1]   Paul Ricoeur. *Memory, History, Forgetting*. Trans. Kathleen Blamey and David Pellauer. Chicago: The University of Chicago Press, 2004. 22.

In this sense hindsight is not necessarily skeptical of the memory-contents themselves, at least in the sense of their accuracy. A consideration of hindsight need not therefore take us into the massive and contested problematic of the memory trace, concerning the very possibility of memory, its accuracy, its object (that which no longer exists), and the mechanisms by which the trace can be laid down and by which it can be recalled. The skepticism of hindsight is directed not at the accuracy of memories but at their adequacy; it may seek to re-order or re-evaluate memories, but not necessarily to undermine their accuracy or remove them to the side of the remembering subject as though they were all the product of the needs of that subject in the present. Hindsight is absolutely a second-order activity in relation to memory-contents (Ricoeur can also use a vocabulary of 'primary' and 'secondary' memory to restate the distinction between memory and its contents), but recognizing this secondariness need not propel us into over-emphasis of its reconstructive power or, for that matter, to discount it in favour of the presumed authenticity of primary memories.

We need however to consider the prompts or occasions for hindsight, if it is not to be thought of as merely another name for memory itself, allowed by the passage of time to look back on a former self. Indeed it is possible to make a distinction between the passage of time and the course of events; the former, the passage of time, is the condition which permits the course of events to occur, while the latter is the predominant instigator of hindsight, and only some courses of events lead to a re-evaluative act of hindsight: obviously enough these include disasters or disappointments, but hindsight can also be prompted by the emergence of knowledge unavailable previously, or by encountering the usual prompts to memory such as old photographs or – in English usage this time – souvenirs. Hindsight in this sense is an activity of the remembering subject which directs attention to the moment or moments surrounding an act of choice or decision, or to moments in a person's life (which might extend as long as their childhood and youth) when many possibilities seemed open. The actual course of events can thus lead one to reflect on alternative possibilities – 'the road not taken' – such that the actual path taken appears as a closing-down of possibilities. But it can also seem as a confirmation of a predominant tendency or bias, or a confirmation of the constraints that have always acted on a life. Hindsight in this context thus entails on the one hand a recognition of alternative possibilities, and on the other a sense of the inevitability of the course actually taken. The former attitude can lead to regret and even a kind of sentimental cynicism – 'si la jeunesse savait' – while the latter can lead to fatalism and a confirmation of a life-time's habits.

Robert Frost's poem 'The Road Not Taken' (1916), alluded to briefly here, is the inevitable reference point here, and does indeed suggest some of the contours of this ambivalence of hindsight at the level of the individual life:

Two roads diverged in a yellow wood,
And sorry I could not travel both
And be one traveler, long I stood
And looked down one as far as I could
To where it bent in the undergrowth;

> Then took the other, as just as fair,
> And having perhaps the better claim,
> Because it was grassy and wanted wear;
> Though as for that, the passing there
> Had worn them really about the same,
>
> And both that morning equally lay
> In leaves no step had trodden black.
> Oh, I kept the first for another day!
> Yet knowing how way leads on to way,
> I doubted if I should ever come back.
>
> I shall be telling this with a sigh
> Somewhere ages and ages hence:
> Two roads diverged in a wood, and I—
> I took the one less travelled by,
> And that has made all the difference.[2]

For the most part the poem concentrates on the moment of existential decision, the hesitation between the two divergent paths in the wood ('Nel mezzo del cammin di nostra vita / mi retrovai per una selva oscura / che la diritta via era smarrita'[3] – Dante is a not too distant reference-point for Frost's poem). Though he suggests in the second stanza that there is a rationale for the decision he takes in the fact that the path chosen 'was grassy and wanted wear', he immediately retracts this to assert that both paths were in reality equally worn, and that anyway it was impossible to tell which was the more worn as both were obscured by as yet untrodden leaves. So the decision to take one path rather than another has something of an existential *acte gratuit*, which has no justification other than its exercise of liberty. Frost wants to retain this sense of liberty ('Oh! I kept the first for another day!'), but instantaneously corrects himself, or rather admits to his more fundamental knowledge that taking one road rather than another is likely to prove irrevocable. It is in the last stanza that the problematic of hindsight becomes most visible; the poet anticipates a moment in the future when this decision will appear a matter of sentimental regret ('I shall be telling this with a sigh'). There is some uncertainty about the time-frame for the last three lines of the poem: are they to be understood as a kind of free indirect discourse, an anticipation of what the poet will be saying 'ages and ages hence'; or are they rather to be understood as the poet speaking in the 'now' of the poem, the deictic present, so that their emphatic sense of the irrevocability of the decision taken is the final impression

---

[2]   Robert Frost. 'The Road Not Taken'. *The Poetry of Robert Frost: The Collected Poems*. Ed. Edward Connery Lathem. New York: Henry Holt, 1975. 105.

[3]   Dante Alighieri. *The Divine Comedy*. Vol 1, *The Inferno*. Trans. John D Sinclair. Oxford: Oxford University Press, 1961. 22. Sinclair translates these opening lines of *The Inferno* as follows: 'In the middle of the journey of our life I came to myself in a dark wood where the straight way was lost').

which concludes the poem. The ambiguity is relevant to the problematic of hindsight. In the former interpretation the stress of the poem would rest on the moment of hesitation, of alternative possibilities leading to different futures; while in the second case the emphasis lies on the momentousness and irrevocability of the decision taken. Frost's poem remarkably reveals this ambivalence that accompanies hindsight: at once insisting upon the prior freedom, the sense that accompanied one of alternative possibilities; but also insisting equally on the irrevocability of the chosen path.

Frost's poem focuses with exemplary clarity on the moment of decision, which is at once a moment of bifurcating possibilities and irrevocable choice. I take it that this is a moment in an adult life; autobiographical hindsight naturally enough deals as much, or even more characteristically, with childhood and youth. It is apparently the founding attitude of autobiographical narrative as such, though such narratives reproduce the problematic of hindsight with more or less insistence. David Copperfield, in a novel that I will discuss more fully in a subsequent chapter, expresses the attitude of hindsight very explicitly when he exclaims at one point 'If I had known then, what I knew long afterwards! –'. [4] Autobiographies, both fictional and non-fictional, can make more or less salient the difference and distance between past ignorance and present knowledge, and thus subject their writers' former selves to more or less degrees of irony. However this is not a book predominantly about the representation of hindsight within writing, but rather a book about the implications of hindsight for us as readers of past texts. The problematics of hindsight at the level of the individual are invoked here as suggestive possibilities for such an examination of reading.

III: From Individual Hindsight to Historical Hindsight

Three analogies or suggestive connections immediately present themselves as we make the transition from the individual experience of hindsight to historical experience more widely, all within the context of a more general analogy which aligns the passage of time within an individual life to the passage of historical time. This general analogy by no means entails any notions of progress, or any sense of a transition from childhood to maturity, in the movement of historical time, though looking back to an earlier historical period is often accompanied by a sense of the superiority of the present moment. Nevertheless, I am interested here in the hindsight of relative historical and social proximity, suggested by the hindsight of an individual life; the distance in time between the nineteenth and the twenty-first centuries certainly permits a suggestive play of continuity and difference within British society, to which I limit myself, such that it is allowable to use the term hindsight in ways which recall its core usage in the problematics of the self. Within this general analogy, three further and more specific analogies

---

[4]   Charles Dickens. *David Copperfield*. Ed. Jeremy Tambling. London: Penguin Books, 2004. 525.

are relevant: the sense of alternative possibilities in an individual life, analogous to alternative social and historical possibilities; the irrevocability of the actual path chosen, analogous to the one true path of historical development; and the irony that surrounds the individual subject in retrospect, dependent on subsequent knowledge – suggestive of the multiple possibilities for historical irony which emerge with the passage of time and its capacity simply to let us know more than the original historical actors.

Taking these analogies in turn, I start with the sense of alternative historical possibilities that hindsight can reveal. It is tempting to call this 'good hindsight', since it opens up possibilities and recognises that the one true line of development was not the only possible one. In this sense it is anti-teleological; like the poet in Frost's poem, it draws our attention to the moment of hesitation when more than one path was available. It also can be said to require recognition of the very existence of differing possibilities in the society of the past: no social or historical order is monolithic, unself-contradictory, or incapable of offering different possibilities that can be inflected in differing ways, though the possibilities for such inflections vary enormously between differing historical agents. This is not a matter of historical contingency, though hindsight can reveal the sometimes adventitious concatenation of events – the 'convergence of the twain', as Hardy memorably put it. Rather it is a matter of hindsight revealing or drawing attention to unrealised possibilities that indicate the multiple, varying, and unclosed nature of all social orders, which are endlessly engaged in the process of reconstructing themselves and in which the social order is always at risk.

But just as this sense of possibilities revealed is accompanied by a knowledge of the path that *was* taken at the level of the individual life, so too the sense of differing historical possibilities is accompanied by a retrospective knowledge of the actual course of events. This is not simply 'bad hindsight', since it is genuinely revelatory: knowing how things turned out can reveal a truth about the balance of forces in the initial state of affairs, or can reveal factors at play that were unknown to the historical agents at the time. But this kind of hindsight can lead to teleological thinking, effectively sanctifying the one true course of events as the only possibility, and marking it out as inevitable. Behaviour, events, attitudes, beliefs, writing are all understood exclusively in the light of their contribution, or otherwise, to the present where we now are. Hindsight of this kind can only understand historical difference either as it leads to the present or as it is relegated to the archive. It can thus exclude the defamiliarising sense of possibility *for the present* that a recognition of historical otherness can provide.

Our third analogy between the problematic of hindsight at the level of the individual life, and a wider sense of historical hindsight, concerns the matter of knowing more *now* than one did *then*. At the level of one's own life this can lead to pathos, regret, even remorse, or it can surround one's earlier life with a greater or less intensity of irony. Translate these into historical attitudes and some of the same possibilities appear: the pathos that surrounds those living in the summer of 1914 is a familiar trope. Regret or remorse seem generally inappropriate historical attitudes other than in those circumstances where there can be thought to be a national continuity between the past and the present which still entails responsibility upon contemporary actors. Simply knowing more than people in the past – that is, knowing more about them than they could know themselves – is indeed one possibility created by hindsight, and is in one sense a normal historical attitude: it is the effort to make sense of, to understand more fully, the course of events when the original actors are implicated in the overwhelming buzz and hum of the contemporary moment. But in certain cases hindsight can permit much more than this clarifying or explicative role: advances in scientific and medical knowledge certainly enable us know to explain matters which in the past were wholly inexplicable. Knowledge of the epidemiology of the Plague, or of cholera, sheds a light on the past which was unavailable until late in the nineteenth century, and it can explain the peculiar inefficacy of the efforts of those at the time to combat these diseases, whether based upon religion and prayer, or inappropriate theories like the miasma theory of disease. But the historical attitude that such a knowledge creates is open to very differing inflexions; it can certainly lead to an ironic attitude at the expense of the people of the past. The Enlightenment attitude to history (Godwin: 'It is an old observation that the history of mankind is little else than a record of crimes'.[5]) may have been most fully expressed in the eighteenth century, but it has remained a possibility ever since; certainly the historiography of the Victorians, not only starting with Lytton Strachey but certainly including him, has been very tempted by an ironic attitude based on a presumption of greater enlightenment.

These are suggestive possibilities, which will be explored more fully in the chapters that follow. In the meantime however we need to consider more fully the nature of the reconstructive historical look, that is to say the inevitability of our contemporary knowledge as we look back on the past, and the way that such knowledge both enables knowledge, and appears to threaten the adequacy of the beliefs, attitudes and actions of historical actors.

IV: Historically Effected Consciousness

So far 'hindsight' has been conceived too exclusively in the domain of knowledge, a matter of knowing now what we did not or could not know then. We need to thicken this conception, to recognise that hindsight, here understood as retrospective historical knowledge, is a much denser, historically richer, and socially and personally more complex matter than has so far been suggested. It emerges, to put it at its grandest, from a whole life-world, where the knowledge that one has is infinitely richer than a mere matter of what one does or does not know. We are situated beings not only in a basic physical and biological sense, but also in terms of the complex and striated set of assumptions and understandings of the world

---

[5] William Godwin. *Inquiry Concerning Political Justice*. Ed. Isaac Kramnick. Harmondsworth: Penguin Books, 1976 [1796]. 83.

that derive from our moment in history and what we inherit from both our near and our distant past. We bring all this to the act of making sense of the past, and hence to our reading of the texts of the past: our sense of what constitutes normal and strange behaviour; myriad assumptions, both explicit and hidden from us, about the way that society works or ought to work; beliefs, therefore, about social hierarchy, gender, class, race, ethnicity, the way to treat children, how to be old, about one's relation to the natural world; generic capacities that fit one or disqualify one from recognising what kind of thing each and every text that we encounter is. These are all the conditions of any understanding, the means by which making sense is possible. This mass of complex knowledge is the equipment we bring to the task of reading, our entry point to any act of interpretation or sense-making. Understanding is thus historical, and there is no weightless Archimedean standing-ground which permits us objective understanding outside our position in history.

The historically dense nature of understanding is central to the tradition of hermeneutics; Gadamer's *Truth and Method* (1960) is an extended meditation upon this perception. Thus Gadamer speaks of understanding as a 'historically effected event'.[6] That is to say, the means by which we are enabled to understand the texts of the past are created by the myriad historical connections which link us to that past:

> Time is no longer primarily a gulf to be bridged because it separates; it is actually the supportive ground of the course of events in which the present is rooted. Hence temporal distance is not something that must be overcome. This was, rather, the naive assumption of historicism, namely that we must transpose ourselves into the spirit of the age, think with its ideas and its thoughts, not with our own, and thus advance towards historical objectivity. In fact the important thing is to recognize temporal distance as a positive and productive condition enabling understanding. It is not a yawning abyss but is filled with the continuity of custom and tradition, in the light of which everything handed down presents itself to us. Here it is not too much to speak of the genuine productivity of the course of events. (297)

In this conception, our immersion in our situation is not only inescapable, it is also productive of understanding, because our situation is the inheritor of, or better still is created by, multiple connections to the past that we are seeking to understand. Gadamer describes these connections as 'custom and tradition', and there is an explicit conservative agenda to be carried by those words; Gadamer wishes to rehabilitate the notion of 'prejudice' as a necessary condition of understanding, making it equivalent to the pre-judgment or fore-knowledge which we bring to all acts of understanding. But the complex chronological to-and-fro which he envisages in this passage, by which the very course of events creates traditions of understanding which then enable us to understand retrospectively that course of

---

[6]   Hans-Georg Gadamer. *Truth and Method*. Trans. Joel Weinsheimer and Donald G. Marshall. Rev. ed. Continuum: New York and London, 1989. 300.

events, can encompass more than the Burkean connotations suggested by 'custom and tradition': we should include in custom and tradition the multiple democratic and egalitarian assumptions and affiliations that connect us to aspects of our nineteenth-century past at least. At all events, understanding is here conceived as inextricably historical, a process in which we are both linked to and distant from the past that forms the object of our attention.

This is an absolutely necessary extension and enrichment of our notion of hindsight, but it provokes its own problems, not least the tendency to eradicate historical difference which the repudiation of historical time as a 'gulf' entails. Gadamer is capable of formulations that sound utopian in their insistence on the possibility of connection between past and present:

> The mode of being of a text has something unique and incomparable about it. It presents a specific problem of translation to the understanding. Nothing is so strange, and at the same time so demanding, as the written word. Not even meeting speakers of a foreign language can be compared with this strangeness, since the language of gesture and of sound is always in part immediately intelligible. The written word and what partakes of it—literature—is the intelligibility of mind transferred to the most alien medium. Nothing is so purely the trace of the mind as writing, but nothing is so dependent on the understanding mind either. In deciphering and interpreting it, a miracle takes place: the transformation of something alien and dead into total contemporaneity and familiarity. This is like nothing else that comes down to us from the past. The remnants of past life— what is left of buildings, tools, the contents of graves—are weather beaten by the storms of time that have swept over them, whereas a written tradition, once deciphered and read, is to such an extent pure mind that it speaks to us as if in the present. That is why the capacity to read, to understand what is written, is like a secret art, even a magic that frees and binds us. In it time and space seem to be superseded. People who can read what has been handed down in writing produce and achieve the sheer presence of the past. (163–4)

This is the 'magic' to which one inflection of, or emphasis within, this tradition of hermeneutic philosophy tends. While it is true that there is an almost mystical insistence on 'sheer presence' in this passage, such moments of transcendence of historical distance are always conditional upon situatedness: to achieve connection with the past is not to abandon one's location in the present, but to inhabit it more fully. Reading at once frees and binds – it liberates us into another historical moment, into contact with a mind from the past; but it binds us also by making such understanding conditional upon a discipline learnt in the present. Nevertheless, historical transcendence understood in this way is not the only terminus of Gadamer's thought, and from our perspective can seem like a version of 'bad hindsight' in over-emphasising the presentist perspective, however 'historically effected' over the self-understanding of the past.

These matters are most fully discussed by Gadamer in relation to the notion of understanding as a 'fusion of horizons', and it is worth dwelling on this aspect of his thought:

In fact the horizon of the present is continually in the process of being formed because we are continually having to test all our prejudices. An important part of this testing occurs in encountering the past and in understanding the tradition from which we come. Hence the horizon of the present cannot be formed without the past. There is no more an isolated horizon of the present in itself than there are historical horizons which have to be acquired. *Rather, understanding is always the fusion of these horizons supposedly existing by themselves.* We are familiar with the power of this kind of fusion chiefly from earlier times and their naiveté about themselves and their heritage. In a tradition this process of fusion is continually going on, for there old and new are always combining into something of living value, without either being explicitly foregrounded from the other.

If, however, there is no such thing as these distinct horizons, why do we speak of the fusion of horizons and not simply of the formation of the one horizon, whose bounds are set in the depths of tradition? To ask the question means that we are recognizing that understanding becomes a scholarly task only under special circumstances and that it is necessary to work out these circumstances as a hermeneutical situation. Every encounter with tradition that takes place within historical consciousness involves the experience of a tension between the text and the present. The hermeneutic task consists in not covering up this tension by attempting a naive assimilation of the two but in consciously bringing it out. This is why it is part of the hermeneutic approach to project a historical horizon that is different from the horizon of the present. Historical consciousness is aware of its own otherness and hence foregrounds the horizon of the past from its own. On the other hand, it is itself, as we are trying to show, only something superimposed upon continuing tradition, and hence it immediately recombines with what it has foregrounded itself from in order to become one with itself again in the unity of the historical horizon that it thus acquires.

Projecting a historical horizon, then, is only one phase in the process of understanding; it does not become solidified into the self-alienation of a past consciousness, but is overtaken by our own present horizon of understanding. In the process of understanding, a real fusion of horizons occurs – which means that as the historical horizon is projected, it is simultaneously superseded. To bring about this fusion in a regulated way is the task of what we call historically effected consciousness. Although this task was obscured by aesthetic-historical positivism following on the heels of romantic hermeneutics, it is, in fact, the central problem of hermeneutics. It is the problem of *application*, which is to be found in all understanding. (306–7)

This passage is remarkable for the way in which it opens up a 'phase' in the process of understanding, in which the historical otherness of its pastness is momentarily recognized, only to close it down again as quickly as possible in order to proceed to the moment of closure in the 'fusion of horizons'. It is possible to untie the organic tidiness of this, in several ways. We can initially assert that we are not tied to the past by one tradition only, but rather by multiple, complex and even contradictory traditions which entail differing and complex negotiations with the past. Gadamer's model of understanding, while insisting on its continuous formation and reformation, makes it too much a matter of assimilation, and too little a process which can involve resistance and repudiation. Secondly, because the goal of the whole process is the furtherance of this benign continuation of tradition, it is in effect threatened by the sense of historical otherness which it nevertheless recognizes as a necessary part of historical understanding. Gadamer describes this as a 'phase' only, brought on by special circumstances which the scholar has to endure; the aim is to move beyond that recognition of historical distance, that projecting of a historical horizon which is different from one's own, in order to reach a fusion of horizons so that the normative activity of the tradition can be resumed. Once we abandon this goal, once, that is, we recognize the plural and contradictory ways in which we in the present necessarily understand the past, we can recognize that the projected historical horizon – the set of presumptions, understandings, beliefs, attitudes and commitments which we recognize as other than our own – is necessarily more than a phase but is rather a characteristic state of the attempt to make sense of the past. We could describe such a recognition, to invoke Bakhtin here, as a carnivalisation of tradition, a putting into play of the multiple resistances, hostilities, willed allegiances and arbitrary affinities which characterize any engagement with the past, and which make the multiple valencies which any past text carries liable to upset or overspill any assimilative effort.

The third way in which I seek to untie Gadamer's excessive tidiness is by pressing on the distinction that he makes here between 'understanding' and 'application'. We could recast this as distinction between 'meaning' and 'force', a distinction however which tends to undo the careful phasing of Gadamer's analysis: first the understanding, then the application. The danger of this sequencing of the process of understanding is that it risks sealing off the texts of the past: the unstable forces locked into the texts of the past are likely to remain there, however well understood. Another Bakhtinian notion is helpful in this context, even if only by way of analogy – his distinction between a linguistics and a metalinguistics, the first capable of understanding language as far as its grammar and vocabulary go, the second seeing the essential fact about language the fact that the meanings that it creates are only ultimately meanings when they are in use in the more or less agonistic situation of a dialogue. Coming to terms with the texts of the past does not only entail understanding without application; not only is an estimation of the force of what we read an essential part of the process of understanding, but coming to terms with it in the present necessarily involves allowing it to act on us, even while we recognize its provenance from elsewhere. That is why the recognition of the otherness of the historical horizon must not be relegated to a phase in the process of understanding because to do so can involve the too ready assimilation of the perspective of the other into one's own. Moreover, recognizing the force of an utterance, or indeed the multiple valencies of a complex artistic product, is to recognize its instability, its particular negotiation of the complex and contradictory range of possibilities in any historical situation. I describe this as a rhetorical economy; this is why hindsight, the looking-back from our inevitable present, so wonderfully described by Gadamer, can have the effect of violently disturbing the rhetorical economy of the texts of the past.

But it is possible to put this more strongly, and, reverting to my earlier vocabulary, assert that it is possible to use one's knowledge of the past to resist the assimilation of hindsight. I am proposing that one aspect of reading material from the past – indeed, of reading in general, of which reading from the past is only a sub-section – is the capacity to put aside or suspend the too-ready judgment that one is aware of emerging from the contemporary moment, or from one's own subject position as a reader. This is no more than the capacity to hear what the other person is saying, and recognizing that it comes from somewhere else. In the case of material from the past, this means recognizing that what one is reading or attempting to understand emerges from a whole life-world as complex as one's own, so that to allow it to act on one – to release its force – is to put into dialogue two historical moments, and the consequences do not seem to me to resemble the 'fusion of horizons' of which Gadamer speaks. On the contrary, such moments of connection are invariably complex and in principle inconclusive, as the multiple historical strands that link us to the past (traditions rather than Gadamer's singular tradition) induce differing and layered responses, agreements, disagreements, outraged rejections and occasional assent.

This is absolutely to remain within the problematic of 'historically effected consciousness', but it is to assert that the history which connects us to the past, and which produces us and our capacity to make sense of the past, is complex both in consisting of multiple strands and in working to different rhythms or temporalities. In the book that follows I shall be describing some of these multiple social and political histories, which are the ground of our connection with, and our capacity to make sense of, the texts from the past. I call these 'Gadamerian continuities', while at the same time recognizing that I am giving a much more historically specific inflection to such continuities than Gadamer's own notion of tradition suggests.

Gadamer, though he speaks of 'historically effected consciousness', is nevertheless hostile to historicism as such, by which he means the belief that it is possible to understand the past in its own terms from a perspective that is in some sense above history. He goes so far as to say that 'the text that is understood historically is forced to abandon its claim to be saying something true' (303). I take it that this means that a certain kind of historicism effectively relegates texts to the archive, explaining them fully in terms of their originating historical moment and consequently preventing them from having a truth *for us*. I think this is a powerful assertion. I nevertheless wish to continue to understand texts historically, but believe it is possible to allow that history to act on us in the present. The condition of this action is indeed the historical continuities that link us to the past, but the action of the past on the present need not be the assimilative meaning that Gadamer sees as the end-point of understanding, but, on the contrary, a defamiliarising recognition that the present can be otherwise. Any productive interchange between past and present involves a multiple negotiation of recognition and unfamiliarity, of sameness and difference, and I hope to put some texts from the past into this productive interchange in what follows. Another way of saying this is that it is possible to hold hindsight in abeyance, and attend to the multiple historically-charged meanings carried by any text. This need not consign such texts to the archive, but, equally, the alternative is not the excessive tidiness of Gadamer's tradition, or indeed the wisdom of the ages. It is, rather, the recognition of the unanticipated force that voices from the past can have as they carry their historical otherness into the contradiction-filled melee of our contemporary moment.

V: Hindsight and the Victorians

If hindsight can be given the substance and thickness that it requires – if, that is, we must recognize that we always look back from somewhere which has its own contours and density – we must recognize the ever-changing historical specificity of the moment from which we look. To draw on an illuminating distinction by Ricoeur, in a discussion of "'our" modernity', we must distinguish between the deictic 'now' of the moment of writing, and the ever-changing modernity to which such deictic references appear to tie us.[7] This distinction is especially important in considering the nineteenth century and subsequent reflection upon its social, cultural, economic and political legacies, since 'modernity' has been a central term in situating and negotiating those legacies. What the distinction points to is the difference between the indifferent passage of time and the historically marked course of events, productive of the cultural, social and political specificity of the moment we inhabit.

If such a distinction is important for our contemporary moment, it is also important for the nineteenth century on which I shall be looking back in this book. The choice of the terms 'nineteenth century' and 'Victorian' precisely captures the distinction between a relatively neutral chronological category, and an ideologically charged historical distinction – irrespective of the obvious non-coincidence of the dates. It is generally around the word 'Victorian' that the multiple cultural battles that characterize twentieth- and twenty-first-century modernity have been fought, even though the content of the word has altered. Successive generations, starting in the nineteenth century itself, have defined their modernity by contradistinction to the Victorians who preceded them, while equally others have sought to make some return to Victorian values, in accents of more or less naiveté and stridency. Hence my usage in this book is to use 'nineteenth century' as the neutral term and 'Victorian' as the term which alludes to this ideologically charged history – and though the latter term should always go in inverted commas to signify its imbrication in contested cultural debates, heavy-handed scare quotes are best perhaps avoided.

---

[7]   Ricoeur, *Memory, History, Forgetting*. Trans. Kathleen Blamey and David Pellauer. Chicago: The University of Chicago Press, 2004. 311.

In the chapters that follow I will be discussing a number of topics where negotiations around this Victorian legacy have been particularly acute. In some respects such topics are easy to name: it is especially around areas of sexuality, class and feminism that negotiations with the Victorians have been enacted. This list can readily be extended, and I shall discuss texts that require us to consider the relationship between nineteenth-century liberalism and neoliberalism; the baleful light cast by subsequent history on late-Victorian utopianism; the specifically parliamentary history in the light of which we now look back on representations of the nineteenth-century process of reform; and the current ecological crisis which illuminates some nineteenth-century texts with a particular brilliance. But in a sense this is almost an arbitrary list of topics unless they are understood as examples only of the multiple connections, and ways of connecting, with the century before last, which are the product of substantial histories and transformations. Such connections are created and carried not only in public histories but also in collective memories, family histories, and genres and discourses whose persistence is only possible because of the substantive social history that persists from then till now.

These are the illuminations of hindsight, the ways in which the backward look throws into relief features of the writing of the past which appeared with less salience at the time. Equally important is the provocative and defamiliarising kind of light cast by the cultural artifacts of the past, whose truth should not be overwhelmed by that backward glance and so have a chance to have meaning for us in the present. What this book seeks to do above all is to mobilize or set in motion this unstable interchange between now and then, in a way which recognizes both the inevitability and the productiveness of the backward look, but also the capacity of the meanings of the past to resist that look and to challenge us now.

A case in point is the complex, highly charged and obsessively discussed question of Victorian sexuality, perhaps the central trope in popular stereotypes of the Victorians. On the one hand it is undoubtedly the case that hindsight can reveal more about the pervasiveness and power of sexuality than was available to certain kinds of inhabitants of the nineteenth century themselves. Here is a small example: in Elizabeth Gaskell's *North and South* (1854), the Northern mill-owner Thornton watches fascinated as the Southern heroine is serving out the tea:

> She had a bracelet on one taper arm, which would fall down over her round wrist. Mr Thornton watched the re-placing of this troublesome ornament with far more attention than he listened to her father. It seemed as if it fascinated him to see her push it up impatiently, until it tightened her soft flesh; and then to mark the loosening – the fall. He could almost have exclaimed – 'There it goes again!'[8]

This is readily decipherable – perhaps too readily decipherable. Elizabeth Gaskell brilliantly suggests Thornton's erotic fascination with the woman he is watching,

---

[8]   Elizabeth Gaskell. *North and South.* Ed. Dorothy Collin. Harmondsworth: Penguin Books, 1970. 120.

in a way which indicates a fuller knowledge perhaps even than he has himself. But this mild irony at his expense is reinforced very powerfully by the retrospective knowledge – shorthand, post-Freudian – which knowingly interprets the symbolism of the bracelet being pushed up and down on the flesh of the woman's forearm. At one level Elizabeth Gaskell must 'know' this, else she would not have chosen this illustration of Thornton's growing fascination with Margaret Hale. But at another level she cannot know this, and it is the privilege of hindsight to make it explicit.

Nevertheless it is the danger of hindsight that it too readily translates this necessary knowledge into a teleological account of the Victorians in which their blindness about sexuality becomes the master perspective from which to view their history, so that only those who are in some ways knowledgeable about sexuality appear as the heroes of the narrative which is told: such people 'anticipate' modern knowledge, are 'surprisingly modern', while the others are relegated to the archive as merely 'Victorian' – fulfilling Gadamer's assertion that 'the text that is understood historically is forced to abandon its claim to be saying something true'. This is especially true when the notion of 'repression' is invoked; Cora Kaplan argues in fact that repudiation of 'repression' is perhaps the dominant attitude in subsequent 'modern' readings of the Victorians. Those people or fictional characters who act therefore in an approved 'unrepressed' or self-assertive way often receive the accolade of posterity and are approved for their surprisingly modern repudiation of the world that surrounds them.

There is a powerful social history of sexuality, in motion since the middle of the nineteenth century, which has been contested at all points, which has unrolled at different tempos in different societies and in different parts of society, and which has characteristically invoked the 'Victorian' at crucial moments; this social history is what underlies, or perhaps could be said to constitute, the varying assessments, re-assessments, repudiations and celebrations that mark post-Victorian attitudes to Victorian material. In a later chapter on *The Mill on the Floss* I trace one strand of this social history and its implications for readings of that novel. This is indeed the Gadamerian continuity which links us to those past texts, but the explosive and fissile nature of this history indicates how much it is necessary to expand his notion of tradition.

However, Kaplan goes on to say that 'our' repudiation of repression is evidence of our own sexual utopianism, our belief that somehow or other sexual fulfillment is a right for everybody.[9] This opens up the possibility of setting in place the productive interchange between then and now which allows each side to provoke and illuminate the other. In other words the point of reading with hindsight, and of acknowledging the attempt to keep hindsight at bay, is not only to illuminate better some nineteenth-century cultural monuments, or indeed to trace their reception history (though this is an important part of my project): it is also to see how the historical otherness of these texts from the past can operate upon us in our present

---

[9] Cora Kaplan, *Victoriana: Histories, Fictions, Criticism* (Edinburgh: Edinburgh University Press, 2007).

moment, and loosen up the deadening grip of the utopianism of the present – our sense that we are the terminus of historical development – to suggest other possibilities and alternatives.

Comparable histories can be traced from the nineteenth century to the present day, which all entail valuations and transvaluations in relation to their starting-points. Thus in subsequent chapters I trace the history of the notion of *bildung* in relation to *David Copperfield* and *The Mill on the Floss*; an important social history in relation to education and gender clearly underlines the way we can now make sense of these novels. A chapter on Trollope's parliamentary novels, especially *Phineas Finn*, traces ideas of reform and progress, and notes the surprising light cast by past histories of parliamentary scandal on the present state of representative democracy. The remarkable resurgence in liberal economic theory in the last forty years, such that the present era is usefully described as neoliberal – surely the most important kind of neo-Victorianism – is contextualized by considering the fortunes of a mid-century critic of liberal economics, John Ruskin, in his powerful tract *Unto This Last*. This requires us to invoke the present ecological emergency as an inevitable context for our understanding of this text, which is also relevant to Morris's *News from Nowhere*; though the subsequent history of the twentieth century, with the profoundly equivocal light that it throws on utopianism as such, is also an inevitable context for our thinking in relation to this text. A final chapter shifts gears to discuss the action of hindsight in writing historical novels set in the nineteenth century, which a convenient scholarly shorthand now refers to as 'neo-Victorian' novels.[10]

In short, I shall be arguing that the particular ways that we respond to and make sense of the exemplary nineteenth-century texts that I shall be discussing have been formed by the multiple and contradictory social and cultural histories that link us to our nineteenth-century past. This is not to say of course that 'we' all respond to these novels and tracts and utopian projections in the same way, but this very diversity is testimony both to the complexity of the history that links and divides us from our past – its multivalent, contradictory and conflict-ridden nature, which positions us all in differing and contradictory relations both to our own present and to our past – but also to the non-monolithic and open-ended nature of any historical moment, which allows multiple subject-positions to those who inhabit it. Nevertheless multiplicity is not infinite diversity, and historically effected consciousness is radically incompatible with simple individualist subjectivism. Everybody, to put it at its simplest, comes from somewhere.

This is in effect to historicize reception history; that is, I seek to find the ground for the reception history of the texts I discuss in the social history that underlies it, in relation to which particular readers position themselves as they read. The implications of this are very different from those which might be deduced from the notion of 'critical heritage'; what is being asserted here is not that the Gadamerian

---

[10]   See Ann Heilmann and Mark Llewellyn. *Neo-Victorianism: The Victorians in the Twenty-First Century.* Basingstoke: Palgrave Macmillan, 2010.

tradition of understanding is carried by the critical histories of texts, but that it is carried by the underlying social history. For this reason it is possible for a new reader to come to a text in complete ignorance of its critical reception and respond to it in ways which 'spontaneously' resemble those of the critical tradition.

But even this way of understanding reception history is too unequivocally placed on the retrospective, hindsight-driven side of the equation, too firmly placed on the side of *la mémoire* and insufficiently capable of recognizing the independent validity of *souvenirs*. For an alternative way of approaching reception history – one which comes from the other side, as it were – I want to draw on the work of Mikhail Bakhtin, and the notion of 're-accentuation' with which he concludes his great book-length essay on the novel, 'Discourse in the Novel'.[11] In this account, which is specific to the novel but is nevertheless suggestive for other modes of writing, the novelistic text undergoes a continuous process of 're-accentuation' as its original context is lost but as other dialogic contexts appear. This process is made possible by the generically specific characteristics of the novel, in which the 'word' or utterance always appears dialogised, in multiply differing possible ways, by the authorial word. The passage of time, that is to say, the transition to new dialogic contexts, can certainly obscure the characteristics of this original dialogic relationship (can deafen subsequent readers, for example, to parody or irony); but it can also release new possibilities of meaning that were always implicit in the original novel. This is not a restatement of humanist pieties about the richness of great art but a recognition of the way that the unstable or multiple meanings of a novelistic text are continuously re-accented in new social-historical circumstances, as these are realized in particular heteroglossic configurations.

Earlier I quoted Gadamer at his most optimistic in relation to the process of reading: 'People who can read what has been handed down in writing produce and achieve the sheer presence of the past'. Characteristically this numinous moment is achieved by the reader in the present; it is an act of transcendence made possible by the magic of reading, and makes available to us now the meanings of the past. A comparable moment of almost mystical optimism – compensatory optimism, we might call it, in the light of the tragic history of twentieth-century Russia – can be found in Bakhtin's writing, though in another essay than 'Discourse in the Novel':

> There is neither a first nor a last word and there are no limits to the dialogic context (it extends into the boundless future). Even *past* meanings, that is, those born in the dialogue of past centuries, can never be stable (finalized, ended once and for all) - they will always change (be renewed) in the process of subsequent, future development of the dialogue. At any moment in the development of the dialogue there are immense, boundless masses of forgotten contextual meanings, but at certain moments of the dialogue's subsequent development along the way

---

[11]   M.M. Bakhtin. 'Discourse in the Novel'. *The Dialogic Imagination*. Ed. Michael Holquist. Trans. Caryl Emerson and Michael Holquist. Austin: University of Texas Press, 1981. The 'discourse' in the title is a translation of the Russian word *slovo*: word or utterance.

they are recalled and invigorated in renewed form (in a new context). Nothing is
absolutely dead: every meaning will have its homecoming festival. The problem
of *great time*.[12]

'Every meaning will have its homecoming festival': it is a utopian hope and offers,
it seems, a finally redemptive promise, that the meanings of the past are waiting
to be re-activated, in transformed ways, in the present. This formulation allows
for a carnivalesque randomness in what Bakhtin calls here 'the development
of the dialogue': it allows, that is, for the sometimes adventitious connections
and frankly implausible rediscoveries that mark literary history and indeed the
history of reading more generally. But perhaps these belong more to 'great time',
which I interpret as the longest rhythms or temporalities of human history, no less
historical for being epochal or even species-long. This study, which is concerned
with the generally shorter rhythms of the historical continuities that connect us to
the nineteenth century, will argue that, despite the apparently adventitious nature
of some of the connections that we inevitably make with the cultural artifacts of
the century before last, in general these connections are absolutely not random and
they are to be grounded on definite and traceable histories. The following chapter
will specify some of these more fully.

---

[12]   M.M. Bakhtin. 'Towards a Methodology of the Human Sciences'. *Speech Genres
and Other Late Essays*. Ed. Caryl Emerson and Michael Holquist. Trans. Vern W. McGee.
Austin, Texas: University of Texas Pres.170.

Chapter 2
Reading with Hindsight:
The Nineteenth Century and the
Twenty-First

I

There is a powerful moment in *Past and Present*, published in 1843, when Carlyle provides a striking image of the process of scholarly historical reconstruction. The 'past' of 'past and present' is the life of the twelfth-century abbey at St Edmunds, which can only be reached by an old monkish chronicle, the *Chronica Jocelini*, recently published by virtue of the antiquarian endeavours of the Camden Society. Carlyle imagines the process of historical reconstruction in these terms:

> Readers who please to go along with us into this poor *Jocelini Chronica* shall wander inconveniently enough, as in wintry twilight, through some poor stript hazel-grove, rustling with foolish noises, and perpetually hindering the eye-sight; but across which, here and there, some real human figure is seen moving: very strange; whom we could hail if he would answer;- and we look into a pair of eyes deep as our own, *imaging* our own, but all unconscious of us; to whom we for the time, are become as spirits and invisible![1]

The process of scholarship is thus one in which we can at best get glimpses of human subjects, who exist not so much *in* the documents as *behind* them. Such glimpses are at once rewarding and unsettling. As we gaze briefly into the unconscious eyes of those people who pre-existed us at such an immense distance of time, we get a momentary sense of our own insubstantiality to them: 'we, for the time, are become as spirits and invisible!'

By comparison with the historical distance that separated Carlyle from the twelfth century, the gulf between us and the nineteenth century is small. The intervening history has however been dramatic and transforming; I explore in this book some of the ways that that history has altered our sense of the nineteenth-century past. To focus that exploration in this chapter I have chosen to discuss a number of moments in the nineteenth century when writers anticipated future responses to themselves and their own society and civilisation. In other words, I wish to read with hindsight, but only when invited to do so. Before doing this, I wish to consider how best to understand the apparent barrier to understanding created by the sheer fact of historical distance, and for this purpose I use some memoirs published in the early twenty-first century which make explicit the apparent continuities and discontinuities between us and that nineteenth-century past.

---

[1]   Thomas Carlyle. *Past and Present*. London: Dent, Everyman's Library, 1978. 48.

Carlyle was divided from his topic by a gulf of seven centuries; he described it as a 'chasm', which it was 'no easy matter to get across' (48). In conceiving his relationship to the historical past in this way, Carlyle showed himself to be a characteristic romantic historian, possessed of a sense of the alterity and historical specificity of the past. Such romantic notions have been the topic of explicit critique in the twentieth century, most notably by Hans-Georg Gadamer, who, in a passage I have already quoted in Chapter 1, writes as though in direct repudiation of Carlyle. It is worth returning to that passage:

> Time is no longer primarily a gulf to be bridged because it separates; it is actually the supportive ground of the course of events in which the present is rooted. Hence temporal distance is not something that must be overcome. This was, rather, the naive assumption of historicism, namely that we must transpose ourselves into the spirit of the age, think with its ideas and its thoughts, not with our own, and thus advance towards historical objectivity. In fact the important thing is to recognize temporal distance as a positive and productive condition enabling understanding. It is not a yawning abyss but is filled with the continuity of custom and tradition, in the light of which everything handed down presents itself to us. Here it is not too much to speak of the genuine productivity of the course of events. (297)

Where Carlyle speaks of a chasm, Gadamer denies the notion that in understanding the past we have to cross a 'gulf' or bridge a 'yawning abyss'. On the contrary, in his account it is precisely the passage of time which permits retrospective understanding, not merely because time allows matters to fall into their true proportions, but because understanding is itself historically effected, and the custom and tradition which join us to the past are the condition of our understanding it.

The obvious difficulty with Gadamer's assertion is his almost mystical idea of tradition, which is hard to specify in terms of real histories or as real and enduring popular memory. It is very much easier to make such a specification for us with respect to the nineteenth century than it would have been in the nineteenth century looking back to the twelfth. But even for us now, seeking to engage with the nineteenth-century past, the nature of our understanding necessarily alters as that past recedes from us. That sense of a past receding beyond personal connection has been reinforced by the passage into the twenty-first century when, to make a point that is not merely numerical, in looking back to the nineteenth century we look back to what is now the century before last. Nobody now alive has direct personal memory of the reign of Queen Victoria. Our sense of a living continuity with the nineteenth century is thus palpably diminished. Nevertheless, the connections that we have with the century before last are clearly of a different order from the sense that Carlyle had of the twelfth century about which he was writing. Partly this *is* a matter of time; to seek to reconstruct the lives, or to seek to get a vivid living sense of lives lived seven centuries ago, is clearly a different matter from trying to do so in relation to lives lived merely two centuries ago. In part also this is a matter of the sheer volume of historical sources available. Carlyle imagines the documents available to him as 'some poor stript hazel-grove'; for the nineteenth century we have vast and luxurious forests of documents which complicate and facilitate our vision. But these are really beside the point from Gadamer's perspective; more importantly there are still powerful continuities, carried by a sense of immediately preceding generations, which connect us to the nineteenth century in ways that could not connect Carlyle to the twelfth. It is these connections which I wish to explore in the first half of this chapter. In doing so it will appear that 'custom and tradition' are characterised by dispute and contradiction in ways that Gadamer himself would perhaps have been unhappy to recognise.

II

I want to suggest no less than the embodied social history, or multiple social histories, that link us to our nineteenth-century past in more substantial ways than the learnt social history of the classroom or the text-book or even the historical 'source', important though these are in forming or framing our sense of the past. This is seemingly an impossible project: not quite a history of everything, but a history of how people make substantial connections with their own more or less distant past.[2] These connections are revealed in autobiographies and memoirs, and rediscovered or excavated by the massive contemporary interest in family history and genealogy. So what follows is in effect merely a sample, which suggests a way in which the Gadamerian connections, to which the philosopher alludes, might be understood in concrete terms. The examples also suggest something of the substance of this history, how in particular the triumph of neoliberalism since the 1980s has put a stop to some of the substantial or institutional connections to our nineteenth-century past even as, in one of its guises, it has posed as a return to 'Victorian values'.

So I consider three early twenty-first-century pieces of writing which are all in effect memoirs, or family histories, and which take us back to the nineteenth century. The first is to be found in Alasdair Gray's *Book of Prefaces*, published in 2000; its postscript, dated December 31st 1999 and thus especially suffused with a sense of the passing of the centuries, contains what is in effect a family memoir. The postscript is a kind of testimony to the education that Gray received, and which was in evidence (self-mockingly) in the elaborate anthology of Prefaces which precedes this concluding moment. He recounts how he had conceived the whole project almost twenty years previously, in thrall still, at that moment in the early 1980s in Scotland, to a notion of progress which he had inherited from his grandparents and parents and which was evidenced in the progress of their own lives and in his own. This is how Gray tells his family history:

---

[2] For this impossible project, see however Raphael Samuel, *Theatres of Memory: Past and Present in Contemporary Culture*. Vol. 1. London, Verso, 1996; and Raphael Samuel, *Theatres of Memory: Island Stories – Unravelling Britain*. Vol.2. London: Verso, 1999. The collective memories embodied in autobiographies can be sampled in, for example, John Burnett, *Useful Toil*. Harmondsworth: Penguin, 1984, and *Destiny Obscure* Harmondsworth: Penguin, 1984.

For my grandparents had been born in the middle of Victoria's reign. My mum's
dad was a foreman shoemaker who brought his wife from Northampton to
Glasgow when English employers blacklisted him for trade union activities.
He also brought his daughters to tears by reading them Hardy's *Tess of the
d'Urbervilles* ... My dad's dad was an industrial blacksmith and elder of a
Congregational kirk: the kirk Cromwell worshipped in because the congregation
chose its own priests. His political heroes were William Gladstone and Keir
Hardie, both of whom wanted Scotland and Ireland to have independent
governments, and British manual labourers to be as healthily and comfortably
housed as their bosses, if not quite as spaciously ... My dad, born 1897, left
school at twelve, worked a weighbridge in a Clydeside dock, and joined the
army in 1914. He survived Flanders, lost his parents' Christian Liberal faith and
became a Fabian Socialist, earning money between 1918 and 1939 by operating
a machine in a cardboard box factory. In his part time he worked without pay for
co-operative outdoor holiday organisations: The Camping Club of Great Britain,
Scottish Youth Club Association and others.

That Trade Union Shoemaker, Liberal blacksmith and Co-operative Fabian box-
cutter were three types who created the first British Labour government: a party
of MPs who preferred Ruskin to Marx and in 1924 passed parliamentary acts
enabling town & rural councils to build the kind of housing scheme where I was
born in 1934 ... [3]

The passage continues with some more directly autobiographical material
concerning Gray's childhood into the 1950s. My point is simply that for Gray there
is a direct continuity between the lives lived by his grandparents' and his parents'
generation with his own life, a life which benefited materially and educationally
from the partial realisation of their political and social beliefs and aspirations. This
was the ground of his own political beliefs, especially in progress. Moreover, that
belief in progress, of a felt benign continuity between the nineteenth century and
the contemporary moment, has now been lost for Gray as he writes on December
31st 1999. The agents of that disruption (briefly 'the world-wide triumph of
international capitalism') have brought to a conclusion one form of continuity
between the mid-nineteenth century and us, which therefore adds a whole new
context to our reading of Ruskin, to our understanding of Gladstonian liberalism,
and to the meanings we attach to nineteenth-century Trade-Unionism and the
growth of socialism.

Another early twenty-first century memoir tells a similar story. In 2001 John
Lucas published *The Good That We Do*, an account of the life of his grandfather,
who lived between 1880 and 1940.[4] It is not exactly a memoir, because his
grandfather died when Lucas was still too young to remember him. The form of
the book is therefore interesting, because it starts with sixty pages or so that read
like a novel; it only becomes a more properly (or more narrowly) scholarly account
and reconstruction when it moves into his grandfather's adult life as teacher and

---

[3]   Alasdair Gray. *The Book of Prefaces*. London: Bloomsbury Publishing, 2000. 628.
[4]   John Lucas. *The Good That We Do*. London: Greenwich Exchange, 2001.

then headmaster in London schools in the twentieth century. The premise of the book is that Lucas's grandfather, H.W.S. Kelly, was in a primary sense a good man; the source of the book's title is provided in its epigraph, taken from an essay by Dickens: 'The good that we do, and the virtues that we show, and particularly the children that we rear, survive us through the long and unknown perspectives of time.' The book thus seeks to make explicit or to substantiate the survival of one good man in the unknown perspective of time that we now represent for Lucas's grandfather.

Lucas also quotes the moving conclusion to *Middlemarch* in his prefatory note to the volume: 'For the growing good of the world is partly dependent on unhistoric acts, and that things are not so ill with you and me as they might have been, is half owing to the number who lived faithfully a hidden life, and rest in unvisited tombs'. One powerful frame for the book, then, is provided by these quotations from Dickens and George Eliot, in which the succession of the generations is the primary means by which 'goodness' is transmitted and our worth as human beings is somehow validated in a secular perspective. The book thus seeks to provide, in a similar way to Gray's postscript, a sense of a meaningful continuity between this figure with his roots thoroughly in the nineteenth century and the life to be lived by his grandchild two generations later.

In Lucas's case, to a greater extent than that of Gray, this continuity is founded upon education. Kelly was headmaster of several schools with very deprived catchments in Fulham. Though Lucas is keen to find political continuities between his grandfather and himself, the evidence for this is slight, and the best evidence that he can muster is the discovery that Kelly had been a friend of Ernest Bevin – at least to the extent of the occasional visit to share tea with him at the House of Commons. A more substantial connection is to be found via Kelly's belief in the possibilities of education for all. For example, he tried to share his love of the English classics with his schoolchildren (especially the novels of Dickens); and he took them, elementary school children from backgrounds so deprived that they often could not attend school because they had 'no boots', to see productions of Shakespeare. Lucas suggests that Kelly's own love of Dickens came in turn from *his* father, a Devonian butcher who might himself have gone to hear Dickens read in Exeter or Plymouth. So Lucas constructs a genealogy which goes straight back to the mid-nineteenth century, in which lower-middle-class self-education, difficult but high-minded state education in the nineteen-twenties and thirties, and his own profession as Professor and educator are all linked. This is perhaps a different sense of 'the growing good of the world' than that envisaged by George Eliot herself, though Lucas obviously wants to include this also. For Eliot, that notion was promoted partly in opposition to the progress understood in an overt political or institutional sense; or at least, she offered it at the end of *Middlemarch* as a consolation for her inability to imagine any such outlet for Dorothea's talents. The influence of good people can be understood as a cumulative set of consequences which sustains social life almost independently of its institutional or political forms. But Lucas wants to make a bigger claim than this, because he does 'believe in' politics in a way that George Eliot did not. That is to say, he wishes to assert that the institutions of public education to which Kelly dedicated his life, and the educational ideals that animated him, are part too of that 'growing good of the world'.

But here too, like Gray, Lucas is conscious of a check to that sense of progress; he also asserts his feeling that the current world marks the high-water mark of those ideals, which are now defeated or at least in retreat. Perhaps there really was such a thing as a twentieth-century *fin de siècle*, but the century whose conclusion it marked was the nineteenth. At all events, for both Gray and Lucas there is a strong sense of continuity back to the nineteenth century, based upon family histories which connect meaningfully to wider social and political histories. Their sense of the nineteenth century – what it means to them, how its various cultural manifestations are judged – inevitably emerges from those central pathways; such continuities seem to me to be precisely what Gadamer means by 'custom and tradition.' And for both of them, there is a sense, which is as much a political as a generational one, that the current moment is one which is losing the benign possibilities of a positive politics linking back to those old nineteenth-century hopes and struggles.

A final example is provided by another professor of English literature, and thus again raising those matters of education and reading which have been present in both the previous two cases. In the *London Review of Books* for 21 August 2003, John Sutherland wrote a Diary piece about his grandmother, born in 1890, and the first in her family to benefit from Forster's 1870 Education Act, just as he had been the first to benefit from the 1944 Education Act. Sutherland's mother in turn had learnt shorthand and typing at the Pitman School; she had taught him five-finger typing. The whole piece is a touching meditation on the meaning of reading to people who have little tradition or context for it; the most poignant aspect of the piece is the discovery that his grandmother had systematically pilfered a local commercial lending library and hoarded the books. Sutherland's piece is about both continuity and discontinuity – about the steady progression that led from the Forster-educated working-class woman to the Butler-educated scholarship boy who became a Professor of English, but also about the anxieties, resentments and petty snobberies that marked that progression. So while there is no sense of the institutional and political affiliations that characterise my other two examples, there is still the capacity, on Sutherland's part, to look back to the nineteenth century and its social history via a substantial and embodied generational connection.

Such examples could doubtless be multiplied, if not indefinitely, then at least without too much difficulty. People in their sixties in the first decade of the twenty-first century tended to have grandparents born at the end of the nineteenth, and can thus claim connection of that substantial and embodied kind with real Victorians. My point is not only that such connections are fading with the simple passing of the generations, but also that the social histories that connect us to the nineteenth century are now also more attenuated – or indeed under actual political threat – and that this inevitably alters the context in which we understand the Victorians. When we gaze back into those eyes (unlike Carlyle, we have the advantage of photographs and the pathos of such acts of connection is that much more acute) we do so from a position that is increasingly removed from the world inhabited by Horace Kelly or Gray's grandparents or Sutherland's grandmother.

These are all millennial stories, which take the arbitrary marking of the passage of time as an occasion for retrospection which is both personal and a matter of embodied social history. All three stories are centrally concerned also with the matter of education; to this extent they bear out the argument of Dinah Birch's *Our Victorian Education*, which sets out the multiple continuities between the educational ideas and dilemmas of the nineteenth century and the twenty-first.[5] But they indicate also what would be involved in taking Gadamer seriously as a guide to social history: the effort to give substance, in the actual lives and memories of historically-existing people, of the historical continuities which, he asserts, are the positive ground for our knowledge of the past.

III

Carlyle's point, in speaking of the distance which separates us from figures in our past, was that those people in a sense gazed back: this is the defamiliarising moment in the study of the past, where a strong connection with that inalienably different figure allows us briefly and even disturbingly to get a sense of the historically determinate strangeness of our seemingly natural selves. In the second half of this chapter I wish to consider some moments when nineteenth-century people are caught in the act of anticipating the judgments of posterity, because in such moments we get an especially vivid sense of the real histories that separate and connect us to the nineteenth-century past. It is of course impossible to read without hindsight; its inevitability becomes especially apparent when those old writers anticipated the future's backward judgment.

There is in fact a substantial literature of future fiction in the nineteenth century, and though its roots go back into the Enlightenment, the nineteenth century could be said to have invented the genre.[6] I glance at this briefly at the end of the chapter, but this is not my substantial interest; my topic is not whether the Victorians predicted the future correctly, but what the subsequent history reveals both about them and us. There is indeed a built-in obsolescence in predictive fiction, which its most famous practitioner, H.G. Wells, acknowledged towards the end of his life, in making a distinction between such fiction and Utopian writing; he wished to exempt Utopias from the 'self-destructive challenge' of 'we prophets for our own time', who 'pass almost before we are dead'.[7] I am not so sure that Utopian

---

5   Dinah Birch. *Our Victorian Education*. Oxford: Blackwell, 2008.

6   See, for examples and discussion, I.F. Clarke, ed. *The Tale of the Next Great War, 1871-1914*. Liverpool: Liverpool University Press, 1995 and *The Great War with Germany, 1890-1914*. Liverpool: Liverpool University Press, 1997; David Seed, ed. *Anticipations: Essays on Early Science Fiction and its Precursors*. Liverpool: Liverpool University Press, 1995.

7   H.G. Wells, 'Utopias' (1939), quoted in Patrick Parrinder. *Shadows of the Future: H.G. Wells, Science Fiction and Prophecy*. Liverpool: Liverpool University Press, 1995. 96–7.

writing is exempt from the destructive hindsight that Wells attributes to predictive fiction, as we shall see in the discussion of William Morris's *News from Nowhere* in Chapter 6. Nevertheless, it is certainly true that certain kinds of future story make themselves vulnerable to simple disproof by the passage of time, and have indeed instigated a minor popular critical genre in which the predictions of the past are shown to have come true or false. Initially, however, I want to consider anticipations of the future which are more inadvertent than conscious attempts at prediction, which are often designed to influence especially defence policy in the most direct way; nineteenth-century writers' glances at posterity are in some ways more revealing than their sustained and conscious glares.

The most famous moment of such anticipation in the nineteenth century was undoubtedly Macaulay's New Zealander; writing, in an essay on Von Ranke, of the extraordinary longevity of the Catholic Church as an institution, the historian speculated in 1840 that 'she may still exist in undiminished vigour when some traveller from New Zealand shall, in the midst of a vast solitude, take his stand on a broken arch to sketch the ruins of St Paul's'.[8] Illustrated in Gustave Doré's *London* (1872), the image of the New Zealander was drawn upon so often in the nineteenth century as to become something of a cliché.[9] It could be used to express a variety of anxieties about the present, triggered by the notion of St Paul's, synecdochically London, in ruins. Hindsight has scarcely vindicated Macaulay in one respect: London is not in ruins and the white settler colonies may be flourishing, but not in ways which promise to echo the way in which nineteenth-century Britain had superseded Rome. On the other hand the Catholic Church still persists.

That moment in Macaulay's essay on Von Ranke, despite its resonance in the nineteenth century, was little more than a rhetorical flourish. More substantial, because deeper rooted in Macaulay's committed sense of the progress exemplified in English history, is the following anticipation in *The History of England* (1849):

> We too shall, in our turn, be outstripped, and in our turn be envied. It may well be, in the twentieth century, that the peasant of Dorsetshire may think himself miserably paid with twenty shillings a week; that the carpenter at Greenwich may receive ten shillings a day; that labouring men may be as little used to dine without meat as they now are to eat rye bread; that sanitary police and medical discoveries may have added several more years to the average length of human life; that numerous comforts and luxuries which are now unknown, or confined to a few, may be within the reach of every diligent and thrifty working man. And yet it may then be the mode to assert that the increase of wealth and the progress of science have benefited the few at the expense of the many, and to talk of the reign of Queen Victoria as the time when England was truly merry England, where all classes were bound together by brotherly sympathy, when

---

    [8]   Lord Macaulay. *Critical and Historical Essays*. London: Longmans, Green, Reader and Dyer, 1869. 548.
    [9]   See Robert Dingley. 'The Ruins of the Future: Macaulay's New Zealander and the Spirit of the Age'. *Histories of the Future: Studies in Fact, Fantasy and Science Fiction*. Ed. Alan Sandison and Robert Dingley. Basingstoke: Palgrave, 2000. 15–33.

the rich did not grind the faces of the poor, and when the poor did not envy the splendour of the rich.[10]

The ironies of this passage, even within its own terms, are complex. The context is Macaulay's demonstration of the extraordinary improvement in the lives of the English people since the end of the seventeenth century, and his impatience with those sentimentalists who looked back to earlier periods of English history as representing more harmonious times. Since we are to assume that the modish thinkers of the future will be mistaken in their estimate of the reign of Queen Victoria, their imputed belief that in that period 'all classes were bound together by brotherly sympathy', and that 'the rich did not grind the faces of the poor' must be false – and therefore that the contemporary (i.e., nineteenth-century) world *is* characterised by these features which contradict the triumphal utopianism of the present to which this passage supplies the conclusion. The ironies only multiply when the passage is read with a knowledge of the actual social history which has supervened between 1849 (when it was written) and the twentieth century which it looks forward to. Macaulay's anticipations of the rising prosperity of the working class has been met and more than met, if one confines one's consideration of this to the traditional working class of the industrialised world – though this class is now itself subject to widespread anxieties. Equally, Macaulay's expectation that the world will have invented 'numerous comforts and luxuries' unknown to the nineteenth century has been fully realised. It is also certainly the case that one version of the Victorian past current in the twentieth century has precisely been to see it as an age where the rich ground the faces of the poor; that might even be described as the predominant image of the period. But there have been historians also who have looked back to the nineteenth century as providing a moralised social order in stark contrast to the demoralised present – though such historians have not by and large praised Victorian Britain for being merry. In short, the complex social history which has succeeded the nineteenth century has doubled and redoubled the ironies of the passage, in ways which both confirm and unsettle Macaulay's Whiggish confidence.

That intervening social history also provides the ground for our response to the following passage by John Stuart Mill. It occurs in his *Principles of Political Economy*, almost exactly contemporaneous with Macaulay's *History*, when Mill is discussing the operation of the New Poor Law and the controversy surrounding it:

> Everyone has a right to live. We will suppose this granted. But no one has a right to bring creatures into life, to be supported by other people. Whoever means to stand upon the first of these rights must renounce all pretensions to the last. If a man cannot support even himself unless others help him, those others are entitled to say that they do not also undertake the support of any offspring which it is physically possible for him to summon into the world. Yet there are abundance of writers and public speakers, including many of most ostentatious pretensions to high feeling, whose views of life are so truly brutish, that they see hardship

---

[10] Lord Macaulay. *The History of England, from the Accession of James II*. Ed. T.F. Henderson. Vol.1. Oxford: Oxford University Press, 1931. 371.

in preventing paupers from breeding hereditary paupers in the very workhouse itself. Posterity will one day ask with astonishment, what sort of people it could be among whom such preachers could find proselytes.[11]

Mill in this instance was of course mistaken. Posterity has tended to side with the writers and public speakers with 'ostentatious pretensions to high feeling', rather than with the defenders and overseers of the workhouse. We can indeed get a strong sense of what posterity thought of such regulations as the enforced separation of the sexes in the workhouse, and the conditions in which hereditary paupers were 'bred' in them, by reading Norman Longmate's book on the subject of the workhouse, first published in 1974 and republished with a new foreword in 2003.

In his first, 1974, foreword, Longmate includes a letter from a nurse who had worked in the hospital at Andover, whose buildings had originally housed the notorious Andover workhouse in which the most famous workhouse scandal of the nineteenth century occurred. The nurse contacted Longmate after the original radio programmes, on which the book was based, had been published. She wrote:

> Both my parents (born in the 1870s) had a terror of the place. When we passed it on walks my mother and father, though by then traveled and well-educated people, still spoke with bitterness of things done there in the past. As children in the 1920s we still ran past its high walls in superstitious fear.
>
> After many years away I regarded the tales as mere legend, but some years ago I returned to nurse for a brief period in the now bright and decorated 'St Johns Hospital'. But the old corridors and chapel, mortuary and yards remained and, on night duty, doing rounds at night across the yards and blocks, one had a presence of evil ... Once when Sister wanted the old mortuary tidied up and various records removed for repainting and modernising the building, I volunteered and glancing at the records of births and rapid deaths of infants in the past century I knew it wasn't all imagination ... [12]

Another continuity then: a vivid personal and social history which sharply connects the still-extant buildings of early Victorian Britain, via an acute sense of their significance, to a nurse and her experiences recalled in the 1970s. Longmate too is part of that sense of an impinging social history; he describes how he himself grew up on a council estate still overshadowed by the local workhouse. Indeed his 1974 Foreword begins with the words 'I grew up in the shadow of the workhouse'. Posterity, in the form of these two people at least, looked back at the operations of the 1834 Poor Law's 'less eligibility' principle and the regulations designed to prevent the survival of hereditary paupers, with little less than horror.

Yet this is not the end of the story, for there is a generational factor at work here too. Longmate was born in 1925; his nurse correspondent must have been at least ten years older. He was of the generation that writes of his 'war service' expecting

---

[11]   John Stuart Mill. *Principles of Political Economy*. Vol. 1. London: Longmans, Green, Reader and Fuer, 1877. 427.

[12]   Norman Longmate. *The Workhouse: A Social History*. London: Pimlico, 2003. 12.

everybody to recognise that that meant service in the Second World War. The sense of a living and still-pressing history to which he testifies is certainly now attenuated. In his new foreword he writes tellingly of the architectural remains of the old workhouses, and of their rebarbative resistance to the 'swords into ploughshares' principle, by which he means their capacity to be converted for more socially acceptable uses. The Andover workhouse, however, is an exception:

> It became, after losing its original role, St Johns Hospital for the elderly, then an annexe to the nearby Cricklade College and Icknield School. In 1997 the 2.5 acre site was offered for sale, with the 'listed' workhouse in its centre. It was duly sold and has been admirably developed The brickwork of the former wards is immaculate, a flight of gleaming white steps leads up to the front door, which is crowned by an elegant fanlight and flanked by grassy banks. The neatly paved area at the front is separated from the road by neatly cropped lawns and a hedge. The only admonitory note is struck by a sign which warns: 'Strictly No Parking. Residents Only.' With the station – 65 minutes by fast train to London – only a short walk away, properties at what is now The Cloisters are in heavy demand. (viii)

Longmate adds that he inquired for one flat advertised for sale but found that it was already sold. At prices already out of date it was on offer at £95,000 or to let at £500 a month.

Posterity has certainly taken a different turn than that anticipated by Mill. At one time the grandchildren and great-grandchildren of those hereditary paupers rose up, thanks to the systems of state education traceable back to the Victorians (Longmate was a scholarship boy), to denounce the workhouse and brood on its banefully persistent aura. Now capital can seize on the happy solidity of those nineteenth-century buildings and transform them, via a fantasy borne out of Trollope rather than Dickens ('The Cloisters'), into two-room apartments with a patina of heritage. I do not say this to denounce the workhouse's new inhabitants, the developers who converted the buildings, the estate agents who sold them, or the condition of postmodernity which might be the explanatory term of first resort when confronted by this striking sign of the times. I much prefer to think of this use of those buildings, much as I prefer the crowds who come to admire the life of 'Upstairs Downstairs' in a hundred National Trust properties to the crowds of servants whose lives are nostalgically recreated. My point is simply that turning the workhouse into 'The Cloisters' is symptomatic of a historical distance that almost puts us out of reach of John Stuart Mill's anticipated posterity.

Or so it would seem if we remain with the lived continuities of a receding social history: the emblematic nineteenth-century response to a perceived crisis of pauperisation represented by the workhouse. John Stuart Mill may no longer be a name to conjure with in economic thought, but less eligibility, anxieties about pauperisation, and desires to prevent the breeding of hereditary paupers all live on strongly in the prospectuses and policies of neoliberalism. Perhaps indeed it is that failure of historical connection which permits such policies to flourish, and which means that Mill's anticipation of posterity may not have been so mistaken after all.

It may be felt that this is to extrapolate unfairly from what is little more than a passing comment on the part of John Stuart Mill. However, there is certainly a particular social history of the workhouse, and its active memory in British social life, forming our responses now, in the twenty-first century, to his apparently insignificant comment.[13] And there is also a wider history of the inculcation of labour discipline, underlying this institutional story, which has a wider resonance even outside these islands. Elsewhere Mill could make the inculcation of labour discipline, and still more the control of reproduction, the key to the probable future of the working class, as the title of one of his most famous chapters in *The Principles of Political Economy* has it: 'On the probable futurity of the labouring classes'. Insofar as there were nineteenth-century notions of 'progress', this is one of the characteristic versions: an improved future based on the diffusion of the self-reliant virtues that fit people (men especially) for the market. Labour discipline is but one aspect of this. Our response to this is bound to be conditioned by the continuing, seemingly never-ending, presence of such notions in the nearly two hundred years that have succeeded Mill's particular, and in general generous-minded, enunciation of them.

However, such sober and disciplinary notions are not ordinarily associated with Victorian ideas of progress. Routinely invoked in this context,[14] and providing a seemingly grander and less untrammelled vision, is Tennyson's poem 'Locksley Hall', with its anticipations of aerial warfare and 'the Parliament of man':

> For I dipt into the future, far as human eye could see,
> Saw the Vision of the world, and all the wonder that would be;
>
> Saw the heavens fill with commerce, argosies of magic sails,
> Pilots of the purple twilight, dropping down with costly bales;
>
> Heard the heavens fill with shouting, and there rained a ghastly dew,
> From the nations' airy navies grappling in the central blue;
>
> Far along the world-wide whisper of the south-wind rushing warm,
> With the standards of the peoples plunging through the thunder-storm;
>
> Till the war-drums throbbed no longer, and the battle-flags were furled
> In the Parliament of man, the Federation of the world.
>
> There the common sense of most shall hold a fretful realm in awe,
> And the kindly earth shall slumber, lapt in universal law. (119–30)[15]

---

[13]   See Simon Dentith. '"The Shadow of the Workhouse": The Afterlife of a Victorian Institution'. *Literature, Interpretation, Theory.* 20 (2009): 79–91.

[14]   Invoked, for example, by I.F. Clarke in *The Tale of the Next Great War, 1871–1914.* 10.

[15]   Alfred Tennyson. 'Locksley Hall'. *The Poems of Tennyson.* Ed. Christopher Ricks. London: Longmans, 1969. 688–99.

The evident ironies of predictive writing, when seen from the position of hindsight, are only too visible here: both the remarkable exactness of the predictions of aerial warfare and the League of Nations followed by the United Nations, and their evident and inevitable insufficiency given the actualities of technological change and the equally pressing actualities of political failures in the world federations that subsequent history has in fact concocted. However a modern reader responds to Tennyson's lines here, their reading is bound to encompass the multiple ironies that gather round this passage and which are created by the sheer passage of time since it was written.

While this passage can be seen as a *locus classicus* of Victorian ideas of progress, what such a reading fails to recognise is that the poem is already subject to the glare of hindsight even within itself – a hindsight compounded by Tennyson's own revisiting of the poem near the end of his life with 'Locksley Hall Sixty Years After'. Hindsight is built into the very structure of the earlier poem, both in personal terms and the wider political themes which are bound up with the personal here, in the way most fully developed in *Maud*. The original model for the poem, the Mu'allaqāt or 'Hanging Poems' which Tennyson read in Sir William Jones's translation, concerns a man revisiting the scene of an earlier love affair and reflecting on it now that it is in the past. The protagonist of Tennyson's poem thus associates his youthful enthusiasm for progress with an earlier love affair that has subsequently ended bitterly. The lines that I have just quoted are therefore immediately followed by a corrected, even sardonically over-corrected, vision of the present, and of the possibilities of a future transformed by the progress of science:

So I triumphed ere my passion sweeping through me left me dry,
Left with the palsied heart, and left me with the jaundiced eye;

Eye, to which all order festers, all things here are out of joint:
Science moves, but slowly slowly, creeping on from point to point:

Slowly comes a hungry people, as a lion creeping nigher,
Glares at one than nods and winks behind a slowly dying fire. (131–6)

This transition, from ecstatic prophetic optimism to 'jaundiced' pessimism about the state of the world (or indeed the Condition of England – these lines were published in 1842, at the height of the crisis of social relations that marked the 1830s and 1840s – provides in miniature a pattern for the poem as a whole, which swings between these moods until the final tempered conclusion.

But the poem is also marked by hindsight in another way, as the poet anticipates a future for the woman who has deserted him, a future to be marked by bitterness and regret. The poem contains perhaps the saddest version of hindsight yet encountered, an epigram taken from Dante:

... this is truth the poet sings,
That a sorrow's crown of sorrow is remembering happier things. (75–6)

There is even some pleasure taken by the protagonist in envisaging this disastrous future for the woman who has jilted him; and the extent that we are able to see this as readers of the poem suggests its status as a dramatic monologue, anticipating again the later and fuller working-through of these themes in *Maud: A Monodrama* from the mid-1850s.

So the poem presents itself to its subsequent reader with its anticipations of the future necessarily subject to the corrections of time, and with these anticipations marked as youthful idealism and subject to correction within the poem. The progress of reading the poem is a sometimes bewildering swing between these perspectives, indicated not least by its complex tenses, shifting, from the temporal position of its presumed deictic now, both forwards and backwards, and with an anticipation of the future for the lost bride which will include her own embittered retrospect. Nevertheless, and for all these oscillations, the poem concludes with a sufficiently ringing declaration of hope for the future, as the protagonist (now less beset with irony) appears to resume his former strength almost by an act of will:

> Not in vain the distance beacons. Forward, forward let us range,
> Let the great world spin for ever down the ringing grooves of change.
>
> Through the shadow of the globe we sweep into the younger day;
> Better fifty years of Europe than a cycle of Cathay. (181–4)

It is perhaps this conclusive tone of personal and civilisational uplift which makes the poem especially appropriate for the hindsight which Tennyson himself cast upon it with his later poem, written nearly fifty years later but entitled 'Locksley Hall Sixty Years After'.

This latter poem, written in Tennyson's old age, is less of a dramatic monologue than the earlier one; that is, the position of the speaker is less subject to the local ironies that we saw marking the earlier poem, both in its phases of youthful idealism and in its matching phases of jaded misanthropy. But to some extent it has a similar structure: the poem rehearses both deeply pessimistic, indeed frankly reactionary opinions, matches them with optimistic opinions attributed to the speaker's grandson and interlocutor, and then concludes with a tempered hope or prayer for the future. My interest here however is the way that the poem, in setting itself up as a reconsideration of its earlier progenitor text, builds into itself the attitude of hindsight, both of a personal life – this is an old man looking back on his young adulthood and reassessing it in the light of the life that he has led – but also in a wider social and political sense, as the hopes of that earlier moment, curtailed as we have seen that they already were, have or have not been realised. Historically we can describe this as a later phase of nineteenth-century life looking back and reassessing an earlier 'age of reform'; our own sense of historical hindsight is necessarily the inheritor of this earlier, 1880s, act of reassessment. Emphatically, since the whole of the later poem turns on the word 'Forward' (taken from the conclusion of 'Locksley Hall') and thus on the sense in which one can continue with a notion of progress, we have to recognise that our sense of posteriority in relation to naive 'Victorian' ideas of progress had been anticipated by the Victorians themselves.

Thus in an early phase of the poem Tennyson argues that the notion of progress is dependent upon a belief in the after-life, and the widespread scientific materialism that he detects in his contemporary world thus challenges the very possibility of his earlier cry:

Truth for truth, and good for good! The Good, the True, the Pure, the Just –
Take the charm 'For ever' from them, and they crumble into dust.

Gone the cry of 'Forward, Forward,' lost within a growing gloom;
Lost, or only heard in silence from the silence of a tomb.

Half the marvels of my morning, triumphs over time and space,
Staled by frequence, shrunk by usage into commonest commonplace!

'Forward' rang the voices then, and of the many mine was one.
Let us hush this cry of 'Forward' till ten thousand years have gone. (71–8)[16]

Hindsight here has overtaken the poem in its guise of pessimistic retrospect, correcting the idealism of youth with its apparently darker knowledge. Even the marvels of technological and scientific change from the 1830s – the railways, the telegraph – have been robbed of their initial glamour by the sheer passage into the commonplace. In this predominant aspect of the poem, the retrospective assessment of the earlier commitment to a notion of progress becomes the cue for a wide-ranging soured survey of contemporary society and politics. But while this may be the predominant mood of the poem, hindsight works in another way also, allowing the aged protagonist to reassess the man for whom he had been jilted, in the light of the exemplary life that he has led – 'I that loathed, have come to love him' (l. 280). This finally allows the possibility of another peroration organised around the word 'Forward', though now, by comparison with the earlier poem, this is more focused on religious notions. The poem concludes with a specific moment of generational transition to the new 'Lord and Master, latest Lord of Locksley Hall' – the synecdoche 'Locksley Hall – England' confirming its status as a 'Condition of England poem'.

In summary, then, we have to recognise that the apparently ecstatic assertions of 'progress' to be found in the first 'Locksley Hall' come to us heavily tempered by hindsight even within their own initial enunciations. There nevertheless remain the rather windy perorations to both poems, which now appear as no more than attitudes towards the future rather than specific anticipations of it. Nevertheless, to anticipate an aspect of the discussions of specific texts in the following chapters, one effect of reading with hindsight is to disrupt the rhetorical economy of a text, as what appeared important or conclusive now appears nugatory, and what seemed minor or just the way things are has loomed into prominence. Sometimes

---

[16] Alfred Tennyson 'Locksley Hall Sixty Years After'. *The Poems of Tennyson*. Ed. Christopher Ricks. London: Longmans, 1969.1359–69.

indeed adventitious coincidences can have the same effect, as when railway vandalism in 'Locksley Hall Sixty Years After' turns out to be the reason for the grandson's delay, leading to a particularly gloomy diatribe from the grandfather. This has the strange effect of robbing the poem of its shock value, or perhaps robbing contemporary instances of such vandalism of their shock value. Raymond Williams, in the famous opening to *The Country and the City*, suggests that ideas of a golden age are infinitely receding, placed by succeeding generations in the generation before. 'Locksley Hall Sixty Years After' suggests a similar receding escalator in which the shocking nature of now is always reinforced by a sense of the previous better time – only that then too, people were convinced of the shocking nature of now.

IV

Tennyson's anticipation of future aerial warfare ('Heard the heavens fill with shouting, and there rained a ghastly dew,/From the nations' airy navies grappling in the central blue,') points to another genre of more systematic futurology in the nineteenth century, famously initiated by George Chesney's *The Battle of Dorking* in 1871. Tennyson's grasp of technical detail was never good; the 'ringing grooves of change' in 'Locksley Hall' were based on a straightforward misunderstanding of the way that railway wheels run. Equally, his future airships seem to be just that – ships of the line floating in air rather than water, and the 'ghastly dew' that they drop is better understood as blood than any kind of chemical weapon. The genre of future fiction that follows *The Battle of Dorking*, however, prides itself on anticipating the consequences of technological innovation in military and naval matters, faithfully imagining the results of each new design, be it breach-loading naval guns, ironclads and dreadnoughts, or changes in military tactics and the advent of the machine gun. This whole genre thus participates in multiple historical series. First, *The Battle of Dorking* initiates a series of anticipations of the next European conflict which reaches its definitive terminus in the First World War; these fictions are subject absolutely to hindsight as the results of the military technologies which they were so keen to imagine proved infinitely more disastrous than even their gloomiest predictions. Secondly, in a manner which makes it less subject to destructive hindsight, the genre has continued ever since as invasion literature of all kinds, reflecting the current fears of each generation as the prospect of warfare looms or recedes. Thirdly, as the genre moves back and forth between popular journalism and the war-planning of the military staff college, it contributes both to the history of war-scares deliberately inculcated for differing purposes (usually increases in military spending), and to the war-games that try to ensure, usually unsuccessfully, that generals fight the next war rather than re-fight the last. And finally, the whole genre, in the period from the 1870s, right through to the First World War, is no more than a specialised type of a more widespread future fiction including utopias, which I will discuss more fully in a subsequent chapter on *News from Nowhere*, but which, to anticipate, is to be viewed as a symptom of blocked or distorted social change in the period. This whole mode, to give it more dignity than the names of George Chesney and William Le Queux might evoke, includes, for examples, the fictions of H.G. Wells and Erskine Childers.

All such fiction, however, might be felt to be subject to the kind of hindsight articulated by I.F. Clarke in discussing future fiction in its more optimistic aspect:

> Optimism came easily to Wells and his contemporaries. Their forecasts of things-to-come had no entries for global warming, shrinking tropical forests, the nuclear winter, future-shock, or ecological catastrophes such as the desolation of the Aral Sea. In their speculations about time-to-come, they assumed that their successors would manage change, even in warfare, as well as their predecessors had controlled the development of the great industrial societies. As new armaments appeared, the imagination raced ahead to the limits of the possible. Dynamite cruisers, electric rifles, giant submarines, vast flying machines – these appeared regularly in the many popular accounts that began in the 1890s.[17]

One objection to hindsight, as we saw in Chapter 1, is that it lends itself to a teleological view of history, viewing history as a series which leads inevitably to the present. Some historical series, however, are wholly willed, and the evolution of military weapons and tactics is one such – each step in the process leading to the next counter-step in a wholly deliberate succession, however subject to chance in the coincidences of technological innovation. This is doubtless why military future fiction of the kind that succeeded *The Battle of Dorking* is so subject to hindsight, especially since these fictions were typically set just a few years in the future. This equally left them subject to twists and turns in diplomatic strategy; William Le Queux's *The Great War in England in 1897*, published in 1894, had the country invaded by the combined forces of Russia and France; twelve years later he rewrote the script in *The Invasion of 1910*, this time with Germany as the enemy, as the various international alliances and counter-alliances had been put in place in the meantime.[18]

These multiple anticipations of the future, especially military, thus cast a particular shadow after the passage of over a hundred years. One series, of narrow military forecast as it shades off into military planning, appears to reach its terminus in the First World War, when the horrors of trench warfare extinguished for ever one kind of military anticipation. On the other hand, it is not as though war-gaming has therefore ceased; from another perspective, the late nineteenth century only proves its modernity by the proliferation of vividly imagined future wars, and in this sense the compulsory trope of the bombardment of London has been repeated ever since with various capital cities imaginatively destroyed in loving detail. Equally, I.F. Clarke's sense that even in its other guise of optimistic anticipation this fiction has been overtaken by the terrible actualities of the late twentieth century, when he wrote about global warming and other contemporary

---

[17]   I.F. Clarke, ed. *The Tale of the Next Great War, 1871-1914*. Liverpool: Liverpool University Press, 1995. 19–20.

[18]   See William Le Queux, *The Great War in England in 1897*. London: Tower Publishing, 1894; and I.F. Clarke, *The Great War with Germany, 1890–1914*. 139.

perils, is perhaps not conclusive; what characterises our sense of the future under
neoliberalism is indeed a 'loss of the future' conceived as an expectation of future
improvement, and its replacement by what Raymond Williams called 'Plan X': the
active planning for short-term competitive advantage in the full expectation that
conditions of extreme danger will persist. In these circumstances an active sense
of possible futures outside of the constraints of Plan X seems wholly desirable.[19]

However, another example of nineteenth-century anticipations of the future,
with quite a different provenance, suggests other continuities and discontinuities
between then and now. Written a few years before Tennyson's late poem 'Locksley
Hall Sixty Years After', and contemporaneous with some of the future fiction
alluded to here, Hardy's novel *The Return of the Native* (1878) has a wholly
dissimilar sense of the future destinies of mankind:

> Haggard Egdon appealed to a subtler and scarcer instinct, to a more recently
> learnt emotion, than that which responds to the sort of beauty called charming
> and fair.
>   Indeed, it is a question if the exclusive reign of this orthodox beauty is not
> approaching its last quarter. The new Vale of Tempe may be a gaunt wasteland
> in Thule: human souls may find themselves in closer and closer harmony with
> external things wearing a sombreness distasteful to our race when it was young.
> The time seems near, if it has not actually arrived, when the chastened sublimity
> of a moor, a sea, or a mountain, will be all of nature that is absolutely in
> keeping with the moods of the more thinking among mankind. And ultimately,
> to the commonest tourist, spots like Iceland may become what the vineyards
> and myrtle-gardens of South Europe are to him now; and Heidelberg and
> Baden be passed unheeded as he hastens from the Alps to the sand-dunes of
> Scheveningen.[20]

One history that has intervened between Hardy writing this by way of introducing
The Return of the Native in 1878, and our reading it now, is of course that of mass
tourism; while it is indeed the case that Iceland and the Alps (the former newly, the
latter for some time when Hardy was writing) have become tourist destinations,
that has by no means prevented tourists from continuing to flock to the pleasure
gardens of Southern Europe. Whether all such tourists are 'more thinking' is of
course open to dispute; but Hardy's more fundamental point is that the appeal of
the landscape will depend upon a consciousness of the nature of human destinies.
Our race is no longer young; as it passes further into its maturity, or even its
senescence, it will find affinity not with classically smiling, pretty and human,
landscapes, but with the 'chastened sublimity' of desolate and uninhabited ones.

It may be argued that Hardy's own cultural history is rather out of date; the
Vale of Tempe, the imaginary landscape of Claude and neo-classicism, was long

[19] For 'Plan X' see Raymond Williams, *Towards 2000*. Harmondsworth: Penguin,
1983. 243–69.

[20] Thomas Hardy. *The Return of the Native*. Ed. George Woodcock. London: Penguin,
1978. 54–5.

since superseded in the tourist itinerary even when he wrote those lines; though he was surely right to say that neither Egdon nor the 'sand-dunes of Scheveningen' featured much upon it either. Moreover, the landscape that he evoked in the account of Egdon Heath no longer existed, already undergoing the process of being ploughed, on the one hand, and forested on the other, when he wrote the 1895 preface to the novel:

> Under the general name of 'Egdon Heath', which has been given to the sombre scene of the story, are united or typified heaths of various real names, to the number of at least a dozen; these being virtually one in character and aspect, though their original unity, or partial unity, is now somewhat disguised by intrusive strips and slices brought under the plough with varying degrees of success, or planted to woodland. (49)

Those strips and slices have now all joined up; I quote from the artist Gordon Beningfield, who wrote in the early 1980s in the following terms:

> The county has suffered terribly from forestry and farming. Heathland, which was such an important element in the landscape of Dorset and consequently in Hardy's novels, has largely been ploughed up or turned into lifeless forests of Christmas trees by the Forestry Commission. When you look behind Hardy's birthplace in Higher Bockhampton hoping to see the heathland that was the inspiration for Egdon Heath in the novels, you see nothing but dreary rows of conifers.[21]

The most significant intervening history, however, which makes our relationship to landscape so differ from Hardy's anticipation of it, is our consciousness of the ecological catastrophe that is unfolding around us. I am not sure about the sand-dunes of Scheveningen; but certainly it is impossible to visit the Alps without being aware of the disastrous effects of global warming, and not merely in reducing the pleasures of those tourists who seek not so much chastened sublimity as ski slopes. In 2003, for the first time ever, Mont Blanc was closed to climbers throughout the summer because the non-stop sunshine made the snow, which gives the mountain its name, permanently liable to avalanches. The glacier at Chamonix – the Mer de Glace admired by Coleridge and Shelley among others – is in near terminal retreat. Egdon Heath has disappeared, and its sublime counterparts in Europe are increasingly unavailable to lead to thoughts of humanity's maturity. The future of humanity that they suggest is even bleaker than that heroic tragism of Hardy's for which he anticipated that these landscapes would provide an affinity.

Which brings me to my final example, from John Ruskin – another admirer of Chamonix and Mont Blanc, for whom indeed the vision of the snow-capped mountain was a vision of and intimation of Paradise. But here is a moment, from *Unto this Last*, when Ruskin, confronting the transformation and the destruction of

---

[21]   Gordon Beningfield. *Hardy Country*. London: Allen Lane, 1983. 16

the English landscape in the nineteenth century, nevertheless confidently assumes a different future for other portions of humanity:

> All England may, if it so chooses, become one manufacturing town; and Englishmen, sacrificing themselves to the good of general humanity, may live diminished lives in the midst of noise, of darkness, and of deadly exhalation. But the world cannot become a factory, nor a mine. No amount of ingenuity will ever make iron digestible by the million, nor substitute hydrogen for wine. Neither the avarice nor the rage of men will ever feed them; and however the apple of Sodom and the grape of Gomorrah may spread their table for a time with dainties of ashes, and nectar of asps,– so long as men live by bread, the far away valleys must laugh as they are covered with the gold of God, and the shouts of His happy multitudes ring round the winepress and the well.[22]

It is impossible to read this now without a terrible consciousness of the intervening history which has both confirmed and disconfirmed Ruskin's prediction here. The prospect of 'all England' becoming a factory or a mine has been extended to the world at large, in precisely the way that Ruskin said it could not. But then he was right to insist on the ultimate unsustainability of such a future – only he was wrong again to underestimate the 'avarice' and the 'rage' of men in preventing them from realising their own worst ambitions. Doubtless different readers will wish to give different names to the economic and political forces which have made greed and anger into active social powers. The whole tradition which Ruskin and Morris represent, and the ways that they speak to our current environmental concerns, are discussed more fully in subsequent chapters.

In the very next paragraph after the one quoted, Ruskin compounds the error of his optimism by asserting that neither have we to fear the spread of intensive agriculture, for men will realise the necessity of the presence of wildlife to make the landscape wholly attractive. This assertion too has its own melancholy, as the briefest Google search under the term 'Sixth Extinction' will make abundantly clear. But rather than concluding on this pessimistic note – that the intervening history has in many ways confounded the best hopes of the nineteenth century, to surround its writing with a particular pathos – I wish to revert to my sense of there being a dialogue between then and now. It is not that Ruskin's hopes have been confounded, though they partly have been, but that they remain to challenge us into recognising that history might have been, and still might be, otherwise. The effect of reading with hindsight need not be to enforce on us a sense of our own inevitably greater insight, derived from our lucky (or unlucky) posteriority. Rather it can remind us of the contingency of history, and that particular histories which have shaped our readings in one direction, can be developed in differing directions to shape them in yet unanticipated ways. This ambivalence is explored more fully below.

---

[22]   John Ruskin. *'Unto This Last'*, *The Works of Ruskin*. Ed. E.T. Cook and Alexander Wedderburn. Vol. 17. London: George Allen, 1905. 110.

Chapter 3
The Mill on the Floss and the
Social Space of Hindsight

I

In the previous chapter we considered how nineteenth-century anticipations of the future, and their various realizations and frustrations, dramatise the links that connect us to that recent history, and how our own position in relation to that history is inevitably created by hindsight. In considering the nineteenth-century novel, obviously live and accessible connections and identifications are still in place which make the canonical texts available to contemporary readers, and put in play the oscillations of hindsight, as it both reveals more clearly that past social and personal history, and demands a reading practice that resists its too-insistent common sense. Multiple social and cultural histories both link us to these texts and divide us from them; in this chapter I consider especially *The Mill on the Floss* as a novel which both offers strong grounds for those contemporary readerly identifications and also frustrates and challenges them.

It is worth reminding ourselves that *The Mill on the Floss* is itself a historical novel, set in the 1820s and 30s some thirty or more years before its publication in 1860. Maggie and Tom's childhoods, to which a large portion of the novel is devoted, occur before the onset of 'reform' in the early 1830s, a historical moment which clearly marks a watershed in George Eliot's historical consciousness. The writer of the novel looks back to that earlier period initially under the sign of intense personal reminiscence, in the opening chapter 'Outside Dorlcote Mill'; however, throughout the subsequent novel the writer's narrative position repeatedly and explicitly reminds us of the historical distance which divides us from the world of the characters. This is describable in the most evident formal terms: 'narrator' and original reader share the same historical space, from which vantage point they look back upon the now distant world of the characters. Many of the novel's basic rhetorical strategies, of solidarity and irony, emerge from this fundamental premise; these are the formal terms through which the social history of provincial England gets to be represented.

The following passage, for example, describes uncle Pullet's surprise at Mr Tulliver's announcement that he is going to send Tom away to be educated by a clergyman:

> As for uncle Pullet, he could hardly have been more thoroughly obfuscated if
> Mr Tulliver had said that he was going to send Tom to the Lord Chancellor: for
> uncle Pullet belonged to that extinct class of British yeomen who dressed in
> good broadcloth, paid high rates and taxes, went to church, and ate a particularly

good dinner on Sunday, without dreaming that the British constitution in Church
and State had a traceable origin any more than the solar system and the fixed
stars. ... I know it is difficult for people in these instructed times to believe in
uncle Pullet's ignorance; but let them reflect on the remarkable results of a great
natural faculty under favouring circumstances. And uncle Pullet had a great
natural faculty for ignorance.[1]

The most visible sign of the narrator's and reader's historical distance from the
characters in a passage such as this is the change of tense: uncle Pullet and the
'extinct class of British yeomen' exist in the past tense; the narrator and her readers
exist in the present. This permits some partial ironies; that sentence alluding to
'these instructed times', for example, is partially ironic, and of course allows
for the possibility that people may be equally ignorant in their own way even in
this age of enlightenment, the early 1860s. Nevertheless, the historical distance
is also what allows the narrator to place uncle Pullet as socially and historically
typical; he is an example of that 'extinct class of British yeomen' who existed
before the age of reform, and whose manners and political opinions have now
been decisively superseded. Behind this partially ironic and comic paragraph
lies a whole historical sociology or anthropology; in it, the knowledgeable or
intellectually instructed reader will be able to detect, perhaps, the writer of the
Westminster Review article on Riehl's *Natural History of German Life* which had
offered a way of understanding the ingrained mentality of the pre-modern social
strata of the peasantry.[2]

But it is also not difficult to see that this historical distance is simultaneously
a social distance; what permits this fundamental formal gesture is the narrator's
social separation from the world that the novel addresses. In the passage concerning
uncle Pullet it would be possible to describe the genre permitted by this social
distance as comedy; elsewhere in the novel a more hostile 'natural history' or
anthropology takes the novel out of the realms of comedy and into something
more like satire:

> You could not live among such people; you are stifled for want of an outlet
> towards something beautiful, great, or noble: you are irritated with these dull
> men and women, as a kind of population out of keeping with the earth on which
> they live – with this rich plain where the great river flows for ever onward and
> links the small pulse of the old English town with the beatings of the world's
> mighty heart. A vigorous superstition that lashes its gods or lashes its own back,
> seems to be more congruous with the mystery of the human lot, than the mental
> condition of these emmet-like Dodsons and Tullivers. (362–3)

---

[1]   George Eliot. *The Mill on the Floss*. Ed. A.S. Byatt. Harmondsworth: Penguin,
1982. 127.

[2]   George Eliot. 'The Natural History of German Life'. *Selected Essays, Poems and
Other Writings*, Ed. A.S. Byatt and Nicholas Warren. London: Penguin, 1990. 107–39.

The irony of 'these instructed times' is scarcely present here; the direct address to the reader which begins this extract seems to me to be less predicated on a willingness to admit that perhaps things have not entirely changed between then and now. The formal space shared by narrator and reader is here constructed not merely to look back to the past of the Dodsons and the Tullivers – it also permits them to be seen as 'emmet-like' (ant-like). At its most extreme, then, the potential comedy generated by historical distance can mutate into an uncomfortable social contempt for the world which the novel sets out to reconstruct.

But this is not the only, perhaps not even the predominant gesture of the novel, even towards those characters which here appear as 'emmet-like'. Elsewhere in the novel those same characters can become the occasion for invitations to sympathetic identification across the lines of historical and social distance. This is most powerfully done in relation to Mr Tulliver's 'downfall'; though 'nothing more than a superior miller and maltster', his life is capable of rising to the dignity of tragedy. So the invitations that the narrator makes to the reader, in viewing the characters or finding the appropriate generic register for them, can vary widely, and turn on the processes of identification and repudiation ('emmet-like') which follow from the internally differentiated historical distance upon which the novel is premised.

The Mill on the Floss, then, relies upon shifting identifications which are the inevitable ground of our reading the literature of the past, as, in the most abstract terms, such identifications depend upon the play of sameness and difference. But the socially-specific nature of those uncertain readerly investments – to be blunt, their class-defined nature – form the reading of this novel, in so far as our own critical reading occupies the same social space to which George Eliot's narrator invites the original reader to inhabit. One of the predominant social histories which connect us with this novel – the Gadamerian ground which permits us to make sense of it, but also predisposes us to make sense of it in certain ways – is that history which has continued to align education with social distance from the 'provincial' and the lower classes. This is the history which Raymond Williams traced so powerfully in *The English Novel from Dickens to Lawrence* (1970). Such an alignment is especially visible, for example, in Virginia Woolf's largely sympathetic and, for her period, untypically laudatory account of her predecessor novelist, in *The Common Reader*.[3] Commenting on George Eliot's life as it was known to her through Cross's biography, she writes as follows:

> The first volume of her life is a singularly depressing record. In it we see her raising herself with groans and struggles from the intolerable boredom of petty provincial society (her father had risen in the world and become more middle

---

[3] For a very positive account of Virginia Woolf's criticism of George Eliot, especially in the light of extraordinarily hostile late nineteenth-century and early twentieth-century critical opinions, see J. Russell Perkin. *A Reception-History of George Eliot's Fiction.* Ann Arbor: U.M.I. Research Press, 1990.

class, but less picturesque) to be the assistant editor of a highly intellectual London review, and the esteemed companion of Herbert Spencer.[4]

Even this formulation is interesting, allotting the 'picturesque' to the same side of the equation which is also described as the 'intolerable boredom of petty provincial life'. But this not-so-coded social judgement leads inevitably to cognate aesthetic judgements:

> Her sympathies are with the everyday lot, and play most happily in dwelling upon the homespun of ordinary joys and sorrows. She has none of that romantic intensity which is connected with a sense of one's own individuality, unsated and unsubdued, cutting its shape sharply upon the background of the world. What were the loves and sorrows of a snuffy old clergyman, dreaming over his whisky, to the fiery egotism of Jane Eyre? The beauty of those first books, *Scenes of Clerical Life*, *Adam Bede*, *The Mill on the Floss*, is very great. It is impossible to estimate the merit of the Poysers, the Dodsons, the Gilfils, the Bartons, and the rest with all their surroundings and dependencies, because they have put on flesh and blood and we move among them, now bored, now sympathetic, but always with that unquestioning acceptance of all that they say and do, which we accord to the great originals only. (199–200)

George Eliot's success as a novelist in these early novels, in this paradigmatic account, is premised upon her earlier escape from precisely the class which here figures as having the unquestioned plausibility of 'great originals'. Woolf goes so far as to adopt the very vocabulary of 'sympathy' and 'ordinary joys and sorrows' which characterises Eliot's own account of her artistic project in one of its most important aspects, as when she writes that 'the greatest benefit that we owe to the artist, whether painter, poet, or novelist, is the extension of our sympathies'.[5] The contrast with Charlotte Brontë is also highly significant; Jane Eyre and Maggie Tulliver have been the two female heroines from the nineteenth-century novel in English around whom intense debates about their 'unsated and unsubdued' desires have swirled most persistently. Woolf in fact is most uncomfortable with the representation of Maggie Tulliver, precisely because she is the figure who is allowed at least a partial progression from the picturesque class to which her family belongs, with her all-too-temporary entry into the drawing-rooms of St Oggs. George Eliot's scathing remarks on 'good society' (' … has its claret and its velvet carpets, its dinner-engagements six weeks deep,' etc [385]), simply make Woolf uncomfortable; where Eliot attempts to explain Maggie's new-found religious enthusiasm by the 'emphasis of want' (385), Woolf sees social gaucherie and resentment:

> There is no trace of humour or insight there, but only the vindictiveness of a grudge which we feel to be personal in its origin. But terrible as the complexity

4   Virginia Woolf. *Collected Essays*. Vol. 1. London: The Hogarth Press, 1966. 198.
5   George Eliot. 'The Natural History of German Life'. 111.

of our social system is in its demands upon the sympathy and discernment of
a novelist straying across the boundaries, Maggie Tulliver did worse than drag
George Eliot from her natural surroundings. She insisted upon the introduction
of the great emotional scene ... (201–2)

In short, Woolf is entirely attuned to the class-alignments of Eliot's writing, and
makes them the basis of her own criticism, though with less willingness than
Eliot herself to allow for the resentment and anger that are generated by what
she concedes is the 'complexity of our social system'. The terms of her criticism
shadow, however imperfectly, the terms in which the novel invites itself to be read,
and the ground of this repetition is the continuing social history which links the
1920s to the 1860s.

This is a history which has persisted into the twenty-first century, most visibly
in the variety of liberal readings of the novel which are premised upon the narrow,
constricting or coercive nature of provincial society, conceived as the background
against which the foregrounded figures of Tom and Maggie, or more usually
Maggie alone, stand proud ('individuality . . . cutting its shape sharply against the
background of the world', in Virginia Woolf's formulation). Before considering
these liberal readings, however, we need also to recognise the inevitable allusion to
George Eliot's own life which the social history that underlies the novel provokes.
The complex matters of the writerly and readerly investment in Maggie's and
Tom's history, their relationship to their 'environment', and the paradoxes and
frustrations associated with the novel's ending, all point beyond the novel itself
to a 'George Eliot' already imperfectly protected by her pseudonym by the time
of the novel's publication. The personal history invoked by Woolf, however
unsympathetic her formulation of it, is indeed the social ground which permits the
metropolitan intellectual to write the natural history of the picturesque and petty
provincial world of the early novels. The social history of St Oggs can only be
written at a geographical distance, and the movement, almost inevitably, is to the
metropolitan centre in London.

However, what Woolf's brief account of George Eliot's life does not foreground,
and yet what seems overwhelmingly obvious to readers eighty or so years later, is
the remarkable nature of Marian Evans's life-story as a woman. Still more when
she discusses Maggie Tulliver, Woolf's embarrassment is provoked by matters of
class and then 'romance'; gender figures in her analysis at most in subordinate
ways. Yet the most striking feature of discussions of *The Mill on the Floss* over
the last thirty-five years has been the absolute centrality of questions of gender in
accounts of the novel. Feminism has become the primary lens through which the
novel is viewed, the Gadamerian ground which, we can now see, has all along
linked us to the narratives which the novel recounts. J. Russell Perkin, indeed,
has argued that *The Mill on the Floss* has been a principal text through which
questions of feminism have been discussed in criticism.[6] We might add that, as in

---

[6]   J. Russell Perkin. *A Reception-History of George Eliot's Fiction*. 141.

Woolf's piece, Maggie's story is almost inevitably twinned with that of Jane Eyre; the rich subsequent history of rewriting of Charlotte Brontë's novel (*Rebecca; The Wide Sargasso Sea*), in addition to the intrinsic power of Jane's story, has made this latter novel a still more salient text for feminist criticism, and one whose very different narrative trajectory makes it an almost inevitable pairing for *The Mill on the Floss*.[7] The concentration on Maggie's story in the novel, and the particular investment in its outcome, are perhaps inevitable consequence of this necessary and historically determined discovery and rediscovery of the 'Woman Question' in George Eliot's fiction.

The peculiarly intense character of this contemporary criticism, which has adopted widely varying positions in relation to the novel, would not have occurred, it is safe to say, without the initial powerful identification, above all with Maggie, that the novel provokes. Maggie's various acts of renunciation and her defeat at the end of the novel – whatever way one assesses it, she's defeated – while they are indeed exemplary, are not matters of inert cultural history, as one might say, for example, of the contemporary usages of Coventry Patmore's poem *The Angel in the House* (repudiated without being read), or of the succession of self-sacrificing heroines in Charlotte Mary Yonge's novels. The canonical account of such an identificatory reading occurs in Simone de Beauvoir's *Memoirs of a Dutiful Daughter* (1958):

> I read it in English, at Meyrignac, lying on the mossy floor of a chestnut plantation. Maggie Tulliver, like myself, was torn between others and herself: I recognized myself in her. ... It was when she went back to the old mill, when she was misunderstood, calumniated, and abandoned by everyone that I felt my heart blaze with sympathy for her. I wept over her sorry fate for hours. The others condemned her because she was superior to them; I resembled her, and henceforward I saw my isolation not as a proof of infamy but as a sign of my uniqueness.[8]

It is because the novel is capable of provoking such intense identifications, and yet concludes by frustrating them, that it now provides both the invitation and the provocation to contemporary readings in which questions of gender are central.

If it is true that feminism makes salient what has always been one of the principal ways in which the novel has been understood, and alerts us to the gendered ground underlying those primitive acts of identification upon which the power of the novel depends, then what is remarkable is that questions of gender should have been so absent from the various efforts at canonical revaluation of George Eliot in the 1940s through to the 1960s. Equally striking is the renewed salience

---

[7]　For a striking account of the critical history of Jane Eyre, and its centrality to feminist debates, see Cora Kaplan, *Victoriana: Histories, Fictions, Criticism*. Edinburgh: Edinburgh University Press, 2007.

[8]　Simone de Beauvoir. *Memoirs of a Dutiful Daughter*. Trans. James Kirkup. Harmondsworth: Penguin Books, 1963. 140.

of the 'Woman Question' in the novel itself in our readings of it, reminding us that the novel was written in a context of prolonged debate about gender in the 1840s and 1850s. Previously Mr Tulliver's views on women – "'a woman's no business wi' being so clever; it'll turn to trouble, I doubt'" (66) – might have been seen as further evidence of his picturesqueness; in one early phase of feminist criticism, by contrast, it fitted into a wider reading of the novel in which sexist norms are rightly seen as prevalent in the society of St Oggs.[9] Still more visible now are the debates about gender in relation to education which are explicitly dramatised in relation to the schooling Maggie and Tom receive at the Rev Mr Stelling's. In one respect George Eliot provides an exemplary account of the false ideas which lead Mr Tulliver and the Rev Stelling to give priority to Tom's education over Maggie's, and to the equally false ideas which lead the pedagogue to force-feed Tom with a traditional classical education to which he is not suited, and to slight Maggie's evidently apter efforts in the same direction. The novel not only dramatises Eliot's progressive ideas on education here (cognate with those of Herbert Spencer); it also powerfully evokes Maggie's sense of exclusion – her actual exclusion, indeed – from one of the legitimating means of authority in her social world. These ideas of education are perhaps surprisingly libertarian; they hark back ultimately to Rousseau and the belief that children should be allowed and encouraged to follow their own bent.[10] Yet it is also clear that, once having perceived the importance of these notions in the novel in relation to debates over the comparative education of men and women, the novel does not conclude from them positions with which contemporary feminism (itself by no means monolithic) will necessarily be entirely comfortable. In particular, the 'natural bents' of Maggie and Tom point them towards, respectively, the learning of languages, and the successful measuring and taming of the physical world: alignments pretty much cognate with traditional expectations of the innate capacities of girls and boys, however much they challenge Tom and Mr Stelling ('Girls can pick up a little of everything, I daresay ... They've a great deal of superficial cleverness; but they couldn't go far into anything. They're quick and shallow.' [158]). So we have here an exemplary sequence, in which the concerns of the contemporary moment turn us back to a text from the past in a way which makes features of that past text more salient, but in the same gesture we discover that those features both confirm and disconfirm the expectations that led to our renewed attention.

---

[9]   Exemplary instance: Elizabeth Ermarth. 'Maggie Tulliver's Long Suicide.' *Studies in English Literature*, 14 (1974): 587–601.

[10]   See for George Eliot's and Herbert Spencer's affiliations to Rousseau on the matter of education, William Myers, *The Teaching of George Eliot*. Leicester: Leicester University Press, 1984; and Simon Dentith, 'George Eliot, Rousseau, and the Discipline of Natural Consequences.' Ed. Francis O'Gorman and Katherine Turner. *The Victorians and the Eighteenth Century: Reassessing the Tradition*. Aldershot and Burlington VT: Ashgate, 2004. 41–56.

II

For all the internal disagreements, successive phases, and diverse theoretical and political alignments of feminist criticism since the 1970s, a version of liberal feminism has, at the beginning of the twenty-first century, established itself as a kind of common sense. The central narrative of this liberal feminism, in which the heroine emerges from a repressive background to establish or realise her own successful identity, is broadly consonant with the social space of the novel already sketched. The failure of *The Mill on the Floss* is to provide a narrative of escape from 'petty provincial' life; whether it be because of the narrative of renunciation which the novel appears to endorse, or because of the fundamentally inauthentic (because arbitrary) ending to the novel, it stands as challenge to one version of contemporary common sense. The remainder of this chapter is concerned with considering the value of this challenge: I seek to put in play, in fact, the capacity of the novel to speak back to the reductive power of hindsight which thinks that it can fully explain and 'place' the novel.

Before doing so, however, we need to pause to consider the peculiar rhetorical economy of *The Mill on the Floss*, which is fundamental to assessing the way in which it stages the debates, character identifications, and narrative procedures and resolutions, which permit us now to reach any judgments concerning it. It is true that the nineteenth-century novel in general, the 'large loose baggy monster' of Henry James's partly affectionate description, is characteristically rhetorically diverse: it dramatises multiple narratives, permits contradictory dogmatic formulations, and concludes in ways which, sometimes naively and sometimes self-consciously, only one-sidedly resolve the personal and ideological possibilities that have been staged.[11] But in *The Mill on the Floss* these tensions are especially visible, and are more likely than in most cases to provoke wholly conflicting interpretations among its readers. Even before the arrival of feminist criticism in the 1970s, John Hagan had prefaced his interpretation of the novel by an account of the contradictory assessments of Maggie's acts of renunciation that already seemed so central to making sense of it.[12] If there are conflicting possibilities already in the novel, how is that possible and how are they realised?

One way of describing the rhetorical economy of the novel is to start by recognising that it emerges from two simultaneous and contradictory investments on George Eliot's part. On the one hand, there is a commitment to an ethic of renunciation, to a dramatisation of moral growth from egoism to altruism, to the whole Positivist and Feuerbachian assimilation of religious to humanist categories. On the other hand, there is an investment, however displaced or subordinated, in Maggie's growth, in the satisfaction of her legitimate needs, cultural and sexual

---

[11]   The classic account of the 'multiplot novel' remains Peter K. Garrett, *The Victorian Multiplot Novel: Studies in Dialogical Form*. New Haven: Yale University Press, 1980.

[12]   John Hagan. 'A Reinterpretation of *The Mill on the Floss*'. PMLA 87.1 (1972): 53–63.

– in short in the possibility of a realised *bildung* for her, as one appears to be promised to Tom. At the level of 'intention', certainly – that is, at the level of explicit authorial belief and narratorial commentary – the former commitment is undoubtedly primary; at the level of visceral narrative interest and consequent readerly identification, it is surely the latter which predominates and productively unbalances the novel – as Simone de Beauvoir's memoir of her adolescent reading testifies, in its triumphant identification with the calumniated Maggie. I am not therefore attempting to adjudicate between these two contradictory emphases in the book, to produce yet another interpretation, but rather to indicate the unstable nature of the novel's rhetorical economy and its capacity to accommodate differing subsequent readerly demands of it.

We have already encountered this instability in relation to the novel's representation of the Dodsons and the Tullivers, appearing at one level as 'emmet-like' and elsewhere, in Mr Tulliver's case, as the genuinely tragic actor who has to confront the reality that he has been 'thoroughly defeated and must begin life anew' (275). This instability is indeed everywhere apparent in the novel. Eliot wishes to insist on the essential honesty and value of the class from which she herself was drawn, while at the same time being led into comical, not to say contemptuous, descriptions of them. She wishes to insist on 'that sense of honour and rectitude which was a proud tradition in such families – a tradition which has been the salt of our provincial society' (197). Yet it is also not surprising – inevitable, in fact – that the most contemptuous description, with which I have had so much difficulty, immediately precedes the following paragraph:

> . . . these emmet-like Dodsons and Tullivers.
> I share with you this sense of oppressive narrowness, but it is necessary that we should feel it, if we care to understand how it acted on the lives of Tom and Maggie – how it has acted on young natures in many generations, that in the onward tendency of human things have risen above the mental level of the generation before them, to which they have been nevertheless tied by the strongest fibres of their hearts. (363)

In short, the most hostile account of the 'picturesque' classes in the novel is justified as providing a sense of the background against which the foregrounded figures of Tom and Maggie need to be seen – though the excerpt does end with the moderating acknowledgement of the 'ties that bind', the 'strongest fibres of their hearts' (note the superlative) which link Maggie and Tom back to the very 'oppressive narrowness' which at the same time they have to transcend.

In this account Tom and Maggie appear together, equivalent protagonists of a double *bildung* which promises no less than the social and moral renewal of the human race. But this is not characteristically how the novel presents them, nor does it describe the relative dispositions of narrative affect within it. Simone de Beauvoir was entirely right to seize on the calumniated Maggie, spurned above all and most hatefully by her brother, as the moment in the novel which invites most strongly the wounded and indignant identification of the reader. It is the moment at which the narrative investment in the figure of Maggie is most intense, when her rightness *against the world* is most visible to the reader. *Our* subsequent investment in Maggie's narrative, as victim of, and partial rebel against the power of the law and of patriarchy, is most vividly established at this moment in the narrative.

The novel contains, then, not merely multiple stories, like any nineteenth-century 'multiplot novel', but also diverse and even contradictory ways of framing and explicating these stories. This has been well described by Susan Fraiman in her account of the novel within the context of the *bildungsroman*, and the possibility of female versions of it. In her reading of *The Mill on the Floss*, there is both competition *between* different versions of the *bildung*, and *within* one predominating narrative: there is Tom's story, an authentic *bildungsroman*, which is nevertheless shunted off to one side by Maggie's story which attempts to enter the genre but is continually rebuffed and slips back into 'something resembling the gothic.' But 'revising an earlier precept, I am now proposing that the distinction between these be thought of not as the space between genres but as the space within a genre for confusion, complaint, critique, and possibly compensation regarding issues of female development.'[13] It is not merely, in other words, that the novel's conclusion fails to allow for Maggie's onward and upward development, as though it were a truncated *bildungsroman*; the novel actually dramatises the costs and frustrations of the heroine's exclusion from this possible and culturally attractive mode of personal development, in one at least of the ways in which the story is told.

Another way of describing the diverse and contradictory valuations that the novel puts into play is by adverting to its evidently dialogic quality, its willingness to put into play competing viewpoints and ideologies. At key moments in the narrative, especially concerning moments of renunciation which in one sense the narrator endorses, both of Maggie's lovers are permitted powerful formulations challenging her decisions. Philip effectively persuades Maggie after her discovery of Thomas à Kempis that her adoption of renunciation is at least a partial mistake:

> 'No one has the strength given to do what is unnatural. It is mere cowardice to seek safety in negations. No character becomes strong in that way. You will be thrown into the world some day, and then every rational satisfaction of your nature that you deny now, will assault you like a savage appetite ... It is less wrong that you should see me than that you should be committing this long suicide.' (428–9)

This is powerfully put, and indeed provokes a couple of pages of narratorial remonstrance. It is not surprising that it is the *locus classicus* for those who wish to argue for a view of the novel which sees Maggie's career of renunciation as a disastrous personal, ethical and political mistake, whether or not it is endorsed by the narrator. Stephen, equally, is allowed to articulate powerful and culturally resonant objections to Maggie's decision to return to St Oggs and her obligations after the elopement to Mudport: 'But there are ties that can't be kept by mere resolution

---

[13]   Susan Fraiman. *Unbecoming Women: British Women Writers and the Novel of Development.* New York: Columbia University Press, 1993. 121–41.

... What is outward faithfulness? Would they have thanked us for anything so hollow as constancy without love?' (602). Again this is sufficiently cogent to provoke one of Maggie's fullest articulations of the philosophy of renunciation. The novel is thus genuinely dialogic, in that it puts into play opposing viewpoints and allows them to stand as authentic expressions of character positions granted full autonomy. What makes this novel so different from the equally dialogic mode of, say, Thackeray in *Pendennis* (1848–50) – a novel which permits the extensive to and fro of competing viewpoints on a variety of topics – is that the disputes between ethical and cultural positions in *The Mill on the Floss* emerge from such deep recesses in Maggie's emotional life and therefore provoke such complex and contradictory readerly identifications.

'Dialogic' – the notion goes back, of course, to Bakhtin. But the term can be used to take analysis beyond the internal formal organisation of the novel, that is, its capacity to structure the differing voices which compete within it. These voices are themselves in dialogue with, or invoke, the multiple competing voices outside the novel, that conflict-ridden and heavily differentiated linguistic space which Bakhtin designated as 'heteroglossia'.[14] Both Philip and Stephen draw upon and give voice to positions that are live within the culture surrounding the novel, even if, in Stephen's case especially, only in an emergent and still very subordinate way – though, as we shall see, Stephen's allusion to the authenticity of their love, and the hollowness of 'constancy without love', will have a long and successful afterlife. Philip's appeal is couched in the language of contemporary liberalism in one of its strongest formulations: John Stuart Mill's, whose *On Liberty* was published in 1859 and therefore almost immediately contemporary with Eliot's novel. It is not that Philip quotes Mill directly – it is rather that his language echoes that of the tradition which Mill resumes and powerfully rearticulates. This is still more the case when, in a passage of *erlebte rede*, Philip expresses this lament about Maggie: 'the pity of it that a mind like hers should be withering in its very youth, like a young forest tree, for want of the light and space it was formed to flourish in!' (404). This is the classic language of the liberal *bildung*, in which individual development is conceived as an organic growth which should be allowed to flourish without artificial constriction; compare Mill in *On Liberty*: 'Human nature is not a machine to be built after a model, and set to do exactly the work prescribed for it, but a tree, which requires to grow and develop itself on all sides, according to the tendency of the inward forces which make it a living thing.'[15] Or still more strongly in *The Subjection of Women*, published ten years later:

---

[14]   See M.M. Bakhtin, 'Discourse in the Novel'. *The Dialogic Imagination*. Ed. Michael Holquist. Trans. Caryl Emerson. Austin: University of Texas Press, 1981. For a comparable reading of the novel as an intervention in the semiotic system contemporary to it, though drawing explicitly on Vološinov rather than Bakhtin, see José Angel García Landa 'The Chains of Semiosis: Semiotics, Marxism, and the Female Stereotypes in *The Mill on the Floss*'. *Papers in Language and Literature*, 27.1 (1991): 41–50.

[15]   John Stuart Mill. *Utilitarianism, Liberty, and Representative Government*. London: Everyman's Library, 1968. 117.

> ... but in the case of women, a hot-house and stove cultivation has always been carried on of some of the capabilities of their nature, for the benefit and pleasure of their masters. Then, ... certain products of the general vital force sprout luxuriantly and under this active nurture and watering, while other shoots from the same root, which are left outside in wintry air, with ice purposely heaped all around them, have a stunted growth, and some are burnt off with fire and disappear ...[16]

The resonance of Philip's formulations for subsequent liberal readings of the novel is therefore founded upon the already-articulate presence of liberalism in the novel, and its persistence and gathering cogency in the history that has succeeded it. In short, to move from Bakhtin to Gadamer, this liberal narrative is one of the historically-persistent grounds which link the early twenty-first century to the moment of the novel's publication.

Stephen's own version of the ethics governing his and Maggie's relationship can equally be described as liberal, and in its appeal to personal authenticity points directly to the characteristic language of Bloomsbury a couple of generations later. In fact, it is hard to overstate the importance of Bloomsbury in rewriting and repudiating the legacy of the 'Victorians' amongst the educated middle class of which Bloomsbury was a fraction, and thus in writing the script for one persistent phase in the meaning of the nineteenth century in the remainder of the twentieth. We have already encountered Virginia Woolf's engagement with George Eliot. Woolf was engaged in her own struggle with her father Leslie Stephen, whose aesthetic choices with respect to George Eliot are not hard to seek in her essay in *The Common Reader*. A cognate generational confrontation is dramatised directly in May Sinclair's *Life and Death of Harriett Frean* (1922), a novel which, without being a direct piece of 'writing back' in the manner of *Wide Sargasso Sea*, nevertheless rigorously explores the consequences for a woman of pursuing the path of renunciation attempted by Maggie. These consequences are disastrous, as the woman's niece takes some pleasure in spelling out. As a young woman, Harriett Frean rejected the advances of her friend's accepted lover, despite the fact that they were both in love with the other; a life of misery has been the consequence for all of them, including the friend to whom the lover was returned. This is the confrontation between aunt and niece; Harriett at first tells her story in the third person:

> 'I knew a girl once who might have done what you're doing, only she wouldn't. She gave the man up rather than hurt her friend. She *couldn't do anything else.*'
> 'How much was he in love with her?'
> 'I don't know *how much*. He was never in love with any other woman.'
> 'Then she was a fool. A silly fool. Didn't she think of *him*?'
> 'Didn't she think?'

---

[16] John Stuart Mill. *The Subjection of Women*. London: Everyman's Library, 1977. 238–9.

'No. She didn't. She thought of herself. Of her own moral beauty. She was
a selfish fool'
    'She asked the best and wisest man she knew, and he told her she couldn't
do anything else.'
    'The best and wisest man – oh, Lord!'
    'That was my own father, Mona, Hilton Frean.'
    'Then it was you. You and Uncle Robin and Aunt Prissie.'[17]

Mona the niece emerges here as the spokesperson for uncomfortable truths which
post-Victorian women speak back to their mothers' generation, mothers who
themselves are in thrall to the specious moral authority of their fathers. What
Harriett had thought of as a morally beautiful self-sacrifice appears in the light of
her niece's impatient common sense as self-regarding foolishness. She proceeds to
spell out the consequences with some relish: sexual misery and hysterical illness
for all concerned, the 'beneficiaries' of Harriett's sacrifice as much as Harriett
herself. At the end of the interview Mona asks, as her parting remark, '"You don't
mind my telling you the truth, do you?"' (147).

    Stephen's strategic question, 'What is outward faithfulness? Would they
have thanked us for anything so hollow as constancy without love?', has now,
in May Sinclair's novel, returned as a full-blown narrative of fruitless self-
denial, self-deception, and pointless subjugation to the law of the father. The
characteristically bourgeois liberal values of Bloomsbury here now appear to
challenge the 'Victorians' in the name of personal authenticity, sexual honesty,
and demystificatory plain speaking. I have been stressing the generational element
in this history; in a suggestive article about Eleanor Rathbone, Susan Pederson
has argued women in the 1920s often fought out their battles about the family via
their struggles with their mothers.[18] It is this generational history, in which the
'Victorians' have figured as all of our parents, that has shaped our reading of the
novel; Stephen was well ahead of the game.

    Nevertheless, neither his voice, nor Philip's, is given the final word in *The
Mill on the Floss*. Indeed, it is precisely the power of the novel to challenge back
– to resist the overwhelming common sense of the present – with which I wish to
conclude. The novel's alternative investment, in a narrative of moral growth, self-
denial, and consequent social progress, is predominantly articulated in passages of
narratorial commentary, as well as in Maggie's faltering but ultimately eloquent
attempts at justifying the positions she has reached with so much struggle. We could
start with the passage which caused Virginia Woolf such embarrassment, George
Eliot's satire on 'good society', which modulates into a defense of Maggie's new-
found religious enthusiasm, based on the 'emphasis of want' which underlies the
wider national life that supports 'good society':

---

[17]   May Sinclair. *The Life and Death of Harriett Frean*. London: Virago, 1980. 144–5.

[18]   Susan Pedersen. 'Eleanor Rathbone (1872-1946): The Victorian family under the
daughter's eye'. *After the Victorians: Private Conscience and Public Duty in Modern
Britain. Essays in memory of John Clive*. Ed. Susan Pedersen and Peter Mandler. Routledge:
London and New York, 1994. 105–25.

This wide national life is based entirely on emphasis – the emphasis of want, which urges it into all the activities necessary for the maintenance of good society and light irony: it spends its heavy years often in a chill, uncarpeted fashion amidst family discord unsoftened by long corridors. Under such circumstances there are many among its myriads of souls who have absolutely needed an emphatic belief, life in this unpleasurable shape demanding some solution even to unspeculative minds; just as you inquire into the stuffing of your couch when anything galls you there, whereas eider-down and perfect French springs excite no question. Some have an emphatic belief in alcohol, and seek their *ekstasis* or outside standing-ground in gin, but the rest require something that good society calls enthusiasm, something that will present motives in an entire absence of high prizes, something that will give patience and feed human love when the limbs ache with weariness and human looks are hard upon us – something, clearly, that lies outside personal desires, that includes resignation for ourselves and active love for what is not ourselves. Now and then that sort of enthusiasm finds a far-echoing voice that comes from an experience springing out of the deepest need. And it was being brought within the long-lingering vibrations of such a voice that Maggie, with her girl's face and unnoted sorrows, found an effort and a hope that helped her through two years of loneliness, making out a faith for herself without the aid of established authorities and appointed guides – for they were not at hand, and her need was pressing. (385–6)

The voice whose 'long-lingering vibrations' have reached Maggie is that of Thomas à Kempis; behind this passage lies an understanding of the meaning of religion in general, and Catholicism in particular, attributable to Feuerbach and Comte. But the power of the passage derives not from these relatively abstract philosophies, but from its grounding in a consciousness of the realities of class-society and poverty. Certainly the passage suggests that religious enthusiasm of the kind that has sustained Maggie springs from human need; but human need is made apparent and immediate to us here in actual not abstract human lives.[19] There is a strong investment on the narrator's part in this passage, as Virginia Woolf's repudiation of it testifies ('the vindictiveness of a grudge which we feel to be personal in its origin'); the power of the passage to provoke also indicates the continuing presence of a class politics which is still active in readings of the novel.

I am not arguing here an abstract defense of the ethics of renunciation; rather, I am contending for the rhetorical force of its enunciation in *The Mill on the Floss*, its complicated entanglement in the class politics of reading (the passage I have just quoted, after all, is all about how Maggie's religious devotion should be regarded by the reader, assuming the latter's comfortable social situation compared to the social misery which is the ground for religious enthusiasm), and thus ultimately the capacity of the novel to challenge the liberal narrative in which it is also invested.

---

[19]   Compare Marx: 'Feuerbach resolves the essence of religion into the essence of *man*. But the essence of man is no abstraction inherent in each single individual. In its reality it is the ensemble of the social relations'. Karl Marx and Frederick Engels. 'Theses on Feurbach.' *Collected Works*. Vol. 5. London: Lawrence and Wishart, 1976. 4.

Nevertheless, we can recognise that, just as in the case of Philip's language having resonances beyond the text, so too it is not hard to find cognate versions of self-denial and self-repression in the culture of the mid-nineteenth century. It is all too easy, in fact; I have only to write the word 'Victorian' and one version of that culture ('repressed'; 'hypocritical': Mona the niece in *Life and Death of Harriett Frean* was an early speaker of this language) is invoked. So to try to avoid that 'bad historicism' which repudiates the past to the past, I want to suggest that not only George Eliot but Charlotte Brontë too could provide eloquent, rhetorically powerful, and individually persuasive versions of renunciation, though they spring from very different intellectual and personal sources.

III

Jane Eyre itself is rhetorically complex, and though the investment in Jane's narrative certainly brooks fewer contradictions than in the case of *The Mill on the Floss*, they are nevertheless present, for example in the figure of Helen Burns and the powerful ethical position that she articulates. But it is Jane's narrative itself which most strongly articulates an ethic of personal integrity that leads, not to the authenticity of gratified desire, but to renunciation itself; Jane, after all, refuses to elope with Rochester after the discovery of his existing marriage, despite his pleading: 'Still indomitable was the reply: "*I* care for myself. The more solitary, the more friendless, the more unsustained I am, the more I will respect myself"'.[20] In other words, in the case of *Jane Eyre*, the very ethic of personal integrity and authenticity that drives the book forward leads also to an act of sexual renunciation on Jane's part. This is a different matter to the equally impressive, but more ambivalent, account by Lucy Snowe in *Villette* of the necessity of self-repression simply as a mode of survival:

> I did long, achingly, then and for four-and-twenty hours afterwards, for something to fetch me out of my present existence, and lead me upwards and onwards. This longing, and all of a similar kind, it was necessary to knock on the head; which I did, figuratively, after the manner of Jael to Sisera, driving a nail through their temples. Unlike Sisera, they did not die: they were but transiently stunned, and at intervals would turn on the nail with a rebellious wrench: then did the temples bleed, and the brain thrill to its core.[21]

In both these novels by Brontë, renunciation figures as a psychological necessity. In the case of Jane Eyre the necessity springs from the demands of her own personal integrity – behind her act of renunciation we can detect a Protestant vocabulary that goes back perhaps to Bunyan. In Lucy Snowe's case, by contrast,

---

[20]   Charlotte Brontë. *Jane Eyre*. Ed. Q.D. Leavis. Harmondsworth: Penguin Books, 1966. 344.

[21]   Charlotte Brontë. *Villette*. Ed. Mark Lilly. London: Penguin Books, 1985. 176.

the renunciation is figured as an extreme act of a self-damaging kind, which is nevertheless required by the pragmatics of survival. In different ways for the two heroines their situations dictate a necessary caution in the demands these women make on the world. This returns us to Maggie, and the demand she has of some doctrine or some mode of belief that will enable her to deal with her shattered life. Renunciation in all these cases is a mode of coping that is born out of desperate social circumstances.

This is a position that is scarcely likely to persuade the doubters, who could legitimately accuse it of being, at most, a kind of 'second-bestism', an accommodation with the existent which in all cases takes the unequal rewards of the world for granted. Mary Jacobus, in a now-canonical article on *The Mill on the Floss*, put the point powerfully:

> Though the fruits of patriarchal knowledge no longer seem worth the eating, can we view Thomas à Kempis as anything more than an opiate for the hunger pains of oppression? Surely not. The morality of submission and renunciation is only a sublimated version of Tom's plainspoken patriarchal prohibition, as the satanic mocker, Philip Wakem, doesn't fail to point out. Yet in the last resort, Eliot makes her heroine live and die by this inherited morality of female suffering - as if, in the economy of the text, it was necessary for Maggie to die renouncing in order for her author to release the flood of desire that is language itself.[22]

This is powerfully put, though we might retort that the whole novel is not to be summed up by considering it 'in the last resort', and that the 'flood of language' released enables many contradictory positions to the 'inherited morality of female suffering' to be articulated. It is worth spelling out two articulations of the morality of renunciation which still carry a real force.

In *Victoriana*, Cora Kaplan argues that the repeated repudiation of the 'Victorian' as the sign of sexual hypocrisy and repression – with all the contradictions, suppressed nostalgia, and libidinal investments that accompany that repudiation – is nevertheless a sign of our (twentieth/twenty-first century) sexual utopianism. Once again *The Mill on the Floss* has managed to anticipate and challenge a utopian belief that it is possible to imagine a world in which there were no conflictual erotic desires; or at least, it is possible to imagine such a world – Maggie is about to do so – but it isn't the one we inhabit. Before the failed elopement, Stephen has come to plead with Maggie while she has escaped to stay at her Aunt Moss's; as he will later in Mudport, he argues the overpowering claims of authentic desire. Maggie replies:

> 'O it is difficult – life is very difficult. It seems right to me sometimes that we should follow our strongest feeling; - but then, such feelings continually come across the ties that all our former life has made for us – the ties that have made

---

[22] Mary Jacobus. 'Men of Maxims and *The Mill on the Floss*.' *Reading Women: Essays in Feminist Criticism*. London: Methuen, 1986.

others dependent on us – and would cut them in two. If life were quite easy and simple, as it might have been in paradise, and we could always see that one being first towards whom ... I mean, if life did not make duties for us before love comes – love would be a sign that two people ought to belong to each other. But I see – I feel it is not so now: there are things we must renounce in life – some of us must resign love. Many things are difficult and dark to me – but I see one thing quite clearly – that I must not, cannot seek my own happiness by sacrificing others. Love is natural – but surely pity and faithfulness and memory are natural too. And they would live in me still, and punish me if I didn't obey them. I should be haunted by the suffering I had caused. Our love would be poisoned. Don't urge me; help me – help me, *because* I love you.' (570–71)

This seems to me to be persuasive in a different way from the earlier passage of narratorial commentary about the 'emphasis of want', largely because you can follow in it the twists and turns of a developing line of thought, which simultaneously tracks transitions of feeling. Maggie explicitly invokes the utopian, or edenic, possibility of a world in which desire would always be triumphant, in which desire and its fulfillment would always follow on from each other as they did for Adam and Eve. This is not a speech that demonises sexual desire, either in men or women – indeed one of the strengths of the book is the explicitness with which it treats Maggie's and Stephen's physical attraction to each other, which is clearly mutual and frequently implied, in fact imagined explicitly, in the Sixth Book of the novel, 'The Great Temptation'. However (and here I am merely following the natural concessions and transitions of the passage) Maggie does not allow the naturalness of 'love' to override other feelings: 'Love is natural – but surely pity and faithfulness and memory are natural too'. The power of the passage (and of the book more generally) is that it does not present Maggie's dilemma as readily soluble, but as one whose resolution is always going to be a matter of intense struggle, suffering and pathos: 'there are things we must renounce in life – some of us must resign love'. This is perhaps an extreme conclusion to draw from her current entanglement, in which the desire she feels for Stephen cuts across her previous commitments both to Lucy and to Philip. Nevertheless the passage powerfully articulates the conflicting currents of feeling that animate the moral dilemma that Maggie is enduring, and in doing so it offers a rejoinder to our contemporary sexual utopianism which, in one version at least, cuts across these dilemmas too readily.

But even this way of considering the matter is to consider it too abstractly as a moral dilemma to which there are contradictory possible resolutions. One of the characteristics of *The Mill on the Floss*, which it shares with other nineteenth-century realist novels, is that all such dilemmas are seen to be embedded in a network of social relationships; vice-versa, social relationships consist of the totality of individually-negotiated transactions between people. In other words, our current, twenty-first-century engagement with the novel is necessarily entwined with the very form of the nineteenth-century realist novel itself, what the form can show, and its social and historical conditions of possibility. George

Eliot conceives of these in particular ways, and her emphases vary at different stages of her writing career; thus in this earlier novel she has not articulated these interweaved individual lives as the 'web' which metaphorically joins all the actors of the provincial town of Middlemarch together. In *The Mill on the Floss*, by contrast, the resolution of her dilemma undertaken by Maggie is conceived as a moral advance for provincial society, in a Positivist spirit; at the same time this moral advance cannot be recognized by the society which it seeks to transform, and Maggie and Tom die in an impasse for which no other resolution can be imagined. Nevertheless, the striking ambition of her realism in both novels is to be able to contemplate both the details of individual lives in all their complexity and minutiae, while retaining a sense of the overall transitions of the society which these individuals make up. This too is to put the matter too simply; rather we should say that there is a synthesis in the best nineteenth-century realist novels, of which this is one, in which, as in the hermeneutic circle, detail cannot be understood without the totality, and the totality cannot be understood without the detail, in a benign circularity in which no axis of comprehension has priority.

This synthesis has been widely described.[23] The point of invoking it here under the sign of hindsight is to ask what value it can have, in the twenty-first century, to name this now classical form. Certainly it cannot be, in the manner of Lukacs, to hope for a revival of the form against the current of one hundred and twenty years of accumulated social and aesthetic history; nor can a newly-achieved realist synthesis of the classical kind be achieved by an effort of will, as Raymond Williams appears to suggest in his fine discussion of realism in *The Long Revolution*, though the formal complexity of his own little-read realist novels does suggest something of the torsions consequent upon any contemporary realist ambitions. Jeannette Winterson has suggested as an axiom that we 'should read the Victorians, but not attempt to write like them'. This modernist or post-modernist injunction may have some aesthetic force, but it fails to suggest on its own quite why it is impossible to write like the Victorians.

The reason, as a properly Lukacsian analysis readily suggests, is that social transformations since the mid-nineteenth century when Eliot wrote *The Mill on the Floss* have made that realist synthesis impossible – as perhaps they already had by the 1920s when Virginia Woolf was writing and when Lukacs began to polemicise against modernism. In particular, the national and provincial character of British society in the nineteenth century, though always of course underpinned by a vast empire, made the social relationships which Eliot dramatises visible within the confines of a small town – even the international trade relations, visibly described in the second sentence of the novel:

---

[23]   See, for example, Simon Dentith, 'Realist Synthesis in the Nineteenth-Century Novel: "That unity which lies in the selection of our keenest consciousness".' *Adventures in Realism*. Ed. Matthew Beaumont. Oxford: Blackwell, 2007. 33–49. This article provides references to the writings of Raymond Williams and Georg Lukacs who provide the twentieth century's most convincing accounts of nineteenth-century realism.

On this mighty tide the black ships – laden with the fresh-scented fir-planks, with rounded sacks of oil-bearing seed, or with the dark glitter of coal – are borne along to the town of St Ogg's, which shows its aged, fluted red roofs and the broad gables of its wharves between the low wooded hill and the river bank, tinging the water with a soft purple hue under the transient glance of this February sun. (53)

So it is not simply a matter of a set of dramatisable face-to-face relationships, though these are significant, but of a whole set of economic and social links and pressures which Eliot has the ambition to capture and for which realism of the kind she practices gives her the technical means. We have seen that her version of this realism is inflected by class and gender perspectives which are built into the formal fabric of the novel, and that an implicit social geography maps St Ogg's in relation to an unnamed cosmopolitan centre, London, which is nonetheless a condition of possibility for the novel. However, these inevitable class and gender distortions, especially visible to us in the early twenty-first century, should not obscure what the whole novel makes visible, an affectively–charged map of social relations caught in their totality, which poses a social and aesthetic challenge to us, not to reproduce the novel's aesthetic strategies, but to find our own. These might make visible, in the necessarily transformed economic and social conditions of the present, the social relations of the present world caught in their individual immediacy, and the grand global economic forces which are tearing apart the world and remaking it, both for good and evil, before our bewildered eyes.

To conclude, then, I have been emphasising the persuasiveness of elements of *The Mill on the Floss* because, if novels are arguments, they proceed by means which are not merely argumentative. For some of its readers at the time of its publication, the provocation of the novel was its too sympathetic identification with the satisfactions available to clever young women like Maggie. I have been arguing that its value now in part lies in the challenge it provides to our too-ready assumption of the liberal narrative which 'cut[s] its shape sharply upon the background of the world'. The continuing force of the novel depends upon the multiple ways in which its constructions of the world – of class and of gender, above all – are cognate with those of its readers now, and are indeed premised upon actual social-historical continuities and transformations. Looking back upon the novel now we see it new, yet we see attitudes and positions which were always there at least *in potentia*, and which the subsequent history – of Bloomsbury, and of feminism – have now made more salient. But that does not mean that we only see what we project, and the capacity of the novel to provoke us now, perhaps in the opposite way to the provocations it offered to its contemporaries, suggests how its capacity to speak to us in the present is dependent upon its emergence from that past which is and is not our own. Finally, and inextricable from these unavoidable negotiations as we read in the present, there is the very realism of the novel itself, founded upon a set of social relations which have been partly transformed, but which the form could make visible and which, in some transformed sense, we now need in order to make visible the altogether more opaque social relations of the present world.

Chapter 4
'If I had known then, what I knew long afterwards! –':
David Copperfield and the Ambivalence of Hindsight

I

One conclusion to be drawn from our discussion of *The Mill on the Floss* is that while our particular responses and judgments in relation to the many characters, incidents and dilemmas in the novel have been in part created by the complex social history that has unrolled since the publication of the novel, these judgements are necessarily inextricable from the form of the novel itself, that extraordinarily ambitious form known as the nineteenth-century realist novel with its totalising social claims. This is true with still greater force in relation to *David Copperfield*, a remarkable attempt at holding together the multifarious details of a life in the context of a fully realised social world. The form itself is the carrier of the power of the nineteenth century to answer back in ways which challenge the ambitions and conditions of our own social and aesthetic situation. But more than this – still more than *The Mill on the Floss*, central site, as we have seen, of contentions about feminism and the whole consideration of gender in the nineteenth century – *David Copperfield* comes bearing now an extraordinary weight of subsequent reading, analysis, adaptation, popular assimilation, schoolroom acquaintance, and writing back. Second only to Shakespeare, Dickens has become a world writer, and *David Copperfield* is perhaps his most well-known book. From all this vast possible subsequent reading history, I choose just one tiny anecdote to illustrate his possible force. A woman who had been brought up in an especially bleak part of the Soviet Union in the 1940s and 50s told me this: 'Dickens', she recounted, 'Dickens was our friend'.

It may seem that the autobiographical character of *David Copperfield* (1849–50) – or at least, the fact that it is written in the first person – should limit the variety and character of the material which it contains. Certainly by comparison with the other great 'multi-plot novels' of the mid-nineteenth century, including those by Thackeray and George Eliot as much as by Dickens himself, the unifying effect of the single perspective undoubtedly appears to simplify the complex and potentially contradictory material that can be included in, say, *Bleak House* (1852–53) or *The Newcomes* (1853–55). Yet even so it is possible to recognise real generic diversity within this unifying perspective. The novel manages to contain, within the apparent confines of David's story (whether or not we describe this as a *bildungsroman*), an element of popular campaigning journalism in the *exposé* of the solitary system of prison discipline, an exemplary moral-sentimental tale in the story of Annie and Dr Strong, and the comic display of 'characters' – drawing on an ancient generic legacy from the drama and the novel's eighteenth-century forebears.

All these genres, and especially the central *bildung* itself, have their own histories which link them to their forebears, and which link them to us, in complex and historically determinate ways. This can be briefly indicated by reference to David's famous list of books, found in an up-stairs room, which sustained him under the tyranny of the Murdstones:

> From that blessed little room, Roderick Random, Peregrine Pickle, Humphrey Clinker, Tom Jones, The Vicar of Wakefield, Don Quixote, Gil Blas, and Robinson Crusoe, came out, a glorious host, to keep me company. They kept alive my fancy, and my hope of something beyond that place and time, – they, and the Arabian Nights, and the Tales of the Genii, – and did me no harm; for whatever harm was in some of them was not there for me; *I* knew nothing of it.[1]

The very first title in the list sufficiently demonstrates both one part of Dickens's generic inheritance and his transformation of it, for Smollett's picaresque novel (*Roderick Random*: the title is sufficient) is at once a forebear of Dickens's own first-person story and an exemplary instance of what it is not. The story of the man catapulted around the world like a tennis-ball, only to return where he began, is precisely what Dickens's story moves beyond, as the later novel insists on the significant interconnections between child and man, in a narrative which is anything but random. Yet by virtue of a familiar historical dialectic, the displacement of the picaresque novel by the *bildungsroman* (still to be agreed on as the appropriate term) has been repeatedly challenged in the twentieth and twenty-first centuries, as the random narrative of the adventure story has seemed to some to offer a truer model of human life than the socially and morally located pieties of the *bildung*.[2] And talking of pieties – Dickens's insistence on the harmlessness of his reading now seems particularly redundant.

These very broad generic continuities and discontinuities suggest something of the complex history which links us to the novel. Still more so, its 'content' can only make sense to us in the light of multiple intervening histories which provide the terms for their understanding. I need mention only some of the most memorable events and relationships of the novel, such as David's episode in the

---

[1]   Charles Dickens. *David Copperfield*. Ed. Jeremy Tambling. London: Penguin Books, 2004. 66. Dickens's disclaimer about the possible 'harm' that such books could do does not mean that they weren't a possible source of sexual knowledge to him; see Holly Furneaux, *Queer Dickens: Erotics, Families, Masculinities*. Oxford: Oxford University Press, 2009.

[2]   Tobias Smollett. *The Adventures of Roderick Random*. With an afterword by John Barth. New York: New American Library, 1964 [1748].

bottling warehouse; his marriage first to Dora and then to Agnes; his relations with Steerforth; the cross-class friendships, and class hostilities, figured by the Peggottys and Uriah Heep; the class and sexual economy indicated by Little Emily, Ham, and Steerforth; and the family dynamics suggested by David, his mother, and the Murdstones. Twenty-first century readers must understand all of these after the transformations in class, sexual and family relations which have supervened over the last century and a half. To take the first of these examples, David at work in Murdstone and Grinby's warehouse. This is complicated, of course, by the autobiographical element, endlessly debated since Forster made it public, so much so that the episode has been declared to be the primary drive of Dickens's career and had books devoted to it to disprove this centrality.[3] But even without this particular *post hoc* but inevitable knowledge, the 'secret agony' of David's soul as he 'sunk into [the] companionship' (166) of Mick Walker and Mealy Potatoes clearly has a particular force of class degradation which the subsequent history of class relations (in Britain, at least) has made it effectively impossible to identify with in an unembarrassed way. But equally, the episode tells a story about child labour and small-scale capitalist economy and thrift (the children are washing bottles for re-use) which now appears relegated to a previous world ('Dickensian' in one of its connotations), when we fail to recognise it in our contemporary 'Planet of Slums'.[4]

The multiple Janus-faced ironies continuously created by such inevitabilities of reading with hindsight will reappear frequently in what follows. They occur at moments when we are tempted to believe that the text emerges from a world that we have definitively put behind us, though as I have been stressing throughout this book, such temptations to a simple discounting of the text should always be resisted as symptoms of 'bad' historicism. Equally interesting, and posing no lesser challenge to our capacity to read historically, are those moments in the novel when we can read with a sense of the comparable immediacy of David's experience as recorded by the 'secret agony of [his] soul', yet are not tempted to relegate such feelings to the archive. The novel is thick with such moments, after all. One such occurs, it seems to me, on the night of David's drunken supper-party with Steerforth and his Oxford friends:

> I went on, by finding suddenly that somebody was in the middle of a song. Markham was the singer, and he sang 'When the heart of a man is depressed with care.' He said, when he had sung it, he would give us 'Woman!' I took objection to that, and I couldn't allow it. I said it was not a respectful way of proposing the toast, and I would never permit that toast to be drunk in my house otherwise than as 'The Ladies!' I was very high with him, mainly I think because I saw Steerforth and Grainger laughing at me – or at him – or at both of us. He

---

[3]   See Edgar Johnson, *Charles Dickens: His Tragedy and Triumph*. Harmondsworth: Penguin Books, 1977; and Alexander Welsh, *From Copyright to Copperfield: The Identity of Dickens*. Cambridge, Mass: Harvard University Press, 1987.

[4]   The reference here is to Mike Davis, *Planet of Slums*. London: Verso, 2006.

said a man was not to be dictated to. I said a man *was*. He said a man was not
to be insulted, then. I said he was right there – never under my roof, where the
Lares were sacred, and the laws of hospitality paramount. He said it was no
derogation from a man's dignity to confess that I was a devilish good fellow. I
instantly proposed his health. (369)

This scene is dense with the rituals of a particular ('dated') form of hospitality
– the singing of a sentimental song, the exchange of toasts, even the brief flaring-
up of a quarrel. The class and gender of the participants are particular too; the
former indicated, if by no more, then at the least by the reference to the Lares (to
labour the point: a reference dependent upon the acquisition of a class-specific
classical education); while as for the gender – this is surely a textbook homosocial
occasion, in which Woman or The Ladies feature as no more than barriers or
conduits for masculine affection. Yet to rest in these necessary recognitions would
evidently be grossly to misrepresent the passage, whose force lies in the particular
way that David negotiates these rituals, and indeed how he remembers himself
making those negotiations. The passage depends on our following the train of
reasoning which leads David and Markham to the brink of a quarrel and then back
again, reasoning that has an absurd logic but which is inhabited with real belief
by the participants. The comedy of the scene depends in part upon the reader's
continuous knowledge of David's drunkenness; but this comedy is itself tempered
by the tenderly realised immediacy with which his inebriation is suggested (the
time-lapses; the quarrelling over trivialities; the undue self-importance). I guess
a teetotal reading of this scene is possible; but it is written with hindsight by a
narrator who recognises and forgives its tipsy absurdity and anticipates a reader
who can share the joke. That anticipation certainly extends into our present
moment; our understanding of the scene and the evaluative accent with which it is
told depends upon this persistence.

Another occasion: David as a younger boy, on his own in London, and deciding
to celebrate some occasion at a pub:

I remember one hot evening I went into the bar of a public-house, and said to
the landlord:
'What is your best – your *very best* – ale a glass?' For it was special occasion.
I don't know what. It may have been my birthday.
'Twopence-halfpenny,' says the landlord, 'is the price of the Genuine
Stunning ale.'
'Then,' says I, producing the money, 'just draw me a glass of the Genuine
Stunning, if you please, with a good head to it.'
The landlord looked at me in return over the bar, from head to foot, with
a strange smile on his face; and instead of drawing the beer, looked round the
screen and said something to his wife. She came out from behind it, with her work
in her hand, and joined him in surveying me. Here we stand, all three, before me
now. The landlord in his shirt sleeves, leaning against the bar window-frame; his
wife, looking over the little half-door; and I, in some confusion, looking up at
them from outside the partition. They asked me a good many questions; as, what

my name was, how old I was, where I lived, how I was employed, and how I came there. To all of which, that I might commit nobody, I invented, I am afraid, appropriate answers. They served me with the ale, though I suspect it was not the Genuine Stunning; and the landlord's wife, opening the little half-door of the bar, and bending down, gave me my money back, and gave me a kiss that was half admiring and half compassionate, but all womanly and good, I am sure. (171–2)

This is an inconsequential and free-standing episode as far as the narrative is concerned: a memory only, though sufficiently vivid to merit an accompanying illustration by Hablot Browne. The way that the episode is recounted is itself interesting: it moves from a simple act of memory told in the past tense, into the historic present ('says the landlord … '; 'says I … ' – this is the tense used in the idiom of verbal story-telling, and provides both some immediacy and a formulaic quality). It then shifts back into the past tense, before assuming the present tense for the central tableau, recorded as an act of intense imaginative recreation in the present of the writer. As the narrative moves away from that tableau or frozen moment, it resumes the past tense, ending, however, back in the narrator's present as he reassures both himself and the reader of the womanliness and goodness of the landlord's wife. The scene thus dramatises the relationship between past and present, in which memory acts to redeem the past by presenting the pathos of the younger, remembered self. This is scarcely a moment to be described as a 'realisation': the affective relationship that eventually concludes the scene is no more than implicit in the tableau.[5] The scene nevertheless gives substance to the child's simultaneous vulnerability and bravado, recognised by the landlord and his wife and rewarded by a womanly kiss. Perhaps the episode is less free-standing after all; it takes its place among several in which the adult narrator imagines moments of womanly recognition for the motherless boy that he was.[6] For all that, it continues to have a powerful affective charge, even as we recognise that it is caught up in a dynamic of psychological and personal need.

Both of these episodes or moments in the novel suggest its continuing comic and affective charge, founded upon sufficient continuities of historical experience for the reader in the early twenty-first century to respond to the text even as we recognise that this is similarity within difference. Reading with hindsight might lead us to recognise the historical particularity of the hospitable rituals of David's supper party, or indeed the specificity of the notion of 'womanliness' enacted in that landlady's kiss. But in recognising these scenes' continuing comic and affective charge, hindsight permits us also to reassess the power of the past in the present.However, it won't have escaped the reader's attention that this is precisely what is dramatised in the Genuine Stunning episode.Not just in this episode, but more generally and throughout, *David Copperfield* is the great nineteenth-century novel of hindsight, and its narration repeatedly enacts its doubleness: at once an

[5]   See Martin Meisel, *Realizations: Narrative, Pictorial and Theatrical Arts in the Nineteenth Century*. Princeton: Princeton University Press, 1983.

[6]   Compare, for example, a similar moment of recognition on Mrs Micawber's part: 'a mist cleared from her eyes, and she saw what a little creature I really was' (186).

act which reminds us in the present of otherwise overlooked aspects of our past experience, whose significance at the time we could not recognise; and an act of retrospective reconstruction, reordering our memories in the light of our current exigencies.In its former guise it permits us to entertain other possibilities than those that actually eventuated, to recognise complexities and contradictions before they were resolved; in its latter guise of retrospective reconstruction it appears as an act of simplifying reduction, cognate perhaps with Freud's secondary revision in making a too-hasty sense of the trajectory of a life in the light of its eventual destination.The novel thus provides a model for the act of reading with hindsight; the doubleness of hindsight within the novel permits it to hold open contradictions and ambivalences which it is later required to resolve.In a cognate way, looking back on the novel and its location within its fractured mid-nineteenth-century cultural and ideological terrain, we can now see both the unresolved complexities of that conjuncture and the one true line of development which resolved them.

The most sustained acts of hindsight in the novel concern, firstly, David's courting of and marriage to Dora and his simultaneous failure to recognise the nature of the affection offered to him by Agnes; and secondly, the whole story of Little Em'ly's childhood and her seduction by Steerforth. In both cases the retrospective narration which is such a feature of the novel – three of its chapters are entitled 'A Retrospect', 'Another Retrospect', and 'A Last Retrospect' - creates for Dickens a particular task: to suggest the narrator's knowledge of the narrative outcome while not allowing this knowledge to overpower with irony the behaviour and beliefs of the characters who are living without that knowledge.

In the first instance, the retrospective narration has to occupy fully the overpowering immediacy of David's feelings for Dora, to suggest the fact that they represent a compulsive repetition of his feelings for his mother, to hint without explicitly stating the eventual narrative outcome, and to permit the reader to share the older narrator's position of privileged knowledge without suggesting any easy ironies at his younger self's expense.Some of these narrational complexities can be seen in the following passage, which culminates in a characteristic exclamation of anticipated hindsight, but throughout attests to the simplifying or reconstructive aspect of the self-correcting backwards glance. It concerns a moment when Agnes is briefly allowed to tend to her father while the two are visiting London:

> I pray Heaven that I never may forget the dear girl in her love and truth, at that time of my life; for if I should, I must be drawing near the end, and then I would desire to remember her best! She filled my heart with such good resolutions, strengthened my weakness so, by her example, so directed – I know not how, she was too modest and gentle to advise me in many words – the wandering ardor and unsettled purpose within me, that all the little good I have done, and all the harm I have forborne, I solemnly believe I may refer to her.

> And how she spoke to me of Dora, sitting at the window in the dark; listened to my praises of her; praised again; and round the little fairy-figure shed some glimpses of her own pure light, that made it yet more precious and more innocent to me! Oh, Agnes, sister of my boyhood, if I had known then, what I knew long afterwards! – (525)

Part of the skill of this passage is to suggest very strongly the eventual narrative outcome of the book, especially in its last sentence; yet it sufficiently avoids doing so to retain at least some sense of the legitimacy of David's feelings for Dora – reinforced and to some extent desexualised here though they are by the light shed on them by Agnes. Immediately following this passage the danger of narrational hindsight is made apparent when David leaves Agnes and is met by a beggar calling 'Blind! Blind! Blind!' (526); too ready a willingness to stress the contemporary perspective can lead the former self over-exposed to a potentially damaging charge of blindness; subject, indeed, to easy ironies. But it might be felt that the longer passage, even as it is, sufficiently demonstrates the dangers of hindsight; in the first paragraph the passage invokes the final retrospection of the narrator's imagined death, while throughout we are offered in summary mode the official conclusions to be drawn from David's relationship with the 'sister of [his] boyhood'.The passage aligns Agnes's influence with the self-disciplining which is, of course, one of the central end-points to which the novel is tending but which David, at this point in the story, has still to learn. 'The first mistaken impulse of an undisciplined heart' (671) has yet to resonate in David's breast, but this passage certainly intimates the process of disciplining.

My second exemplary instance of narration by hindsight in the novel concerns the story of Little Em'ly whose unhappy destiny is announced in the first chapter in which she appears, very near the beginning of the book, and about whom, therefore, the reader is to expect a difficult turn of the plot throughout the first half of the novel, until it duly arrives with the news of the elopement with Steerforth in Chapter 31, halfway through the novel. This is how that narrative foreboding is indicated as early as Chapter 3; David's thoughts are provoked by Emily running along a piece of timber that overhangs deep sea water:

> The light, bold, fluttering little figure turned and came back safe to me, and I soon laughed at my fears, and at the cry I had uttered, fruitlessly in any case, for there was no one near. But there have been times since, in my manhood, many times there have been, when I have thought, Is it possible, among the possibilities of hidden things, that the sudden rashness of the child and her wild look so far off, there was any merciful attraction of her into danger, any tempting towards him permitted on the part of her dead father, that her life might have a chance of ending that day? There has been a time since when I have wondered whether, if the life before her could have been revealed to me at a glance, and so revealed as that a child could fully comprehend it, and if her preservation could have depended on a motion of my hand, I ought to have held it up to save her. There has been a time since – I do not say it lasted long, but it has been – when I have asked myself the question, would it have been better for little Em'ly to have had the waters close above her head that morning in my sight; and when I have answered Yes, it would have been. This may be premature. I have set it down too soon, perhaps. But let it stand. (48)

This is relatively complicated as far as the narrative moment is concerned – the narrator here is looking back not only to Emily's dance over the water, but looking back also to moments in his own adulthood when he has reflected on that moment. Here there are two possibilities, both differing versions of hindsight. The first is the almost mystical – or simply superstitious – speculation that, 'among the possibilities of hidden things', the child's dead father may have been permitted to call her into the sea to join him, and save her from the life that she is about to live. Although the speculation has this superstitious quality, it is expressed with so many qualifiers or expressions of chance or possibility that it reads as much like an assertion of unrealised narrative possibilities, Dickens briefly inhabiting that garden of forking paths which is one of the abysmal dangers surrounding the backward glance when it wishes to entertain alternative narrative outcomes. The second instance of hindsight is more straightforward but perhaps more shocking – the adult David's thought that he should have refrained from saving Emily if he had known the life she was to lead. Hindsight here has led to a radical revision of the valencies attached to the memories that, elsewhere in this chapter, so sweeten his life. The final sentence in the quotation could almost be read as a 'note to self' on the part of the Dickensian narrator – but it certainly has the effect of marking Emily's life to come with the sign of moral disaster.

The possibilities of this marking remain dormant until David revisits Emily and the Peggotty boathouse on the occasion of his return to Yarmouth – which is also the moment when he and Steerforth participate unexpectedly in the celebrations caused by the announcement of Emily's engagement to Ham. This episode is framed by hindsight, particularly in relation to the character of Steerforth, and while it is not allowed to diminish the emblematic character of the scene (marked by an illustration by Hablot Browne), it does suggestively illuminate the otherwise understated possibilities for disaster in it. In fact the hindsight with which the scene is introduced is repudiated by the young David, in a parallel with his refusal to see the predatory side of Steerforth's nature at the end of the scene; characteristically for this novel, the challenge for Dickens is to suggest the destructive power of hindsight while not allowing it to overwhelm the scene itself:

> If any one had told me, then, that all this was a brilliant game [for Steerforth], played for the excitement of the moment, for the employment of high spirits, in the thoughtless love of superiority, in a mere wasteful careless course of winning what was worthless to him, and next minute thrown away – I say, if any one had told me such a lie that night, I wonder in what manner of receiving it my indignation would have found a vent! (318)

What David repudiates here is not exactly hindsight, but a fuller knowledge of Steerforth's character to be confirmed by hindsight. He wilfully refuses to accept the evidence which might have persuaded him of the truth even at the time – as when Steerforth remarks, after the celebratory scene, that '"That's rather a chuckle-headed fellow for the girl; isn't it?"' These intimations are enough to suggest a more disenchanted reading of the scene that they bracket, especially concerning Emily's bashfulness in admitting to having Ham as a husband (read sexual reluctance), and her admiration for the adroitness and charm of Steerforth's manner (read class infatuation). These intimations are all of course to be confirmed by her eventual elopement with Steerforth.

This latter incident too is prefaced by hindsight, but in a different aspect – that which recognises the unalterable finality of what has occurred, the sickening realisation that none of the other possibilities that you can entertain about the past can ever be actualised. David is walking back to Yarmouth after the funeral of Barkis:

> A dread falls on me here. A cloud is lowering on the distant town, towards which I traced my solitary steps. I fear to approach it. I cannot bear to think of what did come, upon that memorable night; of what must come again, if I go on.
> It is no worse, because I write of it. It would be no better, if I stopped my most unwilling hand. It is done. Nothing can undo it; nothing can make it otherwise than as it was. (454)

Since we are to be told the worst that can be told, hindsight in this aspect exacts no irony, but requires David to confront the worst that can be told and to recognise finally not only the truth of Emily's elopement but perhaps still more significantly, in terms of David's own development, the truth about his infatuation with Steerforth. Hence the unmitigable dread with which the topic is approached.

Hindsight within the text, then, both permits the almost ecstatic recreation of recaptured memories as earnest or harbinger of a life in which the past is in meaningful connection with the present; and can also be the instrument of the retrospective reconstitution of that life in line with its ideological destination. The question is, whether our own retrospective criticism need align itself with that latter disciplinary aspect.

II

One way of approaching this question is via the very category of 'Victorian' which appears so necessary in seeking to make explicit subsequent readers' sense of the historical specificity of novels such as *David Copperfield* – that is to say, that historical otherness of which they tend to disapprove. I shall discuss three moments in the novel when it seems appropriate and inevitable to invoke the notion of the 'Victorian' – or at least, when readers have certainly done so. These moments are David's conflict with the Murdstones; his relations with his child-wife and his sister-bride; and the importance of his being earnest. The Murdstones first.

It is scarcely necessary to rehearse again the Oedipal drama of David's eviction from his mother's bedroom by Mr Murdstone; the intense hostility and rivalry between Murdstone and David; the biting; and the part that Murdstone plays in David's employment in the warehouse and consequent class degradation. We can add that Miss Murdstone reappears later in the novel as Dora's chaperone and thus resumes the family role of obstructing David's desire. Why does Dickens focus his Oedipal resentments on this intensely masculine figure ('a squareness about the lower part of his face, and the dotted indication of the strong black beard he shaved close every day ... ' [34]), and yet hive off his actual portrait of his father (or at least, one version of him) onto the culturally distinct and very much more benign figure of Mr Micawber? What cultural resonances do the Murdstones have in nineteenth-century society?

One ready answer to this question is that the Murdstones represent a version of Evangelicalism that Dickens was keen to repudiate:

> As to any recreation with other children of my age, I had very little of that; for the gloomy theology of the Murdstones made all children out to be a swarm of little vipers (though there *was* a child once set in the middle of the Disciples), and held that they contaminated one another. (66)

Indeed, some of the passages cut from the manuscript make the attack on this 'gloomy theology' still more explicit.[7] There is no doubt that Evangelicalism represents an important strand within nineteenth-century society; insofar as it has a history extending well back into the eighteenth century, and *David Copperfield* itself looks back to the 1820s for the period of David's childhood, we cannot simply assimilate the Murdstones to the 'Victorians'.[8] Nevertheless, when Murdstone stands in for (or simply comes to represent) the Victorian patriarch, readers have been consistently repudiating their 'Victorian' father ever since – indeed 'Victorian' in this sense has been invoked over all the generations since the end of the nineteenth century exactly to mean that father figure (firm, stern, unjust, child-beating) exemplified by Murdstone. The novel provides one of the classic ways in which we understand the 'Victorian' and hence our own relationship to patriarchal authority.

Further aspects of the Murdstone regime both at Blunderstone and in Norwood (Dora's home) combine with this patriarchal authoritarianism (in which Miss Murdstone fully participates) to amplify our hostile caricature of the Victorians: their aversion to children ('little vipers', as we have noticed); their insistence on learning by rote; their predation on, and hostility to, innocent sexuality. The intense identification that the novel invites for David's act of rebellion in biting Mr Murdstone, and with his humiliation when he is placarded at his first arrival at Salem House, evidently aligns the reader with its repudiation of this vividly realised embodiment of a particular cultural presence in nineteenth-century England.

Yet it is instantly clear, and from within the text itself, that the Murdstones represent only a fragment or cultural possibility within 'Victorian' society, and

---

[7]   See, for example, the association of Creakle with Calvinism, in the excluded manuscript section quoted by Jeremy Tambling in the Penguin Classics edition, 947–8.

[8]   And see Michael Mason, *The Making of Victorian Sexuality*. Oxford: Oxford University Press, 1994, and *The Making of Victorian Sexual Attitudes*. Oxford: Oxford University Press, 1994, for an argument that disclaims the Evangelicals as responsible for the rigidities of Victorian culture. Nevertheless Dickens – and Charlotte Brontë, in an almost exactly contemporary text, *Jane Eyre* (1847) – was keen to ally Evangelicalism to a kind of moral authoritarianism and repressiveness he was anxious to repudiate.

that other possibilities are present also. Dickens is explicit about some of them: he extols the educational regime at Dr Strong's academy, for example, which puts students on their honour, and thus brings out the best in them. This too has its own problems, perhaps; but the point is that nineteenth-century society, just like our own, was riven with contradictory practices and beliefs, and that this text situates itself within that dissonance. Competing educational ideals; unresolved attitudes towards 'the child'; arguments over corporal punishment; all these are present at mid-century when the novel was written, and in representing the Murdstones as it does the novel intervenes in these debates, or at least seeks to inflect the cultural landscape which surrounds them. It is characteristically Victorian, we might say, in repudiating the Murdstones, and thus provides the initial ground for one powerful way of understanding subsequent repudiations of the 'Victorians' as they have been figured by these characters.

We may therefore notice something of a paradox, which lies in the way of one liberal reading of the novel, and indeed of the apparent liberalism which characteristically identifies with the central character's 'oppression' by an authoritarian social order. Relevant here is the coincidence of *David Copperfield* and *Jane Eyre*, in terms of dates of publication and the fact that both novels feature an episode in which their central characters are made to wear a humiliating placard at school (in both novels, too, the central figure on whom the narrative's hostility is directed is a stern Evangelical: Brocklehurst is Jane's equivalent to David's Murdstone). The paradox is this: the novels are most 'Victorian' in their aversion to 'Victorianism'. At the very least we therefore ought to recognise the fractured and contradictory nature of any complex social order and hesitate to characterise it in monolithic and homogenising ways. This is a scarcely coded way of saying that 'Victorian' may speak to some possibilities within the nineteenth-century social formation but that its too-ready invocation is invariably misleading.

In the novel's representation of the Murdstones it appears that it contests one version of Victorianism, and in doing so has enabled subsequent readers to figure their own opposition to patriarchal authority.But it should be said that one predominant critical position over the last twenty years or so – let us date it from D.A. Miller's *The Novel and the Police* (1988) and from Mary Poovey's (1989) *Uneven Developments* – has been to see the novel as participating in the very structures of domination that the liberal reading had seen it as resisting. Indeed, in both cases, 'liberalism' is part of the problem: *David Copperfield* is classically involved in the creation of the liberal subject, who does not need to be beaten into line because he has internalised that very discipline in the act of resisting it: in Miller's words, '*David Copperfield* everywhere intimates a dreary pattern in which the subject constitutes himself "against" discipline by assuming that discipline in his own name.'[9] For Poovey, the novel contributes to the ideological work of

---

[9]   D.A. Miller, *The Novel and the Police*. Berkeley: University of California Press, 1988, 220. Miller provides the now-canonical exposition of the implications of such internalised systems of discipline.

gender by its notion of the 'literary man' – a mystifying model of autonomous labour which in fact occludes the paradoxical situation of literary work at mid-century, supposed to be free but very obviously, via periodical publication, part of the capitalist system of labour.[10] Many subsequent accounts of the novel, each with their particular emphases but nevertheless consistent in their suspicion of the novel's imbrication in, and furthering of, the ideological work of Victorian systems of domination in the realms of gender, class and the disciplinary order, have endlessly elaborated Miller's 'dreary pattern'.

In some respects this whole line of argument (inadequate characterisation: better to say, this whole ideological and cultural formation) appears to repeat one characteristic twentieth-century response to Dickens from well before Foucault and the New Historicism. In discussing the 'ambivalence' often provoked by Dickens, John Bowen and Robert Patten have remarked that 'perhaps in no other area is this ambivalence felt more strongly than in Dickens's treatment of sexuality and sexual difference. For many critics in the twentieth century, he never seemed more "Victorian" than in his prudishness and sentimentality about sex and the diminished and domestic femininity that saturates his fiction.'[11] We are familiar with this use of 'Victorian' – it is the usage which carries with it our investment in, to use Cora Kaplan's term, sexual utopianism: our hope that in repudiating the Victorians we are asserting our belief in our more liberated ways of conducting our familial and sexual lives. And this perhaps sufficiently indicates what distinguishes Foucauldian accounts from what preceded them; while both are content to see in Dickens repressive systems of representation, the accounts that stem from Miller in particular see no possibility of 'liberation' even in the apparent 'autonomy' that the novel appears to endorse.

We can pursue these questions into our account of David's relationship with Dora and Agnes, *locus classicus*, surely, of the ambivalence provoked by Dickens, especially in relation to the 'diminished and domestic femininity' that the novel offers. Two quotations will be sufficient to indicate the unease that these sections of the novel are likely to provoke. The first concerns Dora's response, after her marriage, to David's persistent efforts to educate and improve her:

> 'I wish,' resumed my wife, after a long silence, 'that I could have gone down into the country for a whole year, and lived with Agnes!'
> 'Why so?' I asked.
> 'I think she might have improved me, and I think I might have learnt from *her*,' said Dora.

---

[10] Mary Poovey. *Uneven Developments: The Ideological Work of Gender in Mid-Victorian England*. London: Virago Press, 1989. See Chapter Four, 'The Man-of-Letters Hero: *David Copperfield* and the Professional Writer'.

[11] John Bowen and Robert L.Patten. 'Introduction'. *Palgrave Advances in Charles Dickens Studies*. Basingstoke: Palgrave, 2006. 7.

'All in good time, my love. Agnes has had her father to take care of for these many years, you should remember. Even when she was quite a child, she was the Agnes whom we know,' said I.

'Will you call me a name I want you to call me?' inquired Dora, without moving.

'What is it?' I asked with a smile.

'It's a stupid name,' she said, shaking her curls for a moment. 'Child-wife.' (651)

Sharp intake of breath – and for so many reasons. That the mild flirtatiousness of the dialogue should end in that shocking association of sexuality with childhood; that Dora should justify herself with this 'diminished femininity'; these combine to produce intense discomfort. It is important to observe that this statement of Dora's – her recognition of her inadequacies and her perverse defence against David's implicit but insistent criticisms of her – is made immediately after her belief in what Agnes might have taught her. So let us turn, as the text invites us, to Agnes:

As I rode back in the lonely night, the wind going by me like a restless memory, I thought of this, and feared she was not happy. I was not happy; but, thus far, I had faithfully set the seal upon the Past, and, thinking of her, pointing upward, thought of her as pointing to that sky above me, where, in the mystery to come, I might yet love with a love unknown on earth, and tell her what the strife had been within me when I loved her here. (849)

Where the characterisation of Dora is strongly but uncomfortably sexualised, that of Agnes is associated here and elsewhere with death; though shortly he will overcome his hesitation to declare himself, at this point, and throughout the novel, Agnes's affection can only be imagined in a bodiless heaven.

This seems then a peculiar blockage or bifurcation on David's part: that his desires should split between a sexually infantilised love-object on the one hand, and a sexually dormant or prohibited object on the other: between a child-wife and a sister-bride. For all that Bowen and Patten are surely right in their reference to the 'Victorianness' which twentieth-century readers have felt in confronting these matters, it is not clear to me that the *pattern* that David follows here has a widespread cultural resonance. On the other hand, considered separately, it is certainly possible to consider both the characterisations, of Dora and Agnes, as participating in established signifying systems of gender and sexuality. Indeed, the novel itself suggests this, especially in relation to Dora, for all that the compulsiveness of David's behaviour, in repeating his father's mistake and in substituting Dora for his mother, is recognised. Perhaps we should say that this compulsion *contributes* to our sense of cultural persistence.

David's courting of Dora, as much as his marriage to her, is recounted under the sign of hindsight, but in its aspect of benign retrospection and tender reminiscence:

When we had our first great quarrel (within a week of our betrothal), and when Dora sent me back the ring, enclosed in a despairing cocked-hat note, wherein she used the terrible expression that 'our love had begun in folly, and ended in madness!' which dreadful words occasioned me to tear my hair, and cry that all was over!

When, under cover of night, I flew to Miss Mills, whom I saw by stealth in a back kitchen where there was a mangle, and implored Miss Mills to interpose between us and avert insanity. When Miss Mills undertook the office and returned with Dora, exhorting us, from the pulpit of her own bitter youth, to mutual concession, and the avoidance of the Desert of Sahara!

When we cried, and made it up, and were so blest again, that the back-kitchen, mangle and all, changed to Love's own temple, where we arranged a plan of correspondence through Miss Mills, always to comprehend at least one letter on each side every day!

What an idle time! What an unsubstantial, happy, foolish time! Of all the times of mine that Time has in his grip, there is none that in one retrospection I can smile at half so much, and think of half so tenderly. (495–6)

The passage demonstrates again the text's capacity to dwell in the very feelings and language of a past time, and to hold off the threat of hindsight in its judgemental or reconstructive guise. These feelings are authentic, though they are couched in a language which is ironically presented: it is at this point that we can see how the text participates in the discursive to-and-fro of its society, as the sentimental language to which Miss Mills in particular is addicted is foregrounded to comic effect. The mild and affectionate irony to which this language is subject is sufficiently indicated by the use of exclamation marks: when the older David wishes to indicate the unironic truth of his current perspective ('think of half so tenderly') he abjures the exclamatory style. In short the passage indicates a more general feature of the book: that the courtship of Dora is conducted in a way which permits us to see its participation in a wider sentimental system, but which is nevertheless not foreclosed in the light of the eventual destination of the writer.

So here in relation to the courtship of Dora, and later in relation to her marriage, the text offers critiques (the word seems far too heavy-handed in the light of its retrospective tenderness) of a particular form of sentimental femininity, and of David's infatuation with it. It does so, however, by contrast to an equally disabling version of femininity; if one can imagine Mary Wollstonecraft's impatience with Dora, we can scarcely suppose any greater sympathy on her part for Agnes. Nevertheless, and this is the point, the text holds open a number of possibilities and resists, while it can, the teleological perspective that always threatens it.

One final example of an element of the text which provokes readers to reach for the category of 'Victorian' in a way which leaves the text especially vulnerable to hindsight: David's insistence on his habits of industry and thoroughness:

I do not hold one natural gift, I dare say, that I have not abused. My meaning simply is, that whatever I have tried to do in life, I have tried with all my heart to do well; that whatever I have devoted myself to, I have devoted myself to completely; that, in great aims and in small, I have always been thoroughly in earnest. (613)

Alexander Welsh, indeed, has offered this as perhaps the characteristic instance of Victorian earnestness.[12] Who, after Wilde, would dare to own up to being persuaded by such language as this? – though the cultural authority of that late nineteenth-century Wildean moment of effervescent release has itself had its vagaries in the twentieth century. Nevertheless, we can notice that David's assertion in this passage acts as a moment of retrospective summary, in which he is seeking to account for his own success, looking back from a position of assurance. Like David's praise of Agnes, which similarly stresses her capacity to strengthen his resolution and settle his purpose, this is the official version of David's own life, the *post hoc* rationalisation which makes retrospective sense of it.

Which is not to say that it is simply contradicted elsewhere in the text, but that a comparable language of spirited resolution and determination is certainly subject to more playful treatment, especially in the immediate aftermath of David's loss of the prospect of his aunt's fortune: 'What I had to do, was, to turn the painful discipline of my younger days to account, by going to work with a resolute and steady heart. What I had to do, was, to take my woodman's axe in my hand, and clear my own way through the forest of difficulty, by cutting down the trees until I came to Dora. And I went on at a mighty rate, as if it could be done by walking' (526). We can certainly see here Miller's 'dreary pattern' of internalised discipline; but we can also see that, thanks to David inhabiting the vocabulary of his former self, he is able to put this language into inverted commas, to indicate some distance from it. This is a classic novelistic moment in Bakhtin's sense, in which the official language of the moment ('perseverance', 'self-help' – the passage invokes these surrounding ideological presences) appears in a 'double-voiced' mode, at once the language of David-at-the-time and subject to the indulgent memory of the narrating David-in-the-future.

There is no doubt, then, that the novel emerges from and speaks to ideological or discursive presences active in the social formation of its time. Equally, in seeking to make sense of it subsequently, readers have negotiated these ideological presences in ways that have depended upon the unfolding social and cultural history that has supervened between the moment of the novel's publication and the moment of its reading. In doing so they have characteristically explained what they have found partly by recourse to the notion of the 'Victorian', a category with all sorts of ideological baggage and which permits and entails a variety of investments and commitments. The danger however is that we homogenise mid-nineteenth-century culture by this recourse, and fail to recognise its fractured and contradictory character – and in that sense we align ourselves with the operations of reconstructive hindsight within the text. But hindsight can operate in another way, to keep open alternative positions and possibilities, and our own reading with hindsight should equally be alive to this more playful and contradictory mode, without aligning itself to the official summaries to which the text nevertheless tends.

---

[12] Alexander Welsh. *From Copyright to Copperfield: the Identity of Dickens.* Cambridge, MA: Harvard University Press, 1987.

III

We can see possibilities of such readings, alert to unresolved possibilities in the text, in the interesting recent history of the novel, and of Dickens's work more generally, on the matter of sexuality and gender formation. One striking and more recent act of reading with hindsight, in relation to *David Copperfield*, has been the proliferation of readings which have bought out its suppressed homoerotic valencies: a classic instance in which the exigencies of the present have led readers to reassess the writing of the past and to find there possibilities and meanings which had been overlooked. Since some of the readings that have been produced in this vein reproduce strongly a pattern of resolved contradiction, it is worth setting them out before coming to a tentative conclusion.

Let us pass over for a moment the apparently straightforward matter of Steerforth and David ("'You haven't got a sister, have you?", said Steerforth, yawning. "No", I answered. "That's a pity"' [99]), and move directly to David's highly charged relationship with Heep. Several readings have drawn attention to the homoerotic element in the attraction and repulsion that draws David to Uriah. One instance within the text will serve to suggest the remarkable ambivalence of that relationship.It occurs when David has been provoked so much by Heep that he slaps his cheek:

> 'Copperfield', he said, removing his hand from his cheek, 'you have always gone against me. I know you always used to be against me at Mr Wickfield's.'
>
> 'You may think what you like', said I, still in a towering rage. 'If it is not true, so much the worthier of you.'
>
> 'And yet I always liked you, Copperfield!' he rejoined. (626–7)

This is partially a moment of frankness between the two young men, provoked by the evident honesty of David's slap. We could read Heep's admission that he 'always liked' Copperfield as a resumption of his hypocrisy; yet the text does not make this explicit, and allows the remark to stand, suggesting some of the intensities and complexities that mark their relationship. David has not merely been wrong-footed yet again by Heep's superior cunning; he has momentarily allowed himself to be exposed to the powerful current of attraction that co-exists with the hostility.

So how does the novel lay to rest or resolve the ambiguities and tensions created by this powerfully evoked current of homoerotic attraction and repulsion? Some recent criticism has consistently suggested a pattern. For Oliver Buckton, 'Dickens's novel offers a significant instance of the coexistence of different narratives of gender identification, and the suppression of deviant desires in order to produce an apparently seamless narrative of heterosexual identity'. Following Miller, Poovey and Butler, he suggests that the novel's disciplinary project is troubled by the homoerotic elements in it which are, following Butler, constitutive of the heterosexual subject but also produce the melancholia or mourning which characterise both the 'unified' heterosexual subject and the novel itself.

Andrew Dowling suggests that a dominant ideal of 'Victorian' manliness is in part constituted by an image of perversity against which it sets itself; he labels as 'hegemonic deviance' a process described as 'difference creating conformity'. And Vincent Newey, in a bravura reading of the homoerotics in play in the relationship between David and Heep, argues that 'David Copperfield himself, who perhaps more securely than anyone assumes the mantle of middle-class-ness', with its privileges and right-minded values, has to fight off and never quite lays to rest the demon of his cruder, uncivilized side, represented in his unworthy but resilient 'double', Heep'.[13] Though these three readers come to the text from different directions, with widely differing critical procedures and commitments, they nevertheless all suggest a pattern in the text by which the ultimately resolved identity of David, in class and gender terms, depends upon entertaining and then expelling the figure which represents his opposite.

These various recognitions of the homoerotic valencies that permeate the novel are undoubtedly within themselves striking instances of reading with hindsight: apparently unthinkable for most of the time since the novel was published, these readings now return to it to reveal previously overlooked possibilities within it. A radically different way of approaching these matters in relation to Dickens, with important consequences for our current reading practices, has been proposed by Holly Furneaux, whose *Queer Dickens: Erotics, Families, Masculinities* (2009), proposes a challenge to delimiting notions of queer sexuality inherited from the late nineteenth century and then projected back onto Dickens's writing in the manner that we have seen. Far from being only a matter of suppressed and tragic subject formation, the multiple queer possibilities in Dickens's texts, including especially *David Copperfield*, can offer various alternatives to the delimiting fixities of late-nineteenth-century sexology. The mid-nineteenth-century text can offer multiple ways of answering back to our present.

Two instances can indicate the multiple possibilities suggested in the novel. The first concerns the evident erotic investments in the relationship between Steerforth and David, passed over briefly before. Furneaux convincingly indicates how this relationship participates in a pattern, indicated by Steerforth's wish that David should have a sister who resembled him, in which same-sex desire is redirected and preserved via 'in-lawing' and displacement onto the loved one's sibling. Still more importantly for this novel, its remarkable familial arrangements, none of which is straightforwardly that of the heteronormative nuclear family, point to all sorts of queer possibilities beyond the retrospectively imposed norm. The most visible of these 'queer spaces' in the novel is the Peggotty house-boat itself, where Mr Peggotty, as a bachelor dad has gathered around him a household based on

---

[13] Oliver S. Buckton. "'The Reader whom I love": Homoerotic secrets in *David Copperfield'*. *English Literary History* 64 (1997): 189–222, 198–9; Andrew Dowling. *Manliness and the Male Novelist in Victorian Literature*. Aldershot: Ashgate, 2001, 48; Vincent Newey. *The Sciptures of Charles Dickens: Novels of Ideology, Novels of the Self*. Aldershot: Ashgate, 2004, 11.

needs and affections undefined by heterosexual norms. This is how Furneaux
describes her project:

> The minor significance of marriage and reproduction as motivators of kinship
> formation in the Victorian period exposes the artifice at work in the modern
> belief that family is a heterosexual institution. As relatively recent history shows,
> there is nothing natural in the near synonymy now attributed to the familial and
> heteronormativity.
>
> I propose, then, that a historicist approach to Dickens's work can open up new
> ways of conceptualizing queer in relation to the domestic. By looking at the
> various literary and actual accommodations and experiences of queer desires
> and lives in the period of Dickens's career and in queer-affirmative twentieth and
> twenty-first-century after-texts, I explore queer spaces that can be inhabitable
> and even enjoyable. It is my hope that this book will present some directions for
> the development of queer optimism, an affect sadly under-represented in a field
> laden with shame and fascinated by the death drive.[14]

So here we have an exemplary sequence: a reading agenda derived from the
present moment, which directs a certain kind of attention to the texts of the past;
in the light of this the texts of the past, allowed to speak in their own terms and
instantiating discernible wider patterns of their culture, can be re-activated in the
present and put to work to transform the very agenda which begins the process.
Furneaux calls that second phase of this hermeneutic cycle 'historicist' – a word
which means here something like that necessary attention to the alterity of the
past, the recognition that the actions, motives, feelings and understandings of the
past can and should be understood in their own terms. The result of this effort,
in the case of the sexual and gender politics of *David Copperfield*, is to reveal
defamiliarising possibilities both for the past and the present which are radically
other than the 'dreary pattern' found in the text by Miller.

   Yet it may be felt that those readings which concentrated on the more violent
and dangerous relationship between Copperfield and Heep also speak a truth
about the novel. Even here, however, we can recognise that in their insistence
on the ultimate formation of the heterosexual and middle-class subject they align
themselves too much with the very process that they reveal, and are in danger
of relegating the novel to a past that, from our perspective, we believe we have
successfully overpassed. One final reference to Miller and Poovey will perhaps
reveal what is at stake here. For the latter critic, the literary text works in this way:

> Because literary texts mobilize fantasies without legislating action, they
> provide the site at which shared anxieties and tensions can surface as well as
> be symbolically addressed. In fact, if one of the functions of literary work is, as
> I have argued, to work through material or ideological contradictions so as to
> produce such symbolic resolutions, then one component or stage of this working

---

[14] Holly Furneaux. *Queer Dickens: Erotics, Families, Masculinities*. Oxford: Oxford
University Press, 2009. 14.

through will necessarily involve exposing to view the very contradictions the
text manages or resolves. (Poovey, 124)

We might compare Dowling's phrase of 'hegemonic deviance'; this ultimately
Gramscian vocabulary suggests that for hegemony to be established, for 'symbolic
resolutions' to be achieved, the dominant position has to acknowledge the very
matters or oppositional forces that it wishes to suppress. From Miller's more
Foucauldian perspective, by contrast, contradiction is exactly what enables the
novel to have the policing function that it does: '"Against" Marxism, then, we
stress the positivity of contradiction, which, far from always marking the fissure
of a social formation, may rather be one of the joints whereby such a formation
is articulated' (Miller, 99, fn 2). The Millerian world is a more seamless one than
that intimated by Poovey, for its very contradictions and ambivalences serve the
purpose of creating and policing the liberal subject.

Both perspectives, however, seem to me to posit too readily an ideological
effect, read backwards into the novel and thus complicit with its own activities
of reconstructive hindsight. This is not the only form that hindsight can take,
however; it is not that some definite or conclusive position can be found in the past
(whether constituted *despite* or *through* contradiction), but that the past provides
a repertoire of possibilities that can be activated in the present in the light of our
equally fractured and contradictory situation. Furneaux's transformative reading
of the novel is an exemplary instance of this process at work: it is not the only
truth to be spoken of the book, but it does point to a real set of possibilities from
the mid-nineteenth century which can be re-activated in the present. The multiple
intervening histories of class, gender, sexuality, work-ethic and social discipline
permit and require us to read the novel in unanticipated ways, and to find therefore
possibilities that had previously been overlooked - though these are really there
and not just found there for our purposes.

This is to propose a reading practice attuned to the faultlines and underdeveloped
possibilities in a text and in a whole complex and contradictory cultural situation,
and insufficiently respectful, perhaps, of its preferred resolutions and destinations.
For there is no doubt that alongside, or even containing, the benign possibilities
indicated by Furneaux's reading, the novel does indicate a process of subject-
formation which requires some exclusions and suppressions. The novel's
remarkable capacity to render these visible, in ways that draw on unrealised or
scarcely visible historical possibilities, should be recognised before the 'dreary
pattern' is too readily invoked.

In addition, the process of bourgeois subject-formation should not so readily
be written off. This is especially so in the case of *David Copperfield*, which holds
out a promise of a meaningful and ultimately redemptive relationship between
past and present, however compromised by the Oedipal struggles and ferocious
exclusions that the passage from childhood to adulthood entails. This too is a
function of its moment in history, the last moment, according to Lukács, when
the bourgeois or liberal subject could propose his own liberation as a general

liberation: David does indeed become the hero of his own life. But we know this only with hindsight; and the book holds open other possibilities throughout.

To conclude, then, *David Copperfield* offers perhaps the exemplary instance of writing with hindsight of the novel in English: it suggests at once the redemptive possibilities of a benign relationship with one's own past as realised in memory, and also allows us to see how hindsight can put under strain, or place under the sign of irony, the authentic understandings and feelings of a past now differently understood. In doing so it allows us also to see the exclusions and suppressions involved in the process of bourgeois subject-formation; yet there is a danger that in placing too much emphasis on the disciplinary aspect of this, we end up failing to recognise the multiple alternative possibilities that the text manages to keep open. These alternative possibilities are themselves the result not only of Dickens's extraordinary power and invention as a novelist, but are themselves grounded in real social-historical eventualities which are the ultimate ground for all writing. The complex and contradictory possibilities of the mid-nineteenth century – falsely simplified as 'Victorian', this simplification exposed by the very novel we have been considering – can be allowed to speak in surprising ways to our no less complex present. We can only allow it to do so if we resist the reductive power of hindsight and draw instead on its capacity to reveal otherwise overlooked 'roads not taken'.

Chapter 5
Trollope and Political Realism

I

David Copperfield is overwhelmingly a novel of private life, though there is of course the public, campaigning or journalistic element in the novel, centring on the prison system and solitary confinement. It is formed by, and contributes to, historical series – of personal development, *bildung*, of sexuality – which are apart, to some extent, from the public discourses of political life. This is of course not true of Dickens's fiction as a whole, any more than it is true of Dickens's life; but it indicates at least a contrast with Trollope's *Phineas Finn* (1867–69), which is concerned with the passing of the Second Reform Act (1867), and thus evidently addressed to public politics in its most visible institutional form, the manoeuvres, dramas and personnel of Parliament and the House of Commons.

Yet it is not difficult to see that one element at least of Trollope's writing about political life shares a common theme with Dickens, that of the rowdiness and public disorder characteristic of elections – what an 1868 pamphlet called the 'corruption, bribery, intimidation, turmoil and disorder' characteristic of General Elections.[1] This chapter will explore some of the contexts in which Trollope's political fiction, especially *Phineas Finn*, is to be understood, including a topos, shared with Dickens, of the rowdy political election. It will ask how this fiction, and the historical series in which it participates, are illuminated by the subsequent history of parliamentary politics and its attendant scandals. Above all it will suggest that the complex rhetorical economy of Trollope's fiction is disturbed by this subsequent history, and the political and historiographical reflection that it has provoked.

There are several elections in *Phineas Finn*, thanks to the extraordinarily lucky, though somewhat peripatetic, political career of its hero. He first gets elected for the Irish seat of Loughshane with the help of the patronage of the local lord who has fallen out with his brother, the sitting MP; then for the English borough of Loughton thanks to the comparable patronage of the local lord, for whom the seat is in effect a pocket borough; and finally, after reform has disenfranchised Loughton, he returns to Loughshane and succeeds again after the timely death of the MP. This little series evidently makes the matter of patronage salient in the novel, but it also takes on in an extended and explicit way the debates surrounding the Second Reform Act, and is thus implicated in a wider history of reform and

---

[1]   Herbert W. Hart. *How to Return Members of Parliament without the Corruption, Bribery, Intimidation, Turmoil and Disorder at present Attendant on General Elections.* London: Simpkin, Marshall and Co, 1868.

democratisation. This longer series ultimately provides the *terminus ad quem* from which we now look back on the novel.

The three elections in *Phineas Finn* are all comparatively tame affairs, though a number of rowdier elections occur elsewhere in Trollope's fiction. *Ralph the Heir* (1871) provides the most memorable of these election episodes, driven as it is by the bitterness of Trollope's own humiliating defeat at the polls in Beverley in 1868. There is also, in a more obviously comic and satirical mode, the election at Barchester in *Doctor Thorne* (1858), which features the election agents Nearthewinde and Closerstil. These names suggest that Trollope was most interested in the 'corruption and bribery' of that list from the pamphlet title; Dickens, writing thirty years before *Phineas Finn*, had been especially exercised by the 'intimidation, turmoil and disorder' that he saw in the election process. When Mr Pickwick, Sam Weller, and Mr Winkle visit Eatanswill, in *Pickwick Papers* (1836–37), they witness scenes of partisan disorder and violence, and of absurd journalistic pomposity and partisan blindness, which provide the classic instance of a topos that will be retold repeatedly in subsequent fiction. Here's the description of the hustings:

> The right was reserved for the Buff party, and the centre for the mayor and his officers; one of whom – the fat crier of Eatanswill – was ringing an enormous bell, by way of commanding silence, while Mr Horatio Fizkin, and the Honourable Samuel Slumkey, with their hands upon their hearts, were bowing with the utmost affability to the troubled sea of heads that inundated the open space in front; and from whence arose a storm of groans, and shouts, and yells, and hootings, that would have done honour to an earthquake.[2]

This is an ambivalent scene, as scenes of carnivalesque popular uproar often are in Dickens's fiction. There is certainly the usual array of comic buffoons and pompous fools that inhabit municipal and small-town life, and they are exposed to the carnival hootings of this crowd. Even Mr Pickwick is not immune; a small act of gallantry to the wife of the editor of the Blue newspaper leads to an enjoyably ribald popular commentary. Yet in another aspect the whole scene is to be understood as a shameful spectacle, evidence of the inherent bad faith of official political life, certainly, but evidence also of drunken popular disorder which is wholly inappropriate to public life. The same ambivalence, with differing emphases, will mark many of the retellings of this scene by other novelists, including Trollope.

Thus when the latter provides an account of the election at Barchester in *Doctor Thorne*, there is a similar scene in which the candidates give speeches to the assembled electors. The crowd throws a dead cat at one of them, and a rotten egg at the other; their differing skill at handling these missiles, and the boisterous heckling which they exemplify, is one simple way of distinguishing them, and, like

---

[2]   Charles Dickens. *Pickwick Papers*. Ed. James Kinsley. Oxford: Clarendon Press, 1986. 191.

Dickens, Trollope is capable of relishing these displays of popular disrespect. But the principal focus of Trollope's chapter is on the forms of bribery and corruption of the voters that characterise the election process; these lead on the one hand to 'treating' the voters, and are the cause of consequent public drunkenness; but most fundamentally they require the candidates to wade through 'dirt and dishonour' to get themselves elected.[3] Indeed, the opening of the election chapter in the novel contains one of Trollope's many statements of his ambivalence in relation to a place in parliament:

> And now the important day of the election had arrived, and some men's hearts beat quickly enough. To be or not to be a member of the British Parliament is a question of very considerable moment in a man's mind. Much is often said of the great penalties which the ambitious pay for enjoying this honour; of the tremendous expenses of elections; of the long, tedious hours of unpaid labour: of the weary days passed in the House; but, nevertheless, the prize is one very well worth the price paid for it – well worth any price that can be paid for it short of wading through dirt and dishonour. (219)

This will be the question that dogs Trollope's writing about politics, whether it is possible to reconcile an admitted, indeed proclaimed, sense that to be a member of Parliament is a matter of the highest honour, with the knowledge that in fact the pursuit of politics is also a dirty business – literally so at election time. There is no simple biographical narrative which can account for how the balance in his feelings on this matter can be explained. So twenty years after writing this passage in *Doctor Thorne*, and long after his own humiliation at the polls in Beverley, he could write in his *Autobiography* that 'I have always thought that to sit in the British Parliament should be the highest object of ambition to every educated Englishman'.[4] It is better to think of there being conflicting currents in Trollope's ideas and feelings about 'politics', which produce unstable rhetorical economies in his fiction, so that the open and explicit commitment to the dignity of the political vocation is always at risk of being undone by another, more sceptical, current.

At all events, the topos of the rowdy and corrupt election gets told most forcefully in *Ralph the Heir*, written shortly after Trollope himself had stood, as a Liberal, as a candidate for Beverley in Yorkshire, and had come in bottom of the poll. What dominates his account of the election is not only the rowdiness – though the defeated candidate, Sir Thomas Bertram, does get a broken arm – but the widespread corruption, by which voters expect to be paid, one way or another, for their votes. As in actuality, the defeated candidate petitions against the result, and as a consequence Percycross (a very lightly fictionalised Beverley) is disenfranchised. One important aspect of the election is the discussion of the

---

[3]   Anthony Trollope. *Doctor Thorne*. Ed. David Skilton. Oxford: Oxford University Press, 1980.

[4]   Anthony Trollope. *An Autobiography*. Ed. Michael Sadleir and Frederick Page. Oxford: Oxford University Press, 1998. 290.

Ballot (i.e., the secret ballot) which it provokes. Trollope was opposed to the ballot though it was enacted by the Ballot Act of 1872; indeed, it was the single measure which did the most to reduce the buying of votes and the rowdiness of the hustings. Trollope's opposition to the measure is explained in his *Autobiography*:

> I hated, and do hate, both these measures [the Ballot, and a temperance-leaning Permissive Bill], thinking it to be unworthy of a great people to free itself from the evil results of vicious conduct by unmanly restraints. Undue influence in voters is a great evil from which this country had already done much to emancipate itself by extended electoral divisions and by an increase of independent feeling. These, I thought, and not secret voting, were the weapons by which electoral intimidation should be overcome. (302)

Trollope tells an opposing story here to the one which has been consecrated by the subsequent history. It remains a liberal story, of the gradual progress of 'independent feeling' to counter electoral intimidation; the key words in his opposition to the Ballot are 'manly' and 'independent'. But it positions him, in this instance, against the direction of Liberal policy, and against a historical current (which I will characterise more fully later) in which 'independence' will be secured by secrecy and not by the public display of manly selfhood.

   Other novelists in the nineteenth century include the topos of the rowdy and corrupt election – other notable instances include George Eliot's *Felix Holt the Radical* (1866) and W.M. Thackeray's *The Newcomes* (1853–55). This secular series, which stretches from Eatanswill in 1837 through to Percycross in 1870, can readily be made into a narrative of progress, to which Trollope himself largely subscribes, though, as we have seen, his opposition to the Ballot puts him at odds with what will prove to be the predominant story told through this sequence. However, the dramatic possibilities of the election process itself provide only one context for both progressive and sceptical accounts of parliamentary democracy in the mid-nineteenth century; another important context is provided by the widespread debates about democracy and the extension of the franchise that surrounded the passing of the Second Reform Act in 1867.

   This is not the place for a full reconstructive account of that debate, which includes such important contributions as Matthew Arnold's *Culture and Anarchy* (1867–68), Thomas Carlyle's 'Shooting Niagara' (1867), and Walter Bagehot's *The English Constitution* (1865–67). It can however be said that the debate around the Second Reform Act can readily be assimilated to a narrative of progress, even where, as is the case with *Culture and Anarchy*, the welcome given to the extension of the franchise is at best lukewarm, as it is strongly counterbalanced by an emphasis on the emollient powers of culture to mitigate the potentially violent and destructive power of the *demos*. The rebarbative exception to the capacity of a progressive history to reconstruct its own antecedents in the light of subsequent historical developments, however, remains Carlyle's 'Shooting Niagara – and After?', first published in *Macmillan's Magazine* in 1867, and subsequently as a separate pamphlet in the same year. Here is a flavour of Carlyle's essay:

Inexpressibly delirious seems to me, at present in my solitude, the puddle of Parliament and Public upon what it calls the 'Reform Measure'; that is to say, the calling in of new supplies of blockheadism, gullibility, bribeability, amenability to beer and balderdash, by way of amending the woes that we have had from our previous supplies of that bad article. The intellect of a man who believes in the possibility of 'improvement' by such a method is to me a finished off and shut up intellect, with which I would not argue: mere waste of wind between us to exchange words on that class of topics. It is not Thought, this which my reforming brother utters to me with such emphasis and eloquence; it is mere 'reflex and reverberation', repetition of what he has always heard others imagining to think, and repeating as orthodox, indisputable, and the gospel of our salvation in this world.[5]

This is in fact rather mild by the standards of most of the essay, which is shot through with racism and class hatred – though this last can be glimpsed here, as the topos of the rowdy and corrupt election appears in the first sentence. Carlyle is radically opposed to democracy as such, convinced that the course on which England is heading will lead to disaster (hence the title 'shooting Niagara'), and holding out faint hope – if there is any to be had – from the actions of a few aristocrats, hereditary or otherwise, to impose order on an otherwise anarchic world. But this mild précis scarcely does justice to the disproportionate violence and rhetorical overload of the essay. So great indeed is the challenge posed by Carlyle to the narrative of progress that has been constructed around the history of parliamentary reform that his essay has been definitively consigned to the archive, deemed to be of historical interest only. Indeed, the electronic version posted in the Bristol History of Economic Thought Archive comes accompanied by this disclaimer:

Texts posted in the Bristol History of Economic Thought Archive are presented as historical documents. Any views contained in these documents are those of the original authors, not necessarily those of the University or anyone connected with the Archive. Some of Carlyle's views, acceptable in many circles at the time, are not acceptable to many now.[6]

Carlyle's text has been assigned to history: a small instance of Gadamer's provocative claim that to historicise is to refuse to take a text seriously. Except that in this instance the disclaimer suggests that Carlyle's text has been taken all too seriously; this *cordon sanitaire* has been put in place because his writing is all too inflammatory, has a continuing capacity to offend and disturb in a way that, say, discussion of Disraeli's 1867 Budget does not. The reason is not far to seek; Carlyle's writing is addressed to matters, especially to do with race, that have a pronounced salience in our own culture. In this instance a narrative of progress,

---

[5] Thomas Carlyle. 'Shooting Niagara – and After?' *Critical and Miscellaneous Essays*. Vol 5. London: Chapman and Hall, 1899. 9–10.
[6] http://www.efm.bris.ac.uk/het/carlyle/disclaim.htm. Accessed 19/01/2012.

based on the sequence of Reform Bills which led from a restricted and corrupt franchise at the beginning of the nineteenth century to universal franchise over a hundred years later, seeks to banish Carlyle's hostile antipathy to this story to the archive, only to find it threatening offensively to re-emerge as it shockingly addresses matters of race which have not been so definitively settled in the present.

We can extend this narrative of Reform beyond the question of the franchise to see that this is only one strand of a wider narrative that can be told in relation to the history we have just been recounting. The gradual diminution of episodes of Election Day rowdiness, drunkenness and violence is surely part of a secular trend, a matter of self-congratulation to the people of the nineteenth century and of historical study ever since.[7] This whole secular transition, including the narrative of reform, can be told with all the necessary reservations of commentators upon it, be they Trollope, George Eliot, Matthew Arnold, or, as a toxic outlier, Carlyle, but our position at the end of this story is what gives it its coherence and significance.

Trollope has his own version to tell of this story, which is indeed predominantly a narrative of progress, but told in such a way that we need not see his opposition to the ballot as an anomaly. In *Phineas Finn* he allows the character Mr Monk considerable space to put forward moderate progressive views, which, though they are subject to their novelistic dialogic context, are not for all that subjected to any radical irony. They are set out in a series of conversations with Phineas himself, and in a letter that is sufficiently important to get a chapter title to itself: 'Mr Monk upon Reform'. The letter is the fullest explicit reflection upon electoral reform in the novel, and though it is immediately condemned as 'downright Radical nonsense' by one of the novel's Conservative characters, it has the authority of a statement with which we assume that the author is largely in sympathy. It begins by discussing some of the technical details of the measures then under discussion – they really were, when the novel was being written in 1867 – and then alludes to two current authorities who have contributed to the debate about representation. They are not named, but are probably Thomas Hare (1806–91), an early advocate of proportional representation, and Walter Bagehot (1826–77), who argued that the representativeness of the House of Commons should be based on the characteristics of the nation, not on an abstract numerical principle. Mr Monk is opposed to the crude version of democracy to be found in the United Sates, based on a mere 'numerical majority'. He continues:

> The nation as it now exists would not be known by such a portrait [as provided by an American-style democracy]; – but neither can it now be known by that which exists. It seems to me that they who are adverse to change, looking back with an unmeasured respect on what our old Parliaments have done for us, ignore the majestic growth of the English people, and forget the present in

---

[7]   See, for example, J.M. Golby and A.W. Purdue, *The Civilisation of the Crowd: Popular Culture in England 1750-1900*. London: Batsford, 1984; or, in a very different Bakhtinian register, Peter Stallybrass and Allon White, *The Politics and Poetics of Transgression*. London: Methuen, 1986.

their worship of the past. They think that we must be what we were, – at any rate, what we were thirty years since. They have not, perhaps, gone into the houses of honest artisans, or, if there, they have not looked into the breasts of the men. With population vice has increased, and these politicians, with ears but no eyes, hear of drunkenness and sin and ignorance. And then they declare to themselves that this wicked, half-barbarous idle people should be controlled and not represented. A wicked, half-barbarous idle people may be controlled; – but not a people thoughtful, educated and industrious. We must look to it that we do not endeavour to carry our control beyond the wickedness and the barbarity, and that we be ready to submit to control from thoughtfulness and industry.[8]

This account of the meaning of progress ('the majestic growth of the English people') is of a piece with that suggested by Trollope in his *Autobiography*, which led him to oppose the Ballot. Progress is not to be achieved by outward institutional means; rather these outward institutions should reflect the inward growth of the people themselves, discernible to those who have looked into the 'breasts of the men' It depends on the growth of thoughtfulness, education and industry among these men, here characterised as 'honest artisans'. Institutional reform, the extension of the franchise, is dependent upon and has to be preceded by the growth of this independent and self-reliant spirit among the people, though the 'people' is here understood as 'men' and the virtues that they require are specifically masculine ones.

Trollope subscribes, then, to his own version of progress, though it is not quite the one that has been consecrated by the actual course of events, so rudely parodied by Carlyle ('The intellect of a man who believes in the possibility of "improvement" by such a method is to me a finished off and shut up intellect'). This version of progress underpins his whole account of the passing of the Second Reform Act in *Phineas Finn*, which, in a kind of counter-factual history, he attributes to the Liberals rather than the Conservatives led by Derby and Disraeli who actually passed the Act in 1867. But there is another and darker perspective at work in the novel also, which speaks of disillusionment with the political process which Trollope is apparently so keen to specify so fully. In this darker vision, political motives are not to be taken at face value; a number of characters are allowed to voice the opinion that what drives political behaviour is not people's professed motives but a less honourable pursuit of party and personal advantage. Parliamentary rhetoric, in particular, is prone to Trollope's scepticism; it can appear as the very epitome of bad faith, since parliamentary actors have to bury their true convictions in order to conform to party discipline. Phineas Finn himself is just about allowed to retain his integrity; but the whole trajectory of the novel is to embroil him in the urgencies and short-term enthusiasms of parliamentary and government intrigue only to pluck him out at the end of the novel as the only way of keeping his faith to his inner convictions – and, it should be said, to his

---

[8]   Anthony Trollope. *Phineas Finn*. Ed. Simon Dentith. Oxford: Oxford University Press, 2011. 268.

Irish sweetheart. Trollope's famous assertion in his *Autobiography* that 'I have always thought that to sit in the British Parliament should be the highest object of ambition to every educated Englishman' persists in the novel; but alongside it, and potentially undermining it, is a sceptical view of politics as an arena of bad faith and low motives.

So we can conclude this phase of the chapter by recognising that *Phineas Finn* contributes to a narrative of reform and progress in the nineteenth century, though Trollope has his own distinctive commitments within that; that this narrative of reform includes not only the matter of the extension of the suffrage itself, but also a subordinate narrative of the civilising process which concerns the conduct of parliamentary elections; and that dissident or sceptical voices, especially Carlyle's, have been consigned to the archive as of 'historical' interest only, since they have been relegated to the sidelines by the actual course of events. Nevertheless, even though Trollope in his writing, including *An Autobiography*, remains committed to a positive and largely admiring portrait of official politics and the British ruling class – he shares some of Phineas's excitement at being admitted to their salons and dining rooms – there is an undercurrent of scepticism and disillusion with the whole political process which surfaces at times in the novel, and which is in turn related to some other sceptical positions available in the 1860s.

II

I have been arguing that the narrative of Reform, though it was one to which people in the nineteenth century subscribed, has been validated, even consecrated, by the subsequent course of events: in this case by the continued extensions of the franchise, culminating in universal suffrage for both men and women – a destination scarcely envisaged by most of the supporters of Reform in the mid-nineteenth century, though John Stuart Mill famously put it on to the agenda in his amendment to the 1867 Reform Bill, and this was widely discussed at the time (it comes up repeatedly in *Phineas Finn* itself). Nevertheless, another narrative of the historical series of parliamentary reform is possible, and indeed has come to dominate the historiography of the Second Reform Act itself: a sceptical, conservative, insistently anti-liberal narrative most memorably adumbrated in Maurice Cowling's *1867: Disraeli, Gladstone and Revolution* (1967). Indeed, Cowling's account is itself part of a powerful tradition in the historiography of Parliament, which we might designate as at least opposed to the Whig notions of progress and reform, and which goes back to the writing of Lewis Namier.

Cowling was addressing a famous historical conundrum: The Second Reform Act of 1867, which marks a watershed in the extension of the franchise and thus in the extension of the democratic credentials of the British state, was defeated when first proposed by the Liberals, but was passed soon after by the Conservatives. How did this come to pass? Here is one broadly liberal story, which can be told with differing inflections but in essence runs like this: the passage of the Second

Reform Act by the Conservatives can be explained as the governing class as a whole responding to the evident will of the British people, expressed by popular demonstration as much as by sustained argument; the Conservatives were doing no more than bowing to the inevitable. More broadly, we can align this story to the liberal or progressive history of the nineteenth century which sees it witnessing the advance of popular and democratic forces. This story coincides with a particular strategy adopted by the extra-parliamentary left during the 1860s, the strategy of 'pressure from without'. Large demonstrations were mounted in 1866 and 1867, which produced some minor scuffles with police, and some minor damage to property: windows were broken, and, most famously, some railings in Hyde Park were broken down. This established, among other things, the right to free speech in Hyde Park, a right and tradition that persists to this day. The logic behind these demonstrations and other actions in provincial cities was to mount constant pressure 'from without' on the parliamentary classes gathered together in their Westminster cocoon. In this account, the Conservatives were forced to adopt a much more radical measure than they themselves believed in because of the pressure of democratic opinion that acted as a constant force upon them.

Cowling tells another and contrary story. The Conservatives acted as they did, not because of any conversion to the fine-sounding phrases of Liberalism, and not because of the 'pressure from without' which was in truth little more than background noise from people whose persons and opinions they despised. Rather, they acted out of a calculation of their own political self-interest; they made the calculation that they could so manipulate the various boundary changes, extensions of franchise to particular sections of the working-class, and voting qualifications, that the hegemony of the British ruling class, especially in its rural-aristocratic strongholds, could be even strengthened by the passage of this apparently democratic Act of Parliament. In a meticulously researched book, which emerged from complete immersion in the parliamentary papers and correspondence of all the actors in the parliamentary drama of 1865–67, Cowling sought comprehensively to annihilate the Whig narrative of reform; in a combatively and provocatively conservative book he set out to debunk and destroy any illusions about a progressive story to be told about nineteenth-century politics, or any nonsense about 'pressure from without'. What drove the Conservative party, led in this respect by Disraeli, but which also explains the actions of the Liberal party, was calculation of political advantage, and behind that calculations of the long-term interests of their order. High-sounding pieties about democracy, or illusions about the political weight of popular demonstrations, simply cannot withstand Cowling's forensic dissection of the actual motives of the actors involved.

What is at stake here is evidently more than the historiography of a particular episode in British parliamentary history, important though that is. Two world-views are at issue: Whig versus Tory, idealist versus sceptical, progressive versus realist. For Cowling, and for Namier before him, to understand British parliamentary history is to address the behaviour of the elites who ruled Britain, and their self-interested motives however cloaked in grander self-descriptions. Though there is an evident debunking impetus here, this view is also that it is finally for the best that such elites should rule in their own interests, and indeed that they always will.

One of the more superficial effects of hindsight, or perhaps simply the passage of time, is to create all sorts of passing and adventitious connections between 'now' and 'then', and history has not been behindhand in creating such connections for us in the early twenty-first century. Where Trollope presented a catalogue of corrupt elections tainted with bribery, political life in Britain in the period since 1990 has seen a succession of scandals, of which the 'sleaze' and 'expenses' scandals have only been the most prominent. From this perspective, the scarcely-concealed bribes, treating and corruption which characterise the election process in Trollope's *Autobiography* and his novels, can be readily paralleled by the cash-stuffed envelopes, payment for access, and fabricated expenses which have marked British political life in the last few years. There is this evident difference of course; while in Trollope's world payments were made by people trying hard to get *in* to the Houses of Parliament, one hundred and fifty years later the payments were made to people already there.

This connection or striking juxtaposition may not be as adventitious as it first appears, however. Gadamer has taught us to be suspicious of treating historical distance as a gulf across which we can only peer; the remarkable-seeming parallels between then and now can be made to subserve such a way of conceiving the historical process. Rather, we should be looking for the Gadamerian continuities which provide the grounds for our present judgements. The most important of these must be the persistence of elites and their domination of the political process; in this Namierian continuity, though the precise details of the corruption will change, the fact of it will be no matter of surprise. Trollope's disapproval, more than his recording of the corrupt practices he observed, is, in the longer term, perhaps the more surprising.

III

How are we to assess *Phineas Finn* in the light of this sceptical, conservative and realist historiographical perspective? Indeed, what are we to make of Trollope's version of British political life, seen with this particular optic, that is, created by the hindsight of a historical reaction against the progressive version of political life to which he broadly subscribed? The novel itself, with its successor *Phineas Redux* (1873–74), certainly offers a substantial account of the political process, and both emerge from a minutely detailed attention to the operation of parliament and the life of the political elite which populates it. In this respect Trollope provides an understanding of the self-understanding of the political class, gives attention, that is, to the relative autonomy of the political world and the alliances, motivations, manoeuvres, attitudes, opinions and calculations that characterise it. Within the terms of its own self-understanding Trollope gives an account which can appear cognate to that provided by Cowling and the historiographical position which he exemplifies.

First however we have to reckon in the strange device or semiotic which marks all of Trollope's political novels, but especially *Phineas Finn* and *Phineas Redux*, whereby the novels play a complex game of recognition and non-recognition of the political characters they contain. They are not *romans à clef*, but they do include recognisable versions of the dominant political figures of the 1860s and 1870s, including versions of Gladstone, Disraeli, Palmerton, Russell, Lord Derby, and John Bright. On the other hand some of the characters who are granted major political roles in the fictional world of the novels, including Palliser himself, but also Mr Monk and Phineas Finn, are not direct portraits or caricatures of actual politicians, though readers have not been slow in seeking to identify these fictions with real figures. There is an element of gamefulness in all this, a kind of hide-and-seek which invites readers to find direct connections and portraits, but which frustrates them also as they attempt to do so. But the effect overall is to create a parallel universe, closely resembling our own but with some of the premises slightly altered – so that this is a world in which the Second Reform Act gets passed by a Liberal ministry and not a Conservative one. This is more *West Wing* than docudrama, and it creates a fictional space in which the actions and motives of actual political actors can be presented and examined. In *Phineas Finn* more than *Phineas Redux* it is also remarkably contemporary, providing an account of the passage of the Second Reform Act which Trollope was writing even as the Bill was being debated and passed, and which came into print within weeks of its final passage.

Within this space Trollope provides a full and even loving portrait of the British political elite at work and in their leisure. There is indeed a chapter of the novel devoted to 'A Cabinet Meeting', which plays on that game of recognition and half-recognition that we have noted, and which sees the business of the cabinet conducted by an unspoken code which all of its members share, and which requires little more than murmured assent for the business to be conducted. But the novel also attempts to show the characteristic political debate of this class, not in its official version, about which it is uniformly sceptical, but in the salons and dining-rooms of its London houses and country estates. Here a greater space for explicit reflection is allowed, as in Mr Monk's letter to Phineas, and greater licence is certainly allowed to the ladies of this elite, as they mingle with their menfolk in various social settings. Here, for example, is a pre-dinner conversation in which Lady Glencora takes a leading part:

> 'I believe, Mr Monk,' said Lady Glencora, 'that you and I are the only two in the whole party that really know what we would be at.'
> 'If I must be divided from so many of my friends,' said Mr Monk, 'I am happy to go astray in the company of Lady Glencora Palliser.'
> 'And might I ask,' said Mr Gresham, with a peculiar smile for which he was famous, 'what is it that you and Mr Monk are really at?'
> 'Making men and women all equal,' said Lady Glencora. 'That I take to be the gist of our political theory.'
> 'Lady Glencora, I must cry off,' said Mr Monk.
> 'Yes; – no doubt. If I were in the Cabinet myself I should not admit so much. There are reticences, – of course. And there is an official discretion.'

'But you don't mean to say, Lady Glencora, that you would really advocate equality?' said Mrs Bonteen.
'I do mean to say so, Mrs Bonteen. And I mean to go further, and to tell you that you are no Liberal at heart unless you do so likewise; unless that is the basis of your political aspirations.'
'Pray let me speak for myself, Lady Glencora.'
'By no means, – not when you are criticising me and my politics. Do you not wish to make the lower orders comfortable?'
'Certainly,' said Mrs Bonteen.
'And educated, and happy and good?'
'Undoubtedly.'
'To make them as comfortable and good as yourself?'
'Better if possible.'
'And I'm sure you wish to make yourself as good and as comfortable as anybody else, – as those above you, if anybody is above you? You will admit that?'
'Yes – if I understand you.'
'Then you have admitted everything, and are an advocate for general equality, – just as Mr Monk is, and as I am. There is no getting out of it, – is there, Mr Kennedy? Then dinner was announced, and Mr Kennedy walked off with the French Republican on his arm. (104–5)

This exchange is certainly suggestive of the limits of the political discourse of this class as the novel represents it. At first glance it is quite adventurous, in proposing a general equality as the ultimate aim of Liberal policy. Moreover the exchange takes the form of a Socratic dialogue, as Lady Glencora takes Mrs Bonteen (a very minor character in this novel) through her beliefs, and leads her reluctantly to a conclusion which appears to follow from her starting-point. This is the novel as symposium, with Peacock and Mallock as close generic relatives. On the other hand this is Lady Glencora speaking, an allowed free speaker who enjoys her power to shock, and whose liberty is in part conferred by her high rank. It is not, in other words, that the novel is unprepared to entertain radical political ideas, rather that it does so within prescribed social limits and in a safe social context.

This then suggests the discursive characteristics of the British elite at their leisure. The novel is altogether more sceptical of the official rhetoric which they employ when on their feet in the House of Commons. Here is a brief example. The situation in parliament is this: the Liberals led by Mr Mildmay (roughly equivalent to the historical figure Lord John Russell) have introduced a Reform Bill which, for party reasons, does not include disenfranchising seven 'rotten' boroughs (i.e., boroughs undemocratically in the gift of local aristocrats). They are opposed by the left of the Liberal Party, and for equally partisan reasons by Mr Daubeny (i.e., Disraeli). Daubeny makes this speech on the topic:

Mr Daubeny made a beautiful speech about the seven boroughs;– the seven sins, and seven stars, and seven churches, and seven lamps. He would make no party question of this. Gentlemen [i.e., other MPs] who usually acted with him would vote as their own sense of right and wrong directed them;– from which expression of a special sanction it was considered that these gentlemen were not accustomed to exercise the privilege now accorded to them. But in regarding the question as one of right and wrong, and in looking at what he believed to be both the wish of the country and its interests, he, Mr Daubeny,– he, himself, being simply a humble member of that House, must support the clause of the honourable gentleman. Almost all of those to whom had been surrendered the privilege of using their own judgment for that occasion only, used it discreetly,– as their chief had used it himself, and Mr Turnbull carried his clause by a majority of fifteen. (345–6)

This is a classic instance of what Bakhtin calls 'double-voiced discourse', in which two value-systems are simultaneously present: that of Mr Daubeny, and a second sceptical voice which is evidently certain that the professed motives of Mr Daubeny are quite distinct from his real motives – which the reader can instantly recognise as purely partisan. This second more judgemental voice is present in the interjected sardonic valuations which the passage contains. The passage turns, in other words, on the revelation of the real motives which underlie the parliamentary rhetoric, which it is easy to see are simply partisan. The heavy irony of the passage is exactly that members of parliament do not habitually vote 'as their own sense of right and wrong directed them'.

This is part of a general case which the novel makes against the practices of party politics: that party discipline requires individual members of parliament to speak and vote against their real beliefs. This indeed will be the sticking point which will eventually propel Phineas Finn out of politics at the end of the first of the two novels devoted to him, since he supports Irish Tenant Right and is forced to oppose his own party on the issue. He can only retain his integrity at the cost of his place in Parliament. So there is some disgust present in the novel alongside that loving portrait of the British governing class; the balance between the prize of being a Member of Parliament, and the 'dirt and dishonour' which the position seems to entail, can tilt in different directions.

A second major plank against the Whiggish or progressive narrative of the Second Reform Act concerns the action of popular politics outside parliament itself. There was a concerted popular mobilisation on behalf of Reform, led by the left of the Liberal party, notably the Reform League and the trade unions. This was the policy, as we have seen, of 'pressure from without', manifesting itself in large demonstrations in London and in some provincial cities in 1866 and 1867. In the Whiggish account, the Conservatives acted as they did in passing the Second Reform Act as a result of this pressure, which was in itself a manifestation of the underlying secular trend towards Reform. Cowling's account by contrast consistently stresses the partisan interests of the Conservatives, and dismisses the Liberal myth that it was pressure from without that acted on their policies.[9] How does Trollope's novel represent this aspect of the reform crisis?

---

[9]   See Maurice Cowling, *1867: Disraeli, Gladstone and Revolution: The Passing of the Second Reform Bill*. Cambridge: Cambridge University Press, 1967. 17.

Trollope conscientiously includes the popular agitation of the mid 1860s in his novel, though he conflates various different demonstrations and the one set-piece account he gives is of a demonstration that did not in fact take place. The popular element of the reform crisis principally appears in the novel via the figure of Phineas Finn's London landlord Bunce, a keen reformer, who is permitted a mildly sceptical commentary on Finn's performance as an MP, and who is briefly arrested for taking part in a disturbance outside the Houses of Parliament. This occurs in a chapter called 'Mr Turnbull's carriage stops the way', which recounts a fictional episode in which a large crowd gathers around the Houses of Parliament while the second reading of the (Liberal) Reform Bill is being debated. The chapter indeed provides a literal representation of the strategy of 'pressure from without' as the Reform League conceived it. In this version of events, the crowd is gathered to present a petition on behalf of the ballot; the demonstration is effectively led by Turnbull (Trollope's version of Bright); the debate is led by Mr Mildmay (Russell), but the reading is opposed by Turnbull on the grounds that its reform measures do not go far enough because they exclude the ballot. In the excitement at the end of the debate Turnbull leaves the House via his carriage, guarded by several policemen, and several respectable members of the crowd who wish to shake Turnbull's hand are arrested – including Bunce.

Trollope's imagination is exercised by the notion of Parliament debating while a crowd ('mob') is gathered directly outside; it provides him with one of the few occasions when parliamentary eloquence is presented in broadly sympathetic terms:

> Mr Mildmay moved the second reading of the bill, and made his speech. He made his speech with the knowledge that the Houses of Parliament were surrounded by a mob, and I think that the fact added to its efficacy. It certainly gave him an appropriate opportunity for a display which was not difficult. His voice faltered on two or three occasions, and faltered through real feeling; but this sort of feeling, though it be real, is at the command of orators on certain occasions, and does them yeoman's service. Mr Mildmay was an old man, nearly worn out in the service of his country, who was known to have been true and honest, and to have loved his country well, – though there were of course they who declared that his hand had been too weak for power, and that his services had been naught; – and on this evening his virtues were remembered. Once when his voice failed him the whole House got up and cheered. The nature of a Whig Prime Minister's speech on such an occasion will be understood by most of my readers without further indication. The bill itself had been read before, and it was understood that no objection would be made to the extent of the changes provided in it by the liberal side of the House. The opposition coming from liberal members was to be confined to the subject of the ballot. And even as yet it was not known whether Mr. Turnbull and his followers would vote against the second reading, or whether they would take what was given, and declare their intention of obtaining the remainder on a separate motion. The opposition of a large party of Conservatives was a matter of certainty; but to this party Mr Mildmay did not conceive himself bound to offer so large amount of argument

as he would have given had there been at the moment no crowd in Palace Yard. And he probably felt that that crowd would assist him with his old Tory enemies. When, in the last words of his speech, he declared that under no circumstances would he disfigure the close of his political career by voting for the ballot, – not though the people, on whose behalf he had been fighting battles his life, should be there in any number to coerce him, – there came another round of applause from the opposition benches and Mr. Daubeny began to fear that some young horses in his team might get loose from their traces. (187–8)

This is a fantasy situation: the House of Commons did not debate the Second Reform Act while surrounded by a mob. Yet it does suggest the way in which the political elite can incorporate popular pressure into their rhetoric. At first sight it seems that Trollope is acknowledging the success of the strategy of 'pressure from without', since he asserts, in a direct first-person statement, that the fact that the Houses of Parliament were surrounded by a mob 'added to the efficacy' of Mr Mildmay's speech. Yet it becomes clear that the way that it lends force to the speech is because Mr Mildmay can afford to repudiate the crowd's pressure, and his very repudiation impresses even his political opponents. In other words while it is certainly the case that the context of crowd pressure affects the rhetorical situation of Mildmay's speech – and of Turnbull's immediately afterwards – its effect is not to change his opinion but to allow him to gain credit for not changing his opinion. Daubeny's (Disraeli's) calculation, after Mildmay has finished, is similarly to assess how he can best use the presence of the crowd outside to his own best advantage.

So Trollope's response to the popular agitation that surrounded the reform crisis of the mid-1860s was to imagine, in very literal terms, what the policy of 'pressure from without' would look like in actuality, and to fantasise a dignified and powerful speech by a Whig Prime Minister (Russell at the end of his career) who can in effect incorporate this situation into a support for his own position. This lends some weight to the view that the British elite had no need to fear this popular agitation, though the mob, at the end of the debate, does go on to smash the windows of obnoxious MPs, and to cause one in particular some considerable damage. There is never any suggestion that the ruling elite is in any real danger from this mob, or that the pressure it exerts causes anybody to change his mind because coerced to do so. On the contrary this elite is shown as remarkably adept at turning this minor popular disturbance to its own advantage.

This is not however quite the end of the matter, because we need also to acknowledge the genuine legitimacy Trollope grants to Bunce, who is arrested in the minor scuffles that accompany Turnbull's exit from the House. Phineas exerts himself appropriately on his behalf, and he is soon released. Bunce's voice is one of many allowed its say in the novel and indicates both the novel's capaciousness and its limits. Bunce is shown as having a limited but tenacious point of view, and is allowed to best Phineas in an argument shortly before the demonstration outside the House of Commons. The argument turns on whether he, as a decent man, should attend the demonstration or leave it to the 'roughs';

this is significant not only in its immediate context but because the whole debate about the extension of the franchise turned on the way it could be extended to include the respectable working-class, and Bunce is clearly one of these. Moreover he is one of the choric voices allowed to point out the hypocrisy of Phineas's position as the MP for the pocket borough of Loughton; more generally he is one of the few characters in the novel shown to be consistently immune to its hero's charms. Nevertheless he remains a comic figure, or at least one subject to condescension and patronage, and the fact that he is made the only representative of a voice outside the political elite suggests the novel's limits. Turnbull is certainly allowed a voice, but he is subject to extensive satire by Trollope, and insofar as he represents the historical figure of Bright, the novel traduces the actual history, because there is no evidence that Bright was in cahoots with the extra-parliamentary left as the novel suggests.

In several respects, then, *Phineas Finn* gives an account of the Reform crisis which is cognate with that subsequently provided by Maurice Cowling. The novel's topic is predominantly the British political class, and it shows this ruling elite, even at a moment of transition, to be supremely confident in its capacity to rule. The novel does allow some real discursive range, but always within safe limits. The novel is very sceptical of grand political rhetoric and when showing politicians at work in an admiring manner, as in its accounts of a Cabinet meeting, imagines them using a language of mildness and understatement – exactly the idiom of a settled ruling class, in fact, with evidently shared beliefs and attitudes. Even when the novel suggests a scene in which the 'pressure from without' is visibly enacted, it shows how the masters of parliamentary rhetoric are capable of strengthening their own positions by virtue of this; at this juncture the speech of one of the novel's political heroes, Mr Mildmay, is reported as successful, but is not even given in free indirect discourse – we are told instead that 'the nature of a Whig Prime Minister's speech on such an occasion will be understood by most of my readers without further indication'. Mr Turnbull's speech, by contrast, is given verbatim.

Nevertheless, it is not the case that the novel can be simply assimilated to that sceptical, anti-liberal, conservative view. Its other commitments to progress and reform, as Mr Monk articulates them, remain intact. The novel is certainly sceptical of the efficacy of popular political agitation and pins its hopes instead on the growth of manly independent feeling on the part of the 'British people'. Perhaps the imaginary portrait that it provides of the British political elite at work and at leisure is best understood in terms of the Althusserian notion of 'limited autonomy' – that is, it certainly has its own modes of behavior and sets of attitudes and opinions that are specific to it, and which are effective in their way in reproducing themselves and the government they conduct, but in the last instance are not wholly independent as Cowling would have it but subject to wider, secular processes which they are only dimly able to articulate but which are certainly now visible to us as we read their story with hindsight.

IV

The novel's continuation, however, in *Phineas Redux* (1873), takes on some similar material but in a darker key ('they are, in fact, but one novel, though they were brought out at a considerable interval of time and in different forms'[10]). The premise of the later novel, as far as parliamentary politics are concerned, is very different: where *Phineas Finn* is addressed, with absolute immediacy, to a current political crisis, *Phineas Redux* is less concerned with parliamentary business, and the substance of debate, the disestablishment of the Church, while current in the 1870s, was never a matter of gripping national concern. The novel has entered a more simply fictional parliamentary world. The plot of the novel provides more dramatic events for its hero also; he is shot at by a jealous husband, and then tried for the murder of a fellow Minister.

It is this latter event which sends Phineas into a depression, and leads to a thorough disillusionment with politics. The earlier novel took Phineas from Ireland, led him through a very successful parliamentary career, and then took him back to Ireland to a life as a civil servant and married to his local sweetheart. The later books brings him back from Ireland, into Parliament again, marries him to a sophisticated heiress, but leaves him turning down the prospect of a ministerial career, the apparent object of his ambition throughout both books. His motives for turning down the offer of a ministerial post remain obscure even to himself, though he is given the opportunity to explain his disillusionment with politics, precipitated above all by his experience while being tried for his life for murder. The immediate aftermath of his ordeal leads him to speak to Lady Laura Kennedy in the following terms:

> 'Things seem to be so different now from what they did. I don't care for the seat. It all seems to be a bore and a trouble. What does it matter who sits in Parliament? The fight goes on just the same. The same falsehoods are acted. The same mock truths are spoken. The same wrong reasons are given. The same personal motives are at work.'[11]

The novel allows you to see that Phineas's attitude here is partly driven by his extreme sense of hurt at his recent experience of being falsely tried for murder – the novel piling on the agony by making his prosecutor a member of the Government that Phineas closely supports and whom he knows well. But this is clearly not the whole explanation for his words, since they echo attitudes that were present if subordinate in *Phineas Finn*, and which get a more prominent exposition here: that Parliament is an inherently dishonest and inauthentic place, and that its practice involves – to revert to the phrase he had used earlier – 'wading through dirt and dishonour'.

---

[10] *An Autobiography*. 320.

[11] Anthony Trollope. *Phineas Redux*. Ed. John Bowen. Oxford: Oxford University Press, 2011. 487.

Shortly afterwards Phineas explains himself more fully, to the same interlocutor, Lady Laura Kennedy, who has acted as one of his principal political mentors and patrons throughout the novels:

> 'Even twelve months ago, when I was beginning to think of standing for Tankerville, I believed that on our side the men were patriotic angels, and that Daubeny and his friends were all fiends and idiots, – mostly idiots, but with a strong dash of fiendism to control them. It has all come now to one common level of poor human interests. I doubt whether patriotism can stand the wear and tear and temptation of the front benches in the House of Commons. Men flying at each other's throats, thrusting and parrying, making false accusations and defences equally false, lying and slandering, – sometimes picking and stealing, – till they themselves become unaware of the magnificence of their own position, and forget that they are expected to be great. Little tricks of sword-play engage all their skill. And the consequence is that there is no reverence now for any man in the House, – none of that feeling which we used to entertain for Mr Mildmay.' (505)

This is now a more considered disillusionment, less easily explicable by Phineas's recent ordeal, and proving sufficiently powerful for him to turn down the ministerial post he has just been offered. There is an element of merely nostalgic disaffection here, with the suggestion that the conduct of the House of Commons has deteriorated recently: this is the mood which will inform a wider backward-looking cynicism in *The Way We Live Now*, to be published in 1875. But there is a profounder categorical unease with parliamentary politics as such expressed in this passage, seeing it as essentially inauthentic and incapable of matching its behaviour to the great patriotic and national responsibilities with which it is entrusted. There is also some softening of partisan feeling, though given that 'Daubeny' is a version of Disraeli, to whom a fiendish capacity to lead the idiots of the Tory party is attributed, it is scarcely a softening to suggest that the Liberal party now seems scarcely better.

This is the predominant feeling with which *Phineas Redux* leaves Phineas's parliamentary career, and the close representation of parliamentary politics with which the diptych of novels is concerned. If Phineas rejects the offer of a ministerial career at the end of *Phineas Redux*, there is the strong suggestion that he will resume it at a later date, and this indeed proves to be the case in *The Prime Minister* (1876). Indeed it is easy to read the ordeal to which Phineas is subjected in the second of the two novels devoted to his career – and the happy outcome of his marrying a rich woman – as a process of tempering by which the idealistic young Liberal is prepared for the duties of high office by taking on the necessary scepticism and stoical indifference which is necessary for it. In that case the overall trajectory of the Palliser series is indeed towards the more sceptical or 'realist' view of politics.

John Bowen remarks of *Phineas Redux* that 'we move into a strangely contemporary, or perhaps perennial, network of political scandal and the tropes of its reporting ... their destructive power to Phineas, once caught in their grasp, is as shocking as it is now banally familiar.'[12] This reminds us that both in this novel and in its predecessor Trollope devotes much attention to the working of the press; in both novels one of the chief satirical targets is Quintus Slide, a fiery pro-Ballot radical in the earlier novel who switches sides to a kind of populist Toryism in the second. Trollope provides some enjoyable parodies of his journalism, just as he had, in the earlier Barchester novels, enjoyed parodying the prose of the 'Thunderer'. Characteristically, in this dialogic writer, Slide's journalism is allowed to carry some real and hurtful truths about the actors in the novels of whom Trollope carries sympathetic portraits, notably Phineas himself. But Bowen's point about the 'perennial' nature of the network of political scandal and its reporting is a strong one; the ground for this continuity is of course the whole nexus of popular journalism, parliamentary politics and scandal which has been in place since the middle of the nineteenth century. Reading with hindsight back to that earlier period in which this network was being established, and which Trollope finds so shocking, serves to remind us of the systemic set of relationships which were being laid down. Bowen's other characterisation of the situation, as 'strangely contemporary', reminds us also of what is sometimes called the 'modernity' of the Victorian period; a reminder, that is to say, that some of the fundamental features of the nineteenth century are shared with ours today, and that the negotiation we make with this particular past must be based on the recognition of this sameness as much as any sense of difference.

However, a dispiriting sense that 'plus ça change, plus c'est la même chose' should not be the terminus of reading Trollope's novels with hindsight, though it might explain their particular appeal to conservative tastes.[13] Though I have described the novels as giving an account of the specific modalities of the governing elite in the mid-nineteenth century, this does not mean that, though there may still be political elites now, they are either recruited or work in the same ways. And the inter-reliance of popular press, scandal and parliamentary politics, though we can trace a broad continuity, clearly is played out using different technologies and with differing grounds for judgement – though the particular tone of outraged morality and common sense that characterises Quintus Slide's journalism does sound horribly familiar. But this is ultimately one of the points of reading with hindsight, to mobilise the defamiliarising power of texts from the past, a power that can only be put into play if recognition of the past, as much as a repudiation of it, acts as the basis of our reading.

---

[12] John Bowen. 'Introduction'. *Phineas Redux*. xxviii.

[13] In the mid 1980s it was reported that over half of Mrs Thatcher's Cabinet were members of the Trollope Society.

Chapter 6
'The things that lead to life':
Ruskin and Use-Value

In the three previous chapters we have been considering some of the complex historical continuities and discontinuities which link us to three of the canonical novels of the nineteenth century. In the following two chapters we turn to two writers, John Ruskin and William Morris, whose writings suggest equally complex relations to current concerns, and who also challenge too easy an assimilation to our present pre-occupations. Both writers can be considered romantic anticapitalists, to use Georg Lukács's helpful categorisation.[1] In this respect, the two chapters go together and are linked by an underlying consideration of the continuing value of that tradition of nineteenth-century thought, especially in the context of current pressing ecological concerns. This chapter on Ruskin centres on perhaps his most famous assault on political economy, one of the dominant strains of thought in his period, in *Unto This Last* (1860). The following chapter on William Morris, Ruskin's most important successor, centres around his utopian text *News from Nowhere* (1890), where the problems and possibilities of reading with hindsight are especially visible.

I: Ruskin's Critique of Political Economy

The story of the publication of *Unto This Last* is well known, if only because Ruskin himself told it himself so powerfully a few years later in the preface to *Munera Pulveris*. He approached Thackeray, then editor of the monthly *Cornhill* magazine, to publish six essays on economic subjects. After the first three essays appeared, the outcry against them was so great, so challenging to the orthodoxies of political economy, that Thackeray was forced to ask Ruskin to curtail the series; the last essay, slightly longer than the others, thus contains the remaining matter in a compressed form.[2] This is a story that Ruskin tells to emphasise his own distance from the dominant opinion of his age; later writers have tended to take him at his word (as I do myself) and emphasised his challenge to Victorian beliefs. The

---

[1]   The developments and complexity of Lukács's account of romantic anti-capitalism are traced in Michael Löwy, 'Naphta or Settembrini? Lukacs and Romantic Anticapitalism'. *New German Critique* 42 (Autumn 1987): 17–31.

[2]   See Francis O'Gorman, '"Suppose It Were Your Own Father of Whom You Spoke": Ruskin's *Unto This Last* (1860)'. *Review of English Studies* 51:202 (2000): 230–47, for a full account of this episode which refutes the widespread view that Ruskin's views were offensive to his parents, especially his father.

irony of our self-satisfaction in this regard, in the early twenty-first century, when the *pensée unique* of contemporary neoliberalism is so evident, needs scarcely to be spelt out – especially since there is a direct line of descent from the political economy to which Ruskin objected, and the dominant economic thought of the present day.

It is only in the lengthy final chapter of *Unto This Last*, 'Ad Valorem' (both extended as to length, and compressed as to thought), that Ruskin turns to the question of value in political economy. His discussion of the topic in this place is distinctive; characteristically, in the whole tradition against which he sets himself, value is the preliminary question, from which all the other conclusions of the science flow. Thus Adam Smith in *The Wealth of Nations*, though he starts with the division of labour, can only secure his fundamental account of the labour theory of value by starting with the crucial distinction between value in use and value in exchange: this crucial distinction allows the labour locked up in the commodity to persist through the operations of barter and then the market. Ruskin however starts at another point, with his categorical repudiation of political economy as it is currently constituted. As we will see, when he tries, in the chapter on value, close reasoning in relation to political economy, it is precisely on the distinction between use value and exchange value that his objections will turn, and this distinction, so vital to his whole outlook in these matters, is the principal topic of this chapter. But at the outset of his argument, he begins with this *a priori* rejection:

> Observe, I neither impugn nor doubt the conclusions of the science, if its terms are accepted. I am simply uninterested in them, as I should be in those of a science of gymnastics which assumed that men had no skeletons. It might be shown, on that supposition, that it might be advantageous to roll the students up into pellets, flatten them into cakes, or stretch them into cables; and that when these results were effected, the re-insertion of the skeleton would be attended with various inconveniences to their constitution. The reasoning might be admirable, the conclusions true, and the science deficient only in applicability. Modern political economy stands on a precisely similar basis. Assuming, not that the skeleton has no skeleton, but that it is all skeleton, it founds an ossifiant theory of progress on this negation of a soul; and having shown the utmost that may be made of bones, and constructed a number of geometrical figures with death's-heads and humeri, successfully proves the inconvenience of the reappearance of a soul among these corpuscular structures. I do not deny the truth of this theory; I simply deny its applicability to the present phase of the world.[3]

Here, wittily and with considerable panache, Ruskin extends the tradition of the romantic critique of capitalism to its principal intellectual support, political economy as is has been formulated since Adam Smith. Though behind a passage such as this we may hear Carlyle's many assaults on mechanism and the dismal science, Ruskin has begun to take the decisive step of formulating an extended

---

[3]   John Ruskin. *'Unto This Last'*, *The Works of Ruskin*. Ed. E.T. Cook and Alexander Wedderburn. Vol. 17. London: George Allen, 1905. 26.

critique of its premises. What is wrong with political economy is that it assumes that human beings act as calculating, utility-optimising machines, whereas in fact they are activated by a host of complex factors which we can summarise under the heading of the 'social affections', though the word that Ruskin uses in this passage is 'soul'. There is an assault here on the basis *in thought* of the understanding of social and economic life. But also implicit in a passage such as this (and explicit through much of *Unto This Last*) is an assault on the nature of capitalist social relations *in actuality* – their tendency, that is, to undermine affective social relationships and substitute purely economic relations for them.

Another way of putting this is to say that Ruskin's assault here on 'economic man' has in its sights both the theory which posits such an abstraction as its basis and the practice of economic agents who only act in their own self-interest. Certainly Ruskin's position can now be seen as one of the classic statements of the inadequacy of 'economic man', though exactly what this abstraction means can also be seen to be undergoing a significant transformation at the period that Ruskin was writing, a transformation to which in some respects he contributed.[4] Since the opposition between 'the economic' and 'the affective' is one of the fundamental antinomies of bourgeois thought, it is not surprising that it has been stated and restated in myriad differing ways during and since the nineteenth century, and that the balance or borderline between economic motivations and social affections has been a subject of negotiation and contestation. The inadequacy of a simply economic way of thinking about people has recently re-emerged, for example, in current debates about the contemporary economy, given especial force by the financial crisis of 2008 onwards, but not simply triggered by it.

Ruskin's line of argument (or at least, an aspect of it), has been notably revived in an unexpected way by Richard Bronk in his book *The Romantic Economist* (2009), which, as its title suggests, returns to the nineteenth-century Romantic critique of capitalism and the dismal science and asks what implications it holds for contemporary economics. The central intellectual figure in the book is John Stuart Mill, Ruskin's *bête noire*, who figures as a precursor of Bronk's own attempt to marry seemingly opposite intellectual traditions. But Ruskin figures prominently also, and Bronk's critique of economics in many ways echoes Ruskin's own. The problem with classical economics, in his account, in its currently dominant forms, including especially natural equilibrium theory, is that it is an abstraction that scarcely fits the realities of economic life. Economics assumes rational utility-optimising individuals acting, if not consistently, then in the long run overwhelmingly, in their own economic interest. Economics ignores the complexity of motivations that cause people to act even as economic agents, and ignores also the imagination, creativity and sympathy which are required by

---

[4] See Regenia Gagnier, *The Insatiability of Human Wants: Economics and Aesthetics in Market Society*. Chicago: University of Chicago Press, 2000, for an account of the way that 'economic man' became transformed in the transition from classical political economy to a later neoclassical economics.

economic agents of all kinds to be successful. For both thinkers economic life always-already needed the social and personal qualities excluded in principle by economics. But there is this large difference between Ruskin and Bronk: for the former the inadequacy of political economy *in thought* is potentially a reflection of the problem of social and economic relations *in actuality*; for Bronk this is not the case: even capitalist economies, in his account, actually need the human qualities ruled out of consideration by classical economics, and he specifically repudiates any critique of capitalism (i.e., Marxism) based on its tendency to reduce people to mere economic agents.

This means that for Bronk, the evocation of the romantic critique of capitalism ultimately serves both as a necessary corrective to the inadequacies of economics and, potentially, as a palliative or softening adjunct to the profit-maximising calculations of capitalist managers. This leads to the remarkable spectacle of Ruskin being recruited for management advice:

> Hazlitt well understood that our capacity for imaginative projection and identification is not infinite, and that this entails that 'the circle of our affections and duties' cannot extend across the globe. In a modern context, this observation might suggest more than the limits of altruism and moral judgement: it might also suggest where we should expect to find the boundaries of an effective firm (or other organisation). Ronald Coase has argued that the boundary of a firm is set by reference to where the firm structure is more or less effective in reducing the transaction costs of exchange (for example, of labour) relative to arm's-length transactions. Now if Ruskin was right that affections and duty are the most effective means of reducing such transaction costs, it may suggest that the limits of sympathetic identification and affection dictate where the optimal boundary of a firm will be. Firms or other organisations that are so large that employees cannot identify with each other or their bosses (and hence cannot trust them or feel a sense of duty towards them) may be relatively inefficient. Similarly, a firm is likely to have an effective marketing and production strategy only if it is close enough to its customers emotionally and physically to be able to identify with their wishes and needs, and tailor its product range accordingly. In other words, the practical limits of the sympathetic imagination may constitute both the effective boundaries of loyalty within a firm, and the boundaries of a firm's empathetic understanding of its customer base.[5]

This is a remarkable piece of reading with hindsight, in which the vocabulary of the present has been substituted without apology for the actual vocabulary of the past: Ruskin of course never asserted that 'affections and duties are the most effective ways of reducing ... transaction costs'. What he actually said in relation to this is more interesting, and he cast it in the form of a paradox when discussing the right way for masters to treat their domestic servants:

---

    [5]   Richard Bronk. *The Romantic Economist: Imagination in Economics*. Cambridge: Cambridge University Press, 2009. 251–2.

Treat the servant kindly, with the idea of turning his gratitude to account, and you will get, as you deserve, no gratitude, nor any value for your kindness; but treat him kindly without any economical purpose, and all economical purposes will be answered; in this, as in all other matters, whosoever will save his life shall lose it, whoso loses it shall find it. (31)

It is clearly a long way from here to the transaction costs of firms, and that way would have to travel via the analogy between a firm and a domestic household, and a discussion of the paternalism that in Ruskin's case is unavoidable in any discussion of social relations. But all this has been foreshortened in Bronk's account, and Ruskin's social affections, which for him rendered nugatory the account of the real world of economic activity offered by political economy, now find themselves invoked to guide the management accountant in determining the most effective ways of reducing the transaction costs of labour.

But perhaps there was always this possibility in Ruskin's thought, or to put it another way, the romantic critique of capitalism always had built into it this swing between the rejection of capitalist social relations, and the possibility, even the inevitability of being recruited as a means of palliating them. Or to put it another way again: insofar as the romantic critique of capitalism stresses the importance of affective relationships against the anonymity of the market it was always going to be drawn to the small-scale and the local enterprise against the large and corporate – as indeed we see in that paragraph from Richard Bronk. Ruskin is the progenitor, in this view, of a long tradition which, parallel to the descent through Morris and the Arts and Crafts movement, leads through Chesterton and Belloc to Philip Blond, who does indeed make reference to Ruskin in tracing the intellectual lineage of his Red Toryism.[6] Ruskin himself was repeatedly drawn to directing his conclusions towards advice that the employer could use in managing his servants and his work-force; in this perspective Ruskin being recruited for contemporary management advice does not look so remarkable after all.

However, it is possible to trace another inheritance from *Unto This Last* which does not have this disconcerting conclusion. Ruskin's extended grappling with notions of value in 'Ad Valorem' provides the basis for a different critique of political economy less susceptible to being co-opted for the purposes of management advice. It was in some respects an accident that Richard Bronk's book should be published in 2009, in the immediate aftermath of the credit crisis of 2008, just as the themes of Blond's Red Toryism and the 'Big Society' notions that it supported in the British election of 2010 were brewed long before the credit crunch and the meltdown of financial institutions. Ruskin's stress on use-value, however, speaks both directly to our present circumstances and to the longer-term environmental crisis which threatens humanity.

---

[6]   Philip Blond. *Red Tory: How the Left and Right Have Broken Britain and How We Can Fix It*. London: Faber and Faber, 2010. Ruskin appears, along with Cobbett and Carlyle, on page 28.

In the fourth chapter of *Unto This Last,* Ruskin starts to work his way through the classic definitions of wealth and value, starting with Mill, and, finding him unsatisfactory, going on to Ricardo:

> There appears to be some hitch, I think, in the working even of Mr Ricardo's principles; but let him take his own example. 'Suppose that in the early stages of society the bows and arrows of the hunter were of equal value with the implements of the fisherman. Under such circumstances the value of the deer, the produce of the hunter's day's labour, would be *exactly*' (italics mine) 'equal to the value of the fish, the product of the fisherman's day's labour. The comparative value of the fish and game would be *entirely* regulated by the quantity of labour realized in each'. (Ricardo, chap. 1ii, On Value.)
>
> Indeed! Therefore, if the fisherman catches one sprat, and the huntsman one deer, one sprat will be equal in value to one deer; but if the fisherman catches no sprat, and the huntsman two deer, no sprat will be equal in value to two deer?
>
> Nay; but – Mr Ricardo's supporters may say – he means, on an average – if the average product of a day's work of fisher and hunter be one fish and one deer, the one fish will always be equal in value to the one deer.
>
> Might I inquire the species of fish. Whale? Or whitebait? (82–3).

Ruskin's objection has real force, but not in the way that he thinks: this passage too closely resembles logic-chopping, and is anyway based upon selective quotation. Ricardo is arguing that exchange value – that is, the value of one commodity relative to another – is determined by the labour taken to produce the commodity; the relative value of commodities is not therefore affected by a general rise or fall in the price of labour. The sentence from Ricardo's *Principles*, quoted by Ruskin, continues thus: '... quantity of labour realized in each; whatever might be the quantity of production, or however high or low general wages or profits might be.'[7] The phrase 'whatever might be the quantity of production' might also be thought to anticipate Ruskin's comic *reductio ad absurdum* – 'Whale? Or whitebait?' It is indeed the case that, were the labour costs of producing either whale or whitebait equivalent, then their exchange value in relation to the produce of the hunter would be equal. Ruskin has argued himself into something of a corner here – it might be said that 'Mr Ricardo's supporters' had a point, and the concession relating to 'an average' is one that Ruskin cannot afford to make.

On the face of it, it seems strange that Ruskin is not more sympathetic to the labour theory of value, as it is articulated in this instance by Ricardo, but which is after all a central tenet of classical Political Economy from Adam Smith through to John Stuart Mill. But the problem for him is not the assertion that value is created by labour, though he does have quite another notion of value, but that the labour theory of value sets out to explain not the intrinsic value of things but their relative value. It is a way for economists to explain how commodities get to have the values that they hold in relation to other commodities. What the theory seeks to explain is not use value but exchange value; what Ruskin objects to,

[7]   David Ricardo. *On the Principles of Political Economy and Taxation.* Ed. R.M. Hartwell. Harmondsworth: Penguin, 1971 [1817]). 69.

despite the triumphant air of having logically demolished his opponents' case, is the very transition from one to another. Classical political economy is actually a powerful way of explaining values in exchange, that is, it is a way of explaining how commodity production and the market work. Ruskin believes himself to have logically demolished these explanations, when what he has really done is to point to one of the limits of such explanations.

At all events Ruskin gets disgusted with the whole process of consecutive economic reasoning and launches into his own preferred way of thinking about the question of value:

> It would be a waste of time to pursue these fallacies further; we will seek for a true definition ...
>   The value of a thing, therefore, is independent of opinion, and of quantity. Think what you will of it, gain how much you may of it, the value of the thing itself is neither greater nor less. For ever it avails or avails not; no estimate can raise, no disdain depress, the power which it holds from the Maker of things and of men. (85)

One way of reading this act of definitional *fiat* would be to see it as an effort by Ruskin to fix the terms of debate, to secure the foundational term by removing it from the instabilities created by the ever-changing values created in exchange – a classic case, it would seem, of the logocentric being secured by the theocentric. But this would be a mistake, as the next paragraph makes clear:

>   The real science of political economy, which has yet to be distinguished from the bastard science, as medicine from witchcraft, and astronomy from astrology, is that which teaches nations to desire and labour for the things that lead to life; and which teaches them to scorn and destroy the things that lead to destruction. And if, in a state of infancy, they suppose indifferent things, such as excrescences of shell-fish, and pieces of blue and red stone, to be valuable, and spend large measure of the labour which ought to be employed for the extension and ennobling of life, in diving and digging for them, and cutting them into various shapes, – or if, in the same state of infancy, they imagine precious and beneficent things, such as air, light and cleanliness, to be valueless – or if, finally, they imagine the conditions of their own existence, by which alone they can truly possess or use anything, such, for instance, as peace, trust, and love, to be prudently exchangeable, when the market offers, for gold, iron, or excrescences of shells – the great and only science of Political Economy teaches them, in all these cases, what is vanity, and what substance ... (85).

The argument now turns less on the invocation of our 'Maker' than it appeared to at the end of the previous paragraph. It no longer rests on divine *fiat*, but on a remarkably creaturely invocation of the conditions of human existence. The invocation of use value here by Ruskin is being deployed to measure the indifference of the market to the ends to which human economic activity is directed, and, in the references here to 'air, light and cleanliness', points effectively to one of the ecological limits of unfettered commodity production.

II: Intrinsic Value and the Real Science of Political Economy

Ruskin's argument here pushes him towards an intrinsic theory of value; later, especially in *Munera Pulveris*, he will be quite explicit that this is his central assertion: the true understanding of value must be an intrinsic one, and is quite independent of people's estimation of it. This conception of value is related in turn to the way that Ruskin understands the natural world, and the peculiar and in some respects eccentric way that he has of representing it.

Use value had always in fact had a disturbing place in the systems of classical political economy. John Stuart Mill effectively concedes as much when he writes as follows in his *Principles of Political Economy*:

> Political economy has nothing to do with the comparative estimation of different uses in the judgment of the philosopher or a moralist. The use of a thing, in political economy, means its capacity to satisfy a desire, or serve a purpose. Diamonds have this capacity in a high degree, and unless they had it, would not bear any price. Value in use, or as Mr De Quincy calls it, *teleologic* value, is the extreme limit of value in exchange. The exchange value of a thing may fall short, to any amount, of its value in use; but that it can ever exceed the value in use, implies a contradiction; it supposes that persons will give, to possess a thing, more than the utmost value which they themselves put upon it as a means of gratifying their inclinations.[8]

There are two aspects to this assertion, to one of which Ruskin would object, and to the other he might tentatively agree – were it possible to conceive of Ruskin agreeing with anything said by John Stuart Mill. The definition of 'the use of a thing' as meaning 'its capacity to satisfy a desire, or serve a purpose', already concedes far too much to the subjective estimation of value, and the 'value of a thing', Ruskin has told us, is 'independent of opinion'. It should be said that this will prove to be a productive line of reasoning post Mill, and will lead to marginal utility theory and the neoclassical revolution.[9] However, when Mill says that 'value in use ... is the extreme limit of value in exchange', he is approaching a position with which Ruskin could agree. For the latter, the intrinsic value of a thing is fixed, and its immutability renders the whole of Political Economy nugatory. For Mill in this paragraph, however, use value puts a limit on exchange value; it is not that it *determines* exchange value, rather that it is one of the conditions which holds the whole system in place. In this sense it is a necessary condition for accounting for value in exchange, but not a sufficient explanation of it. This is perhaps a destabilising admission, since it means that usefulness of an object both does and does not enter into its value.

---

[8]   John Stuart Mill. *Principles of Political Economy. Collected Works* Ed.J.M. Robson. Vol. 3. Toronto: University of Toronto Press, 1965. 456–7.

[9]   See Gagnier, *The Insatiability of Human Wants.*

Exactly contemporaneous with Ruskin, another discontented critic of nineteenth-century capitalism, Karl Marx, also published his *Contribution to the Critique of Political Economy* in 1859; this would become the basis of his much fuller *Capital* in 1867. For Marx, like the classical political economists whom he is critiquing, use value acts as a limit to the operations of exchange value in commodity production:

> When the use-values of commodities are left out of the reckoning, there remains but one property common to them all, that of being products of labour. But even the product of labour has already undergone a change in our hands. If, by our process of abstraction, we ignore its use-value, we ignore also the material constituents and forms which render it a use-value. It is no longer, to us, a table, or a house, or yarn, or any other useful thing. All the qualities whereby it affects our senses are annulled. It has ceased to be the product of the work of a joiner, a builder, a spinner; the outcome of some specific kind of productive labour. When the useful character of the labour products vanishes, the useful character of the labour embodied vanishes in them as well. The result is that the various concrete forms of that labour disappear too; they can no longer be distinguished one from another; they are one and all reduced to an identical kind of human labour, abstract human labour.[10]

Marx is here pursuing the notion of abstract human labour, as a way of defending the labour theory of value in a context which recognises the separation between use value and exchange value (or value in commodity production, which is a form of exchange value but not the only possible form). This is a different way than the notion of labour value retained by a notion of the 'average', the point at which Ruskin gives up on political economy. However, Marx's acceptance of the distinction between use-value and exchange-value does not preclude his recognition that the whole system of exchange value is nevertheless underpinned by the existence of use-value: 'Finally, nothing can have value unless it has utility. If it is useless, the labour embodied in it has been useless; such labour cannot be counted as labour, and therefore cannot produce value'. (1, 10). But even here, in this rigorously pursued argument for the labour theory of value which seeks to account for the special nature of labour as it is preserved in commodity production, use value persists; it is the necessary limit to the operations of such production, even if 'it is no longer, to us, a table, or a house, or yarn, or any other useful thing. All the qualities whereby it affects our senses are annulled'. Use value remains to permit the whole system to operate, even as the system proves itself indifferent to the intrinsic qualities of the commodities that are produced within it.

It should be said that both the classical economists and Marx were right about this and that Ruskin was wrong: if you want to account for the value of a commodity as a commodity, reference to its intrinsic or use value is not sufficient.

---

[10]   Karl Marx. *Capital*. Trans. Eden and Cedar Paul. 2 vols. London: Everyman's Library, 1957. I, 6.

Ruskin is therefore of little help in understanding the workings of actually existing capitalism. Ruskin's radicalism, however, is to make the use-value of an object the basis of a critique of the system. It is not that exchange-value doesn't in some sense account for the value of commodities – it is the value of the commodities themselves, in this profounder sense, that is at issue. Ruskin's insistence on the creaturely value to humanity of the various elements of the material world provides an essential measure of the proliferating productiveness of the commodity system.

It may seem strange to invoke 'creatureliness' as a value in discussing Ruskin, but his reference to 'precious and beneficent things, such as air, light and cleanliness', in defining the 'great and only science of Political Economy' is not the only moment in the chapter 'Ad Valorem' when the creaturely impact of the environment becomes prominent. In two famous paragraphs Ruskin seeks to offer an alternative vision of the future to that offered by J.S. Mill in his chapter on 'The Probable Futurity of the Labouring Classes' in his *Principles of Political Economy*. Ruskin prefaces these considerations by another moment when he explicitly abandons his active engagement with the details of economic argument and seeks once again to find an appropriate context or perspective by which the operations of economic life can be measured:

> Leaving these questions to be discussed, or waived, at their pleasure, by Mr Ricardo's followers, I proceed to state the main facts bearing on that probable future of the labouring classes which has been partially glanced at by Mr Mill. That chapter and the preceding one differ from the common writing of political economists in admitting some value in the aspect of nature, and expressing regret at the probability of the destruction of natural scenery. But we may spare our anxieties on this head. Men can neither drink steam, nor eat stone. The maximum of population on a given space of land implies also the relative maximum of edible vegetable, whether for men or cattle; it implies a maximum of pure air; and of pure water. Therefore: a maximum of wood, to transmute the air, and of sloping ground, protected by herbage from the extreme heat of the sun, to feed the streams. All England may, if it so chooses, become one manufacturing town; and Englishmen, sacrificing themselves to the good of general humanity, may live diminished lives in the midst of noise, of darkness, and of deadly exhalation. But the world cannot become a factory, nor a mine. No amount of ingenuity will ever make iron digestible by the million, nor substitute hydrogen for wine. Neither the avarice nor the rage of men will ever feed them; and however the apple of Sodom and the grape of Gomorrah may spread their table for a time with dainties of ashes, and nectar of asps,– so long as men live by bread, the far away valleys must laugh as they are covered with the gold of God, and the shouts of His happy multitudes ring round the winepress and the well. (110)

The question of value has now been extended in such a way that Ruskin's understanding of inherent or intrinsic value can be appropriately invoked to indicate the limits of industrial production: 'No amount of ingenuity will ever make iron digestible by the million, nor substitute hydrogen for wine.' Even though

Ruskin concedes that England – at the time of writing the most industrialised society on the planet, with a majority urban population from the 1850s onwards – might become completely obliterated by its continuing industrial expansion, the very nature of human creaturely existence will ensure that continuation, in some portions of the globe, of an environment unspoiled by industrial production and devoted to agriculture.

Ruskin is perhaps too sanguine in this matter, and his further confidence that the world will not be ruined by 'mechanical agriculture' has also proved to be misplaced:

> As the art of life is learned, it will be found at last that all lovely things are also necessary:– the wild flower by the wayside, as well as the tended corn; and the wild birds and creatures of the forest, as well as the tended cattle; because man does not live by bread only, but also by the desert manna; by every wondrous word and unknowable work of God. Happy, in that he knew them not, nor did his fathers know; and that round about him reached yet into the infinite, the amazement of his existence. (111)

The reference to God appears again, as it did in the earlier passage on the intrinsic and unchangeable value of things, as a way of securing Ruskin's own judgements. Mill's comment remains pertinent: 'Political economy has nothing to do with the comparative estimation of different uses in the judgment of the philosopher or a moralist.' Ruskin's determination to fix or hold down his 'comparative estimation of different uses' – in this case, of productive agricultural land, and how much of it should be preserved as wilderness – has led him to invoke 'the unknowable work of God'. There is in fact a deep materialist logic uniting these two paragraphs, the first relying on the immutably creaturely or biological nature of the human animal, and the second secured finally by a reference to the deity; for while it is true that a planet inhabited by human beings cannot solely be given over to industrial production, such a planet can indeed do without 'all lovely things' if their eradication will help feed its population. Use value absolutely leads to Ruskin's powerful assertion of the limits of industrial production; but it can never be sufficient to determine the balance within a productive system, other than by reference to a standard outside itself.

Nevertheless, Ruskin's reliance on use value, and his refusal to countenance the notion that value can be affected by 'opinion' or 'quantity', still leaves us with a powerful repudiation of the priorities of industrial production, and an equally powerful assertion of the limits to it provided by humanity's creaturely nature. The seemingly metaphysical idea of intrinsic and immutable value resolves itself, in some of Ruskin's most impressive formulations, into an assertion of the intrinsic biological and social dispositions of elements of the environment to do good or harm to human creatures.

This conclusion, in different forms, has been reached by different readers of Ruskin as they sought to make him speak to their own social and intellectual priorities. In fact there has been a persistent strain of scientific or materialist criticism of Ruskin which has found in his insistence on use-value a point of entry to permit assimilations of his thought, against its declared intentions, to Darwinian thinking. As early as the 1880s, Patrick Geddes provided a notably materialist reading of Ruskin in his eccentric but enjoyably polemical pamphlet *John Ruskin, Economist* (1884). In an argument with the orthodox political economists, who in his view absolutely fail to provide any substantive definition of utility, Geddes asserts that Ruskin, by contrast, provides a definition which is entirely in line with contemporary science:

> Let us however leave the inmates of the academic cloister; walk out into the world, look about us, try to express loaf and diamond from the objective side in terms of actual fact, and we find that physical and physiological properties or 'values' can indeed be indefinitely assigned: the one is so much fuel, its heat-giving power measurable in calorimeter, or in actual units of work, the other a definite sensory stimulus, varying according to Fechner's law. This is precisely what our author means in such a passage as the following, which, however absurd to the orthodox, is now intelligible enough to us:–
>   'Intrinsic value is the absolute power of anything to support life. A sheaf of wheat of given quality and weight has in it a measurable power of sustaining the substance of the body; a cubic foot of pure air, a fixed power of sustaining its warmth; and a cluster of flowers of given beauty, a fixed power of enlivening or animating the senses and heart.'[11]

Geddes's purpose is to assimilate Ruskin to the latest science. Fechner's law, appropriately for the context, relates the intensity of sensation to the intensity of stimulus in mathematical terms. Geddes does not stop at this physiological assimilation of Ruskin; he goes on to assimilate him to Darwinism also, in a way evidently at odds with Ruskin's own antipathy to evolutionary thinking:

> For it is to be observed if these Darwinians are indeed to draw full consequences from their greatest law – that organism is made by function and environment, then man, if he is to remain healthy and become civilised, must not only aim at the highest standard of cerebral as well as non-cerebral excellence, and so at function healthy and delightful, but must take especial need of his environment; not only at his peril keeping the natural factors of air, water, and light at their purest, but caring only for 'production of wealth' at all, in so far as it shapes the artificial factors, the material surroundings of domestic and civil life, into forms more completely serviceable for the Ascent of Man. (35)

The ambivalent nature of assimilations of this kind becomes apparent here: the social Darwinism that emerges is perhaps more marked by Ruskinism, than Ruskin is marked by the Darwinism. The immediate point, however, is that it is possible to read Ruskin in directly materialist terms, though Geddes in the 1880s made that

---

[11]   Patrick Geddes. *John Ruskin, Economist*. The Round Table Series, 3. Edinburgh: William Brown, 1884. 26–7. Geddes quotes from *Munera Pulveris*.

move in order to bolster his critique of the classical political economists and further his claims for the social relevance of the scientific understanding of human life.

This is perhaps to read Ruskin too unequivocally against the grain, or at least to seize only on those of his expressions which lend themselves to a materialist interpretation – genuinely there – and to leave out much else which might be thought to be valuable in Ruskin. James Clark Sherburne, in his virtuoso playing-off of Ruskin's economic thought with and against the whole tradition of European economics, is evidently unsympathetic to Geddes's materialist assimilation of Ruskin, on the wholly plausible grounds that Ruskin's cast of thought is overwhelmingly idealist in orientation.[12] Nevertheless, Geddes's line of thought was continued by J.A. Hobson in a very much fuller way. In *John Ruskin, Social Reformer* (1898), he also argued that Ruskin's insistence on the intrinsic theory of value – Hobson calls it 'vital use' – is the most profound and also scientific aspect of his thinking: 'Mr. Ruskin's adoption of vital use as the standard and measure of value must therefore be regarded as the most revolutionary of his positions. It may be summed up in this eloquent but strictly scientific formula: "THERE IS NO WEALTH BUT LIFE... '.[13] Hobson, despite Ruskin's declared antipathy to Darwin and indeed to most of his contemporary biology, seeks to align this notion of 'vital use' with the latest advances in biological science. He thinks that Ruskin's theories need supplementing by a further consideration on the 'cost' side of the value equation, and by a fuller consideration of the science of biology which he deliberately flouts, in order to get a better sense of the evolving relation of man to his environment, necessary for a full sense of the values implicit in this relation. For all that, Ruskin still provides the basis for a genuinely scientific political economy:

> It has been humorous to hear the dull drudges of commercial economics speaking contemptuously of an economist whose logic is far keener than their own, and whose work will hereafter be recognised as the first serious attempt in England to establish a scientific basis of economic study from the social standpoint.
> Upon this human basis the fuller economic theory of the future will be built. In America and upon the continent of Europe not a few professional economists of note are engaged in working out the biological factors involved in the various forms of "cost" and "utility," so as to throw fuller light upon the economy of production and consumption. (106–7)

In this view it certainly no longer seems eccentric to use Ruskin to think about the creaturely nature of human existence, and to invoke this to understand more fully the true costs of economic activity and the true values that such activity might create.

This line of thought can also be pursued in relation to Ruskin's own relationship to his contemporary political economists, especially those who began to challenge classical political economy and to shift the discipline (a description

---

[12] See James Clark Sherburne, *John Ruskin or the Ambiguities of Abundance.* Cambridge, Mass: Harvard University Press, 1972.

[13] J.A. Hobson. *John Ruskin, Social Reformer.* London: James Nisbet, 1898.78.

already recognising a narrowing of the topic) towards neoclassical and marginalist versions. Though many commentators on Ruskin have rightly pointed out his actual ignorance of most actual economic writing,[14] he did engage with some economic thought beyond his lifelong antipathy to the works of John Stuart Mill. His response to William Stanley Jevons's attempted mathematisation of economics is instructive, and points to some of the ambivalence of his invocation of intrinsic value, despite the efforts of Geddes and Hobson to give this a scientific cast.

Ruskin makes explicit reference to Jevons early in *Fors Clavigera*, in 1872. In fact Jevons had first published a version of his theory early in the 1860s, and he can thus be aligned with Ruskin and Marx in the remarkable break that was then being made with classical political economy – though all three thinkers pointed in widely different directions. Ruskin however did not perceive Jevons as distinct from Smith, Ricardo and Mill, but as a further symptom of the radical inadequacy and wickedness of the Liberalism to which he assigned them all. He therefore takes time to ridicule the mathematical description of demand proposed by Jevons, and continues:

> But the Professor appears unconscious that there is a third dimension of pleasure and pain to be considered, besides their duration and intensity; and that this third dimension is, to some persons, the most important of all – namely, their quality. It is possible to die of a rose in aromatic pain; and, on the contrary, for flies and rats, even pleasure may be the reverse of aromatic. There is swine's pleasure, and dove's; villain's pleasure, and gentleman's, to be arranged, the Professor will find, by higher analysis, in eternally dissimilar rectangles.

> 4. My friends, the follies of Modern Liberalism, many and great though they be, are practically summed up in this denial or neglect of the quality and intrinsic value of things. Its rectangular beatitudes, and spherical benevolences, – theology of universal indulgence, and jurisprudence which will hang no rogues – mean, one and all of them, in the root, incapacity of discerning, or refusal to discern, worth and unworth in anything, and least of all in man; whereas Nature and Heaven command you, at your peril, to discern worth and unworth in everything, and most of all in man.[15]

The materialist aspect of this is certainly present, even excessively so, as Ruskin, in scarcely veiled terms, draws our attention to the inherently contrasting physical attractiveness of roses and ... the matter to which flies are attracted (the phrase 'to die of a rose in aromatic pain' is a quotation from Pope's *Essay on Man*, I, 200. A few lines earlier Pope also refers to flies, which might have sent Ruskin off in

---

[14]   James Sherburne's 1972 account remains the fullest and in many ways the richest account of Ruskin's relations to economics, and his sympathetic account of Ruskin, even given his deliberate eschewal of economic reading, is noteworthy. See Sherburne, *John Ruskin or the Ambiguities of Abundance*.

[15]   John Ruskin. *Fors Clavigera, The Works of Ruskin*. Ed. E.T. Cook and Alexander Wedderburn. Vol 27. London: George Allen, 1905. 247.

their direction). But the passage immediately lays itself open to liberal objection on two counts – though since this is an assault upon Modern Liberalism, this is not surprising. In the first instance, Ruskin assumes a social hierarchy of pleasures, indeed he states it explicitly, and in that contrast between 'villain' and 'gentleman' he alludes to the social etymology of villain/villein which is implicit in the word. To that extent he immediately lays himself open to the charge of 'elitism' which has been the standard liberal rejoinder to any effort to distinguish between the value attached to different kinds of demand. Related to this is the evident objection to the authoritarianism so visible in the second paragraph's allusion to capital punishment, and Ruskin's unfortunate willingness to use Carlylean rhetoric at moments. So the question which a passage like this poses is whether an insistence on the intrinsic qualities of the goods which surround humanity and which humanity manufactures, does not inevitably lead to elitism and authoritarianism.

This is a crucial question, and I do not wish to avoid it. However, it is a question where our situation of hindsight leads us in different directions. The complex social history which has tended to position readers in the West against the authoritarianism explicit in the passage, has unrolled in the context of an environmental catastrophe in response to which questions about the intrinsic value of production become unavoidable. However, Ruskin's relevance for our current environmental anxieties, already anticipated, will be postponed for one last time while we consider the typological thinking which is also just visible in this passage, and is very much more visible in Ruskin's writings elsewhere. For the meantime we can assert that a materialist reading of Ruskin's notion of intrinsic value is possible, and that it was attempted even in Ruskin's own lifetime by readers with Darwinian sympathies; and that such a reading depends on a sense of the creatureliness of humanity, and an understanding of the intrinsic qualities that make for a benign or noxious environment.

III: Ruskin's Typology of Nature

In that earlier passage from *Unto This Last*, in which Ruskin ecstatically anticipates areas of the world in the future saved from the degradations of a mechanical agriculture, he assures himself of the necessity of a landscape rich in wildlife. The surest sign of that richness will be the sound of birdsong: 'No air is sweet that is silent; it is only sweet when full of low currents of under sound – triplets of birds, and murmur and chirp of insects, and deep-toned words of men, and wayward trebles of children' (111). Birdsong, the first in this list for Ruskin, is the token and promise of a benign human relation with nature, and human consciousness of birdsong figures here as one of the central ways in which the moral and therefore creaturely values of nature impress themselves upon us. Is it possible to sustain this connection between the 'moral' and the 'creaturely' in other areas of Ruskin's writing? Is it possible, that is, to make a comparable assimilation of Ruskin's typological reading of nature that readers such as Geddes and Hobson made of his intrinsic account of value – what Hobson called his notion of 'vital use'? This question can conveniently be pursued by following the sound of birds.

Jeffrey Spear's account of Ruskin's typological thinking is a good starting place. He argues that this kind of thought – with its emphasis on the moral significance of nature – was a result of Ruskin's Evangelical upbringing and is cognate with what Ruskin found in his reading of Carlyle. An argument such as the following is certainly hard to square with Geddes's appropriation: 'The natural science of Ruskin's late years was deliberately archaic and Linnaean in conscious opposition to Darwinism, and designed to sustain his faith in the moral significance of nature so deeply rooted in Ruskin's early life.'[16] Following Spear, we can pursue this typological thinking into a characteristic late book of natural history written by Ruskin, his account of the birds to be found in *Love's Meinie* (1873–81). What are we to make, for example, of a passage like this about the swallow?

> To-day, then, I believe verily for the first time, I have been able to put before you some means of guidance to understand the beauty of the bird which lives with you in your own house and which purifies for you, from its insect pestilence, the air that you breathe. Thus the sweet domestic thing has done, for men, at least these four thousand years. She has been their companion, not of the home merely, but of the hearth, and the threshold; companion only endeared by departure, and showing better her loving-kindness by her faithful return. Type sometimes of the stranger, she has softened us to hospitality; type always of the suppliant, she has enchanted us to mercy; and in her feeble presence, the cowardice, or the wrath, of sacrilege has changed into the fidelities of sanctuary. Herald of our summer, she glances through our days of gladness; numberer of our years, she would teach us to apply our hearts to wisdom;—and yet, so little have we regarded her, that this very day, scarcely able to gather from all I can find told of her enough to explain so much as the unfolding of her wings, I can tell you nothing of her life—nothing of her journeying: I cannot learn how she builds, nor how she chooses the place of her wandering, nor how she traces the path of her return. Remaining thus blind and careless to the true ministries of the humble creature whom God has really sent to serve us, we in our pride, thinking ourselves surrounded by the pursuivants of the sky, can yet only invest them with majesty by giving them the calm of the bird's motion, and shade of the bird's plume:—and after all, it is well for us, if, when even for God's best mercies, and in His temples marble-built, we think that, "with angels and archangels, and all the company of Heaven, we laud and magnify His glorious name"—well for us, if our attempt be not only an insult, and His ears open rather to the inarticulate and unintended praise, of "the Swallow, twittering from her straw-built shed."[17]

The first three sentences are unproblematically materialist: the benign nature of the swallow is explicable because of the function that the bird serves in purifying the air of insects. This makes it a 'domestic' bird. The overarching intellectual

---

[16] Jeffrey L. Spear. *Dreams of an English Eden: Ruskin and his Tradition in Social Criticism.* New York: Columbia University Press, 1984. 51.

[17] John Ruskin. *Love's Meinie. The Works of Ruskin.* Ed E.T. Cook and Alexander Wedderburn. Vol. 25. London: George Allen, 1905. 71–3.

framework even of this passage is nevertheless that of a divine Natural History rather than evolutionary biology; the 'at least four thousand years' for which swallows have served their benign mission to humankind is suspiciously close to the timetable of Biblical history, though Ruskin's equivocation over the exact length of time leaves open the possibility of a longer time-scale. More seriously the 'loving-kindness' attributed to the birds implies some benign human-centred design in their patterns of migration; I read this as a theistic 'just-so story' of a kind familiar from evolutionary biology even if I wish to replace the extraordinary complexities of evolutionary and ecological history for the action of the divine.

With the phrase 'type sometimes of the stranger', Ruskin shifts into an explicitly typological reading of the swallow; the values that this scrap of the natural world have for us must be read via its symbolism. This is to say that the value and significance of the swallow is inexplicable to us outside of the human history in which the bird has appeared. This is not necessarily to assert that the swallow's significance is only to be understood in these terms; but rather that its meanings for us – Ruskin makes several suggestions – are inextricable from the human history in which the swallow has appeared, and indeed they are also inextricable from the passage of the seasons on which they depend and of which they are the sign. Ruskin's assertion of the ignorance of actual scientific knowledge with respect to the swallow is in fact an attack on the misdirected science of his own age; the passage of time has in part corrected this, and we are now certainly more knowledgeable about the structures of the swallow's wing, about how the bird builds its nest, and the mechanisms which enable it to performs its extraordinary migration back and forth to Africa. There is even the possibility that we can explain the avian compass which enables migratory birds to navigate, thanks to an extraordinary capacity of birds actually to *see* the earth's magnetic field.[18] This position of hindsight with respect to Ruskin however works benignly both for us and for him; this is a science of which he would approve, since we are no longer 'blind and careless to the true ministries of the humble creature' – or at least, we may not be blind but whether we are careless remains to be established.

The final third of this remarkable passage provides a flight of typological fantasy as Ruskin embarks on some thoughts about angels, led there by the inadequacies of the science of wings and feathers, and by the fact that human imagination has sought to elevate its conception of the angelic by endowing the human figure with the wings of birds. From there to prayer, and the notion that God might find the twittering of birds more acceptable than our own impertinent acts of worship. We now seem to be in a realm of reasoning well beyond anything approachable by Geddes's or Hobson's rationalist assimilations. But even here, in this unlikely territory of speculation about the anatomy of angels and the grateful feelings of the deity, we can read Ruskin as taking us beyond the human-centred

---

[18]   See Robert MacFarlane, *The Old Ways: A Journey on Foot*. London: Penguin Books, 2012. 77. This research is not as yet conclusive; for a report see http://www.ks.uiuc.edu/Research/cryptochrome/.

concerns of the passage so far, and to a recognition of the value of the swallow and its song intrinsically beyond human purposes.

Typology is not therefore merely random, but, in a passage such as this, can be used to suggest the material conditions which govern human interactions with the environment, the inevitable entanglement of such interactions with human history and the meanings that have accumulated in its course, and, via an allusion to human history seen *sub specie aeternitatis*, a suggestion of the absolute indifference of natural processes to human meaning. I make these interpretative moves, in fact, in a determinedly secularising spirit, though I absolutely do not think that this is to read with hindsight, since both in Ruskin's time and our own there is no consensus on the matter of a divine Natural History. However, hindsight does make most salient the sophistication and seriousness with which people in the nineteenth century discussed matters which are now also the subject of rancorous debate.

Let us hear the rancour in action:

> I have just listened to a lecture in which the topic for discussion was the fig. Not a botanical lecture, a literary one. We got the fig in literature, the fig as metaphor, changing perceptions of the fig, the fig as emblem of pudenda and the fig leaf as modest concealer of them, 'fig' as an insult, the social construction of the fig, D.H. Lawrence on how to eat a fig in society, 'reading fig' and, I rather think, 'the fig as text'. The speaker's final *pensée* was the following. He recalled to us the Genesis story of Eve tempting Adam to eat of the fruit of the tree of knowledge. Genesis doesn't specify, he reminded us, which fruit it was. Traditionally, people take it to be an apple. The lecturer suspected that actually it was a fig, and with this piquant little shaft he ended his talk.
>
> This kind of thing is the stock-in-trade of a certain kind of literary mind, but it provokes *me* to literal-mindedness. The speaker obviously knew that there never was a Garden of Eden, never a tree of knowledge of good and evil. So what was he actually trying to say? I suppose he had a vague feeling that 'somehow', 'if you will', 'at some level', 'in some sense', 'if I may put it this way' it is somehow 'right' that the fruit in the story 'should' have been a fig. But enough of this. It is not that we should be literalist and Gradgrindian, but our elegant lecturer was *missing* so much. There is genuine paradox and real poetry lurking in the fig, with subtleties to exercise an inquiring mind and wonders to uplift an aesthetic one. In this book I want to move to a position where I can tell the true story of the fig. But the fig story is only one out of millions that all have the same Darwinian grammar and logic – albeit the fig story is among the most satisfyingly intricate in evolution.[19]

I presume that Ruskin's meditation on the meaning of the swallow falls exactly under the ban imposed here by Richard Dawkins on 'a certain kind of literary mind'. So what is at stake in seeking to retain the validity of Ruskin's style of meditation in the face of this contemporary re-run of the debate between science and religion? 'Swallow as text' rather than 'fig as text' – the formulation is revealing in that while Dawkins clearly wishes to use the phrase to discredit

---

[19]   Richard Dawkins. *Climbing Mount Improbable*. London: Viking, 1996. 1.

postmodernist nonsense (his piece is contemporaneous with the Sokal affair), if we think of the phrase 'swallow as text' in the context of Ruskin's writing we are rather reminded of his origins in homiletics. Dawkins's scientific reduction ('the fig story is only one out of millions that all have the same Darwinian grammar and logic') is performed to indicate what his literary lecturer has left out – the genuine scientific basis for 'real poetry' and aesthetic 'uplift'. But we may legitimately ask what such a reduction in turn leaves out, without in the least being tempted into any version of the two cultures debate which nevertheless underpins Dawkins's paragraphs. It excludes precisely what Dawkins wishes it to exclude – what the meanings of natural phenomena are and have been in human history, which can include the scientific understanding of them but whose value is in part conferred by these human meanings.

This is a necessary preliminary for the final section of this chapter, which considers the re-working of the rhetorical economy of Ruskin's writing, especially *Unto This Last*, in our contemporary moment of ecological danger. Ruskin intimates something of the value *for us* of the natural world, inextricable from the intrinsic values of the things we produce and the human beings who are produced in the process. A last look at Ruskin's swallow, however, will make a suitable introduction: one hundred and fifty years after Ruskin wrote about the little bird, this is how the Royal Society for the Protection of Birds sums up the health of the European population of the species:

> Independent of weather-related fluctuations, there have been widespread declines in swallow numbers across Europe since 1970. The cause(s) of these declines is unknown but potential factors are discussed below.
>
> Climatic changes in the swallows' African winter quarters and on migration routes may be having a serious impact. Research has shown that swallows are returning to their breeding areas in poor condition and are laying fewer eggs than previously.
>
> Adverse climatic conditions in Europe may also be having a detrimental effect. Cold springs with late frosts can cause problems for swallows, as do exceptionally hot and dry summers. In the latter case, pools dry out, reducing the numbers of emerging insects, and nestlings die from heat exhaustion and dehydration. The expansion of the Sahara desert may be making this formidable barrier increasingly difficult for swallows to cross.
>
> Changes in farming practices throughout Europe may be reducing the numbers of nest sites and the quantity of flying insects. Swallows like to forage over grazed pastures, and the loss of cattle grazing has negatively affected swallows in some regions of Europe.[20]

Our reading with hindsight necessarily includes these intractable facts.

---

[20]   http://www.rspb.org.uk/wildlife/birdguide/name/s/swallow/population.aspx

IV: Ruskin and Ecology

As we have seen, the attempt to assimilate Ruskin to an understanding of humanity's relationship with its environment was first made in the nineteenth century. In that sense there is nothing new in his being recruited for our contemporary environmental concerns, except of course for the sense of urgency and ongoing catastrophe which characterises the present moment, compared to, say, the confident scientific outlook of Patrick Geddes. As Jeffrey Spear put it in the early 1980s, 'if certain of Ruskin's proposals have gained in cogency, it is because the rejection of industrialism as we have known it by nature itself has begun to seem a real probability rather than the logical, but remote, possibility it was in Ruskin's time.'[21] In short, our present circumstances lend a salience and emphatic immediacy to what in the nineteenth century appeared only as the limits or interesting premises of his writing.

Spear, writing in the 1980s, was not the first to recognize the importance of Ruskin to environmental concerns. Sherburne, writing ten years earlier, had already asserted that 'the point has been reached when Ruskin's calls for retreat in technology, urbanization, and population are no longer the counsels of nostalgia or aesthetic preference but the demands of necessity if man is to avoid an ecological catastrophe.'[22] Since then, Ruskin, along with the whole tradition of Romanticism, has been recruited for Green concerns, figuring, for example, in *The Green Studies Reader* of 2000 (sub-title: 'From Romanticism to Ecocriticism'); Ruskin's essay 'The Storm-Cloud of the Nineteenth Century' has emerged to take a central place in anthologies of nineteenth-century literature as its evident relevance to concerns about climate change has been noticed. Indeed, this whole emerging tradition of criticism is a classic instance of reading with hindsight, as the writing of the late eighteenth and nineteenth centuries is reconstituted and re-assessed in the light of our contemporary concerns and priorities.

Nevertheless, there is a question to be asked about the specific importance of Ruskin to us, beyond this general rediscovery of the ecological implications of Romanticism, and in particular of the Romantic critique of capitalism which is the sharply polemical version of romanticism to which Ruskin belonged. Jonathan Bate, for whom Ruskin figures both in *Romantic Ecology* and *The Song of the Earth*, rightly argues that there is no necessary connection between a concern for nature and a particular politics: 'Nature is so various that no consistent political principles can be derived from it. Of course they cannot. To describe an ecosystem you have to stand imaginatively outside it ... politics is what you get when you fall from nature.'[23] But this is perhaps too Heidegerrian a way of putting things,

---

[21]   Spear. *Dreams of an English Eden*.197.

[22]   Sherburne. *John Ruskin or the Ambiguities of Abundance*. 299.

[23]   Jonathan Bate. *The Song of the Earth*. London: Picador, 2000. 267–8. See also Jonathan Bate, *Romantic Ecology: Wordsworth and the Environmental Tradition*. London: Routledge, 1991.

or simply too ready to assume that we inhabit a fallen world. Bate makes the argument in order to make some space for ecology, to detach it from the limiting political labels which have historically threatened to frame it. In particular, as far as Ruskin is concerned, it enables him to put a wedge between Ruskin's commitment to nature and the neo-feudal politics that deformed his outlook. However, we need to ask whether Ruskin's concern for intrinsic value, which unites both his critique of political economy and his attitude to the natural world, points to a distinctive orientation in the fraught and necessarily political world which we actually inhabit – to quote appropriately from Wordsworth in this context, 'Not in Utopia – subterranean fields, – … But in the very world, which is the world/Of all of us, – the place where, in the end,/We find our happiness or not at all!'[24]

Here are three areas where Ruskin's thinking now speaks with a force conferred by the peculiar social and economic history that has unrolled – with massive disruptions, violence, and environmental degradation – since his death. In the first instance Ruskin's emphasis on the intrinsic qualities of both the natural world and the goods that we produce is essential. This is a different matter from the question of comparative quality, though there is always the temptation of some slippage here, as in the following quotation from Sherburne:

> Ruskin's crude refashioning of economic doctrines in terms which encourage a concern for quality is his great achievement, an achievement evident in the chaos of his later work where the question of how the consumer will spend his money is the unifying theme. This achievement is due partly to the success of a production-oriented economy in creating an abundance which makes plausible a concern for quality.[25]

Another aspect of Ruskin's thinking, most fully developed by Morris and then the Arts and Crafts movement, was certainly concerned with quality in this sense, and the limitations of this approach (niche production for elite consumers) have been only too happily pointed out by the movement's critics ever since. Rather, Ruskin's insistence on intrinsic value or intrinsic qualities, and their inevitable impact for good or ill on the well-being of humanity, provides the inevitable perspective in which to place both economic production and human impact on the environment.

Secondly, and closely related to this, the emergence of a creaturely way of understanding the limits of economic production – however intermittently it appears in Ruskin, and however often it appears on its head, as a matter of divine ordinance – precisely critiques the multiple industrial and agricultural processes that tend to the poisoning of human life and not to its sustenance. Incredible that this should require saying, but Ruskin's support here is unequivocal.

Finally, drawing on the more imaginative and typological aspects of Ruskin's writing as it relates to the natural world – 'as the art of life is learned, it will

---

[24] William Wordsworth. *The Prelude: A Parallel Text*. Ed. J.C. Maxwell. London: Penguin Books, 1971. 1850 text, 11. 140–44.

[25] Sherburne. *John Ruskin or the Ambiguities of Abundance*. 178.

be found that all lovely things are also necessary' (*Unto This Last*, 111) – we can find in Ruskin's writing support for aesthetic and historical statements of humanity's response to the natural world which are not merely supplementary to more narrowly practical or economic terms.

These then are some of the implications of Ruskin's critique of political economy, and of his refusal to enter into the analysis of value in exchange. I have stressed the limits that his insistence on use value entails in environmental terms; as we have seen, it is no coincidence that, not only in *Unto This Last*, but also in such lectures as 'The Storm-Cloud of the Nineteenth Century', it should be Ruskin who articulates a consciousness of environmental degradation. But Ruskin's understanding of value has a more punctual relevance also, in the aftermath of the credit crunch and the financial meltdown of 2008. Ruskin can serve to remind us of the ever-increasing distance between the world of finance and the world of production – or more properly, the ever-increasing subordination of the world of production to financialisation. The world of collateralised debt obligations and credit default swaps, of derivatives of various kinds, is a world created purely out of exchange value and has become completely divorced from use value, though we have seen its spectacular capacity to destroy value of all kinds. The shadow banking system and off-balance-sheet accounting are effectively ways of siphoning off the surpluses created in production and add nothing of value in themselves. Ruskin's insistence on use value – 'the things that lead to life' – is at least one measure of the gravity-defying economics of capitalism in its neoliberal phase.

Chapter 7
Utopia Under the Sign of Hindsight

Ruskin's greatest successor in the nineteenth century was William Morris, and in this chapter I discuss his writing, especially his 'utopian romance' *News from Nowhere* (1890). Morris too is a significant contributor to the romantic critique of capitalism, though this did not prevent him coming to an accommodation with Marxism in his later life. Indeed, the following chapter partly turns on the question of the continuing value of his utopian thought insofar as it was distinguished by the particular intellectual and political trajectory that led him to it.

I

If any mode of writing seems subject to the destructive effects of hindsight, it must be the utopian, whose manifold anticipations and projections appear to make it especially vulnerable to the knowingness provided by the backward glance. Still more than the particular datedness that infests all futurist science fiction, whose charming paraphernalia of gadgets and contrivances have been so often superseded by the fantastic actuality, late nineteenth-century utopian writing even comes with its own self-disproving timetable, as *News from Nowhere*'s 1952 date for the onset of the revolution has long since come and gone, and *Looking Backward*'s Boston in the year 2000, that convenient millenarian year, proves to be just as dystopian as the city that Bellamy's time-traveller escaped. Conversely – or perhaps equally - in the dystopian mode, Orwell's *1984* too has come and gone, though it should be said that this has not prevented that particular text from continuing to have 'prophetic' status.

But the operation of hindsight with respect to these texts – *News from Nowhere* in particular – is much more profound than even these not entirely superficial and arbitrary timetables indicate. Situated at the onset of the revolutionary socialist upheavals of the twentieth century, Morris's text (first published in the weekly journal of the Socialist League, *Commonweal*, in 1890) comes to us charged with an extraordinary pathos, as the locus and expression of innumerable hopes and dreams for a transformed future, hopes which appear to have been comprehensively mocked by the terrible history that has succeeded. Indeed, the situation is worse than this; it is not merely that *News from Nowhere* is the innocent expression of such hopes, but that, in a now dominant account, utopianism itself is seen as the cause of the problem. The very fact of seeking to make plans for the future which go against the grain of 'human nature', defined as that which fits us all for the operations of market capitalism, makes texts such as Morris's 'chapters from a utopian romance' vulnerable to the charges of authoritarianism and potentially disastrous social planning, as socialists and communists seek to straighten the 'crooked timber of humanity' in the text's image. Looking backward to the moment of *Looking Backward* and *News from Nowhere* is to see them across a historical cataclysm for which, in one account, they are partly responsible.[1]

An initial way of defending Morris's text from this corrosively sceptical backward look is to recall its own location in its historical moment, to see how and why it was able to articulate those particular desires in that particular form. In one sense this is no more than a necessary phase in making sense of the text, as an inevitably partial and provisional act of attention to it. But it is also a specific question about the utopian imagination, which asks what kind of purchase utopia has on the world to which it is addressed, and on what possible resources of thought and fantasy the utopist can draw in articulating utopian dreams. In leading us to the particularity of Morris's text the question will begin to make clearer how *News from Nowhere* is after all not a merely generic utopia, and thus will begin to specify the distinctive weight that the text has had and might continue to have in relation to that terrible twentieth-century history to which I have gestured.

This is not, for all that, an attempt somehow to absolve Morris's utopia from the general questions about the utopian mode which need to be put to it. This is especially the case because it is so clearly tied to its utopian opposite, Bellamy's *Looking Backward*, to which it is famously a rejoinder. Indeed, Fredric Jameson has suggested, as one initial characterisation of the historicity of utopia, its incidence at moments immediately preceding epochs of historical upheaval, so that the utopias of the 1890s, which include Bellamy's and Morris's writings, fall uncannily before the actual transformations which in multiple ways they anticipate. Perry Anderson has added to Jameson's pairing Hertzka's *Freiland* (1890) and Kang Youwei's *Great Consonance* (1888–1902), and we can also add in a more parochial vein Ebenezer Howard's *Garden Cities of Tomorrow* (1898).[2] From this grand perspective, the specificity of utopian texts tends to get erased, though their particular immersion in the grand currents of history is suggestively indicated.

We can specify the historicity of this *fin de siècle* utopian moment more precisely, and give it a more specific national colouring, by drawing on Matthew Beaumont's account of this phase of English utopianism in *Utopia Ltd: Ideologies of Social Dreaming 1870-1910*.[3] In this account, the proliferation of utopian texts in the period between 1870 and 1910 (he has many more to discuss even than the

---

[1]   Some of these arguments are directly confronted by Russell Jacoby, *Future Imperfect: Utopian Thought for an Anti-Utopian Age*. New York: Columbia University Press, 2005.

[2]   Fredric Jameson. 'The Politics of Utopia.' *New Left Review*, 25 (Jan/Feb 2004): 35–54; Perry Anderson. 'The River of Time.' *New Left Review*, 26 (Mar/Apr 2004): 67–77.

[3]   Matthew Beaumont. *Utopia Ltd: Ideologies of Social Dreaming 1870-1910*. Leiden: Brill, 2005. See also Matthew Beaumont, 'To Live in the Present: *News from Nowhere* and the Representation of the Present in Late Victorian Fiction'. *Writing on the Image: Reading William Morris*. Ed. David Latham. Toronto: University of Toronto Press, 2007. 119–36.

well-known texts by Lytton, Morris, Bellamy, Wells and Howard), needs to be understood in the particular nature of the social and economic crisis in England at the end of the nineteenth century, briefly summarised under the heading of the Great Depression which set in during the 1870s. Widespread awareness of a sense of social crisis, manifested in the extraordinary proliferation of social movements of various kinds, from socialism through feminism, vegetarianism, anti-vivisectionism, Theosophy, 'Back to the Land' and New Lifeism, was accompanied by uncertainty and apprehension about imminent social changes. Beaumont characterises this situation as one of 'expectancy', and it is out of this social soil that utopianism grows, allowing various imaginary escapes and resolutions of the social crisis. Matthew Arnold's account of religious uncertainty earlier in the nineteenth century, 'wandering between two worlds, one dead,/The other powerless to be born',[4] could be used to capture this state of expectancy, and would allow us to relate Beaumont's account to Jameson and Anderson's more epochal one, in which the new world waiting to be born arrives unmistakably twenty-five years after Morris's text.

Nevertheless, all historical moments are complex, and enfold within themselves multiple social and cultural possibilities, all with their own histories, understood here as embodied social and ideological antecedents. It is this very complexity which contributes to the possibility of some ideological distance from one's own moment, which gives historically embedded people, in other words, a capacity to formulate critiques and utopias. The particular character of Morris's utopianism in *News from Nowhere*, which distinguishes it from the many utopias which surround it, depends upon his particular inheritance and positioning in the complex and contradictory conjuncture of the *fin de siècle*. This is a different thing to say than to repeat his own insistence, in his review of Bellamy's *Looking Backward*, that 'the only safe way of reading a Utopia is to consider it as the expression of the temperament of its author.'[5] This is doubtless true, and no temperament or personality is ultimately reducible to its historical environment, however complex. But any conjuncture throws up differing possibilities and opportunities that can be exploited in different ways by the various and irreducible temperaments alive at that moment. Morris's socialism is of course crucial to *News from Nowhere*, but he shared this with many others in the late nineteenth century. It is the particular character of his socialism which makes it distinctive, and this derives from his whole formation as a writer, artist, craftsman and thinker. In short, his particular inheritance from Ruskin, and with him the whole romantic critique of capitalism, evidently suffuses his writing, and makes it a distinctive presence in the retrospective assessment of utopia. Morris's allegiance to this tradition and his practice as a craftsman, which in turn depended upon actually-existing social

---

    [4]   Matthew Arnold. 'Stanzas from the Grande Chartreuse'. *Poetical Works*. Ed. C.B. Tinker and H.F. Lowry. London: Oxford University Press, 1969. ll. 85–6.

    [5]   William Morris. 'Looking Backward'. *William Morris: Artist, Writer, Socialist*. Ed. May Morris. Vol. 2 (New York: Russell and Russell, 1966. 502.

possibilities in his own day, determined the character of his utopia, and thus its particular trajectory through the twentieth and twenty-first centuries.

This tradition of thought, which, following Lukács, I have described as the 'romantic critique of capitalism', characteristically stresses the alienating nature of social relations under the market (Carlyle's metaphor in *Past and Present* was of people frozen into ice-blocks), the destructiveness of industrial production both to those who produce and to the environment, and the destruction wrought by the market on all traditional modes of life. Against this is evoked 'nature', both a notion of human nature in all its affective fullness, and external nature as a measure of the organic by which human constructions can be measured. *News from Nowhere*'s utopianism is evidently marked by this intellectual and cultural inheritance, especially in its repudiation of industrial production, its celebration of the small-scale and the local, and its envisioning of the clearing of the cities and a reconceived relation between the country and the city. Indeed it is this aspect of the text – its reconfigured imagination of the rural, with an effective abolition of the great cities – which most visibly distinguishes it from its utopian contemporaries, and marks its peculiar entry into twentieth-century utopianism.

We can get a measure of this by considering two turn-of-the-century reassessments of the utopian tradition in the twentieth century, by Susan Buck-Morss and David Harvey.[6] In *Dreamworld and Catastrophe* (2000), Buck-Morss impressively indicates the massive and popular utopian investments in modernity in both the Soviet Union and the West in the twentieth century, to the extent that she can claim that 'the Bolshevik experiment, no matter how many specifically Russian traits it developed, was vitally attached to the Western, modernizing project, from which it cannot be extricated without causing the project itself to fall to pieces – including its cult of historical progress' (68). Her own project is to rescue some of those utopian investments from the rubble left by the collapse of the Soviet Union. Morris's utopian project, however (springing from Ruskin), is founded on a rejection precisely of the technological modernity that the Soviet Union invested in. If utopia is indeed a 'critique of what is present' (Bloch), then we can look back to Morris's late nineteenth-century utopianism as providing us with one scarcely realised possibility for critique only partly discredited by the discrediting of progressive modernity. Similarly, David Harvey provides a powerful critique of the way that contemporary urban space has been degraded by the operations of capital and its penchant for the 'spatial fix': degraded, but also providing suburban utopias of a privatised kind, the numerous gated communities that now characterise the urban American landscape (Harvey's case-study is Baltimore). Against this he evokes the utopian tradition, going back indeed to the sixteenth century, but stopping off at Bellamy's *Looking Backward* and Ebenezer

---

[6]   Susan Buck-Morss. *Dreamworld and Catastrophe: The Passing of Mass Utopia in East and West.* Cambridge, Mass: MIT Press, 2000; David Harvey. *Spaces of Hope.* Edinburgh: Edinburgh University Press, 2000.

Howard's *Garden Cities of Tomorrow* which it partly inspired.[7] In the course of the book his critique of contemporary American urbanism is supplemented by a defence of utopianism located in the human capacity to plan; he repeatedly recalls Marx's distinction between the architecture of bees and that of humans. But the striking thing from a Morrisian point of view is his complete excision of Morris from the utopian tradition he evokes, most notably from his reference to Ebenezer Howard who drew equally on Bellamy and Morris in imagining and planning his garden cities. The good space of utopia for Harvey is therefore exclusively an urban space, and the multiple efforts to imagine it in the twentieth century, from Howard through Le Corbusier and Frank Lloyd Wright up to the latest prospectus of urban renewal all repeat this excision of Morris, and with him the tradition of the romantic critique of capitalism which he embodies.

One possible reason for this curious excision from current discussions of utopianism, though not for the distinctive trajectory of *News from Nowhere* through the twentieth century, has been powerfully articulated by Fredric Jameson:

> The weaker alternative, in our time at least, is the term standing in for nature, affirmed unacceptably as human nature in the free-market idiom. Ecology seems to count ever more feebly on its power – unless it be in the form of the apocalyptic and of catastrophe, global warming or the development of new viruses. Everything that today seems outmoded in traditional utopias seeks to redress this balance – to strengthen versions of Nature that are no longer persuasive, in an age when lawns and landscapes and other archetypes of natural beauty have become commodities systematically manufactured (and when the former 'human nature' has proven equally malleable and fungible).[8]

In this account, it is the wholesale commodification of the natural world that has increasingly prevented us from being persuaded by the evocation of nature in texts like *News from Nowhere* – though, as I have just indicated, this is far from a traditional utopia. If Jameson's account were true it would be a signal instance of hindsight disturbing the rhetorical economy of a text, operating, that is, to rob the text of its original force: insofar as the social and geographical realities to which Morris could point, on which he drew, and which any of his contemporary readers can be presumed to know about – that is, the continuing existence of both global wilderness and non-intensively farmed landscapes – have simply disappeared, then to this extent his strengthened version of Nature would indeed no longer be persuasive.

As we saw in the last chapter, this eventuality – of a world consumed by industry and utilitarian farming – is one which Ruskin partly anticipated and which Morris also, in some of his propagandist writing, felt obliged to confront (Ruskin: 'All England may, if it so chooses, become one manufacturing town …'). It is only

---

[7]   Ebenezer Howard. *Garden Cities of Tomorrow*. Builth Wells: Attic Boooks, 1993 [1898].

[8]   Fredric Jameson. 'The Politics of Utopia.' 49.

a world finally exhausted by globalisation – by which is meant the extension of capitalist social relations to every last corner – that there are no longer the spaces left which give Morris and Ruskin grounds for hope, and which therefore lends weight to Jameson's gloomy assertion that all such evocations of the natural world as utopian counterweight to the depredations of actually existing urbanism are doomed to nostalgia. While it is certainly the case that the contemporary ecological crisis provides an inescapable context for our current readings of *News from Nowhere*, there is more to be said on this matter than even Jameson has managed. This chapter will return to this topic after a necessary detour through other aspects of the text, which will also cast light on the 'malleable and fungible' 'human nature' which Jameson alludes to, a topic on which Morris has much to say.

It may be the case, therefore, that Morris's capacity to imagine a world of ecological husbandry is partly dependent on the co-existence of intimations of such a world in traditional farming practices. Something similar needs to be said at the cultural level also. That is, the capacity to imagine alternatives to the existing social world draws upon the repertoire of social and historical forms which come down from the past. Anticipation in this sense depends upon hindsight; in Morris's case, notoriously so, as the very form of his utopianism – literally dressed in medieval clothes – is dictated by his near-total immersion in the cultural forms of the medieval world. Morris is an extreme case of this 'back to the future' element of utopianism, and the romantic critique of capitalism makes a recourse to the medieval world always a likelier option for him than the Greek or Roman clothes with which, in Marx's famous discussion of the Brumaire, the French revolutionaries acted out their historical transformation.[9] This is to suggest our more benign version of hindsight, which need not only mean the recognition of the one true path of development, now visible as the only viable historical possibility; it also means the ability to find in the retrospective view both undeveloped social and cultural possibilities (a hindsight of the losers, so to speak), and, in the very superseded forms themselves, modes of being which challenge the present. The romantic exaltation of the social relations of the medieval world entails its own problems, as are evident for example in Carlyle's or Ruskin's authoritarianism, and as we shall see with a further examination of *News from Nowhere*; but it also provides a model of unalienated work and powerful affective social bonds. In short our reading of Morris with hindsight always entails his own multiple acts of hindsight both in his explicitly utopian writing and extensively in his other romances.

II

The famous opening sentence of Gabriel García Márquez's *One Hundred Years of Solitude* provides a relatively tame example of the temporal complexities that we are about to consider: 'Many years later, as he faced the firing squad, Colonel

---

⁹   Karl Marx. *The Eighteenth Brumaire of Louis Bonaparte. Surveys from Exile*. Ed. David Fernbach. Harmondsworth: Penguin Books, 1973.77.

Aurelio Buendía was to remember that distant afternoon when his father took him to discover ice.'[10] Early in the twenty-first century, we look back to that distant late-nineteenth-century moment when Morris anticipated the twenty-first century, from which imaginary standpoint he could critique his own historical situation, drawing on the imaginative resources of a distant past to do so. The passage of real historical time since the composition of *News from Nowhere* has set up all sorts of complexities, as we have seen, in the way we might come to terms with that original act of imagination on Morris's part. But the interplay between present and future also plays a constitutive role in the text itself, since the possibility of a transformed future is dependent on the acts of historical agents in the present, and the defamiliarising effect of the view from the future provides one of the central aesthetic strategies of the text. Matthew Beaumont, indeed, argues that this defamiliarising effect, created by what he calls 'anamorphic' vision, is the central aesthetic strategy of future utopias; by virtue of imagining a future perspective, inhabitants of the present are able to look back upon their present moment with transformed eyes:

> Utopian thought is an attempt to attain this 'higher intellectual vantage-point' [Lukács], this transcendental perspective: it projects a fictional future from which it defamiliarizes the present state of society and reconceives it as an objective historical totality rather a subjective way of life. In Utopia, the present is the past of a specific fictional future. Time-travelling to the future, it turns out, is about the return journey to the present traced by the forward motion of the time machine itself.[11]

In the terms of this book, utopia in this account is capable of creating artificial hindsight, in which one of the benefits of hindsight, the ability to see things in the round, as an 'objective historical totality', is created as it were by the capacity of utopists to see themselves by squinting out of the corner of their eye. As we have seen, this is a capacity which is dependent on the contradictory possibilities implicit in any complex historical conjuncture.

This defamiliarising capacity applies in the largest way, therefore, to the wider sense of a whole way of life, a cluster of mutually-reinforcing social practices and relations, that are revealed in the present by the perspective of the future. In the case of *News from Nowhere*, this wider perspective provides the context for the many acts of defamiliarisation which cluster around the figure of William Guest himself, wandering bemusedly around Nowhere, and constantly provoking misunderstandings and embarrassments as he tries to carry the customs of the

---

[10]   Gabriel García Márquez. *One Hundred Years of Solitude*. Trans. Gregory Rabassa. London: Picador, 1983. 9.

[11]   Matthew Beaumont. 'To Live in the Present: *News from Nowhere* and the Representation of the Present in Late Victorian Fiction'. *Writing on the Image: Reading William Morris*. Ed. David Latham. Toronto: University of Toronto Press, 2007. 119–36. 123.

nineteenth century into the twenty-first – by seeking to pay for services which are rendered freely, or by being surprised at the beauty and longevity of the people he meets. The function of this artificially created hindsight is made explicit especially in Ellen's much-quoted concluding message to William Guest, as he fades from the consciousness of the people of Nowhere, a message which suggests something of the paradox of the view from the future:

> 'No, it will not do; you cannot be of us; you belong so entirely to the unhappiness of the past that our happiness even would weary you. Go back again, now you have seen us, and your outward eyes have learned that in spite of all the infallible maxims of your day there is yet a time of rest in store for the world, when mastery has changed into fellowship – but not before. Go back again, then, and while you live you will see all round you people engaged in making others live lives which are not their own, while they themselves care nothing for their own real lives – men who hate life though they fear death. Go back and be the happier for having seen us, for having added a little hope to your struggle. Go on living while you may, striving, with whatsoever pain and labour needs must be, to build up little by little the new day of fellowship, and rest, and happiness.' (210–11)

Primarily this provides a justification for the propagandist purpose of this utopian text; it encourages its readers (originally the purchasers of the Socialist League weekly campaigning newspaper *The Commonweal*) to lift their eyes from the daily struggle and be inspired by the view at the far horizon. But it also suggests the dependence of the existence of the future upon our actions in the present, so that the perspective of the future, in this formulation at least, needs the very imagination that creates it. If this takes us towards the various paradoxes of time travel, beloved of science fiction writers, more importantly it points to the change of perspective to be wrought on Guest when he returns to the present of the 1890s and sees it with new eyes: 'you will see all round you people engaged in making others live lives which are not their own, while they themselves care nothing for their own real lives'.

In this respect *News from Nowhere* provides a mirror-image for the operations of hindsight in Morris's *A Dream of John Ball*, first published in *The Commonweal* between November 1886 and January 1887. In this earlier text, Morris's avatar travels backward rather than forward in time, and concludes not by having the future explained to him, but rather by having to explain the future to John Ball himself, the ideologue of the Peasants' Revolt. In this poignant encounter, the Friend has to explain to Ball both the success and the failure of the action in which he is engaged; how, that is, the struggles of the present, for all the necessity which requires them to be fought, and for all the heroism with which they are fought, will eventuate in a future in some ways the opposite from that which was intended. Hindsight in this text risks being totally disabling, just as in *News from Nowhere* it was designed to be inspiriting.

This complementarity of the two texts springs naturally from Morris's conception of the passage of historical time, which cannot be represented as a simple linearity, but is indeed genuinely dialectical, so that no stage in the historical process is simply passed beyond, but in the nature of its supersession permits past historical forms to be carried over into the future in transformed ways. This gives a particular force to the backward glance, as in this prefatory poem to *The House of the Wolfings*, first published in 1888 and thus a near contemporary of both *A Dream of John Ball* and *News from Nowhere*, and emerging indeed from comparable concerns:

> Whiles in the early winter eve
> We pass amid the gathering night
> Some homestead that we had to leave
> Years past; and see its candles bright
> Shine in the room beside the door
> Where we were merry years agone
> But now must never enter more,
> As still the dark road drives us on.
> E'en so the world of men may turn
> At even of some hurried day
> And see the ancient glimmer burn
> Across the waste that hath no way;
> Then with what faint light in its eyes
> A while I bid it linger near
> And nurse in wavering memories
> The bitter-sweet of days that were.[12]

This is a poem literally about 'hindsight': the backward glance across the dark to a lighted homestead, which figures the retrospect on previous historical times permitted us by the passage of history. The danger of hindsight in this sense, or at least as Morris expresses it in this poem, is that it can become a mere exercise in nostalgia, the past 'nursed in wavering memories' to provide some imaginary consolation in the present. But in a stronger reading, the social forms of the past can be activated in the present to indicate its inadequacies.

Several features of *News from Nowhere* are especially subject to the complex plays of anticipation, defeated hopes and persistent critique which this situation sets in motion. All the questions raised in the text about labour, handicraft and self-fulfilment through work have developed multiple accretions of significance since the text's publication, as have issues of design which the text raises. And naturally the text's provocative attitudes towards gender relations have been materially complicated by subsequent history.

Morris's Ruskinian inheritance is especially visible in relation to his insistence on pleasure in work as the defining feature of his utopia; it distinguishes him initially from Bellamy, but also from a whole tradition of socialist thought which has sought to organise and minimise labour. In Ruskin's case this springs above

---

[12]   William Morris. *The House of the Wolfings. The Collected Works of William Morris.* Vol. 14. New York: Russell and Russell, 1966.1.

all from his hostility to the dehumanising routines of the industrial division of labour, to which he opposes most memorably the free expression of the human spirit to be found in the details of the great Gothic cathedrals. Morris continues this tradition, of course – he asserted that in future days 'The Nature of Gothic' 'will be considered as one of the very few necessary and inevitable utterances of the century'[13] – but massively extends and deepens Ruskin's thought by his lifetime spent practicing, re-discovering, and where necessary re-inventing craft traditions. When translated into the utopian mode, this means that he imagines a world of small-scale, craft-based production in which people take intense pleasure and pride in the ordinary activities of life.

The social ground for this act of imagination was already tenuous in Morris's day, though perhaps not cripplingly so. In his own craft practice, he was able to consult practitioners in a number of trades – dyeing, printing, ceramics, weaving, glass-making, furniture-making and so on – who still either practiced or remembered pre-industrial modes of production. And his own extraordinary energy and facility always provided him with a model of what re-energised craft production might resemble. Nevertheless it remained the case even in his own day that the kind of craft-making that characterised Morris and Co was a kind of niche production, serving, as he himself disgustedly put it, the 'swinish luxury of the rich'. Indeed, one of the inevitable contexts for our reception of *News from Nowhere* now is our consciousness of the whole history of the Arts and Crafts movement which Morris did so much to inspire, and whose whole existence has been marked by this contradiction: that the utopian possibilities built into craft production in an age of industrial capitalism are only accessible to a tiny minority of workers, whose products are simply too costly to provide the basis for mass consumption.[14]

This was true of the various utopian projects that Morris inspired, for example the Arts Guild led by Ashbee which decamped en masse to Chipping Campden in 1901 and persisted there for several years – indeed founded a tradition of craft production in the area which persists to this day.[15] If craft production was already anachronistic and destined for a niche in Morris's day, that is of course still more the case in our own; the niche or even hobbyist status of craft production is now

---

[13]   William Morris. 'Preface to "The Nature of Gothic"'. *William Morris: Artist, Writer, Socialist*. Ed. May Morris. Vol 1. New York: Russell and Russell, 1966. 292.

[14]   The scholarship on the Arts and Crafts movement is of course substantial. For Morris's sometimes ambivalent inspiration of the movement, see Peter Stansky, *Redesigning the World: William Morris, the 1880s, and the Arts and Crafts*. Princeton: Princeton University Press, 1985. For an impressive survey and history of the movement, especially strong on its international developments, see Rosalind P. Blakesley, *The Arts and Crafts Movement*. London: Phaidon, 2006. Blakesley sets out the contradictions built into the movement very clearly, and how they were resolved, or not, in different national contexts.

[15]   See, for a full account of this venture, Fiona MacCarthy, *The Simple Life: C.R. Ashbee in the Cotswolds*. London: Lund Humphries, 1981.

more fundamentally removed from the predominant basis upon which human life is supported, and has become relegated to the innumerable artists' colonies which exist in the interstices of the contemporary world. The classic statement in relation to this remains that of Raymond Williams, in an essay on 'Socialism and Ecology':

> The association of that notion of deliberate simplification, even regression, with the idea of a socialist solution to the ugliness, the squalor and the waste of capitalist society has been very damaging. All it leads to, really, is a number of individual and small group solutions, such as the arts-and-crafts movement, or people like Edward Carpenter and a whole succession of good plain-living, honest and honourable people who have found this way of coping with and living through the twentieth century, damaging nobody, helping many. But in general they have fostered the notion that somehow this would solve the problem of the whole social order, in effect by cancellation of all the other things that have happened.[16]

This is doubtless true. Nevertheless it ignores the element of critique carried by the Ruskinian and Morrisian emphasis on pleasure in labour, which need not have the regressive or simple-life implications that Williams sees here as its inevitable outcome.[17]

For the imaginative embodiment of Morris's ideas about pleasure in labour remains, for all the problematic intervening history of the Arts and Crafts movement, impressive in *News from Nowhere*. These perhaps achieve their fullest expression in the episode of the 'obstinate refusers' in the text, encountered by the Guest and his companions as they make their way up the Thames intent on finding work in the hay-making. The refusers are so intent on completing their work (they are building and decorating a house) that they won't leave their labours to join others in the hay-making festival. Chief among them is the stone-carver Philippa:[18]

> She fell to work accordingly on a carving in low relief of flowers and figures, but talked on amidst her mallet strokes: 'You see, we all think this is the prettiest place for a house up and down these reaches; and the site has been so long

---

[16] Raymond Williams. 'Socialism and Ecology'. *Resources of Hope: Culture, Democracy, Socialism*. Ed. Robin Gable. London: Verso, 1989. 210–26. 217.

[17] For a persuasive argument in favour of the continuing relevance of Morris's notion of work, see Peter Smith, 'Attractive Labour and Social Change: William Morris Now'. *William Morris in the Twenty-First Century*. Ed. Phillippa Bennett and Rosie Miles. Oxford: Peter Lang, 2010. 129–50.

[18] Philippa, the best stone-carver among the obstinate refusers, has sometimes been seen as a reference to the historical figure of Philippa Fawcett (1868–1948), who obtained the highest result in the Cambridge Mathematical Tripos exams in 1890, at the time that *News from Nowhere* was being written. See, for example, Florence Boos, 'An (Almost) Egalitarian Sage: William Morris and Nineteenth-Century Socialist-Feminism'. *Victorian Sages and Cultural Discourse*. Ed. Thaïs Morgan. New Brunswick: Rutgers University Press, 1990. 187–206.

encumbered with an unworthy one, that we masons were determined to pay off fate and destiny for once, and build the prettiest house we could compass here – and so – and so'

Here she lapsed into mere carving, but the tall foreman came up and said: 'Yes, neighbours, that is it: so it is going to be all ashlar because we want to carve a kind of wreath of flowers all round it; and we have been much hindered by one thing or other – Philippa's illness amongst others, – and though we could have managed our wreath without her –'. (174–5)

This is an image of free labour, undertaken under ideal conditions and therefore driven only by considerations of design and pleasure in execution. Ruskinian design principles are in evidence: the details of the carving are in accord with natural forms but are also the expression of the particular bent and skill of the workman – or, in this case, the workwoman. There are perhaps problems with the detail of this design, since the 'wreath of flowers' will not be to everybody's taste, but for all that this aspect of Morris's utopia still has genuine powers of critique; that is to say, his starting point in the notion that art is the expression of man's pleasure in labour still has the capacity to lead to a wide-ranging critique of current conceptions of labour and current labour practices – indeed, of the whole contemporary system of labour.

There are of course problems with it, and in the world subsequent to the publication of *News from Nowhere* some of these became apparent. The building of Rodmarton Manor in Gloucestershire ('the last manor house in England') was undertaken on such strict Arts and Crafts principles that the sawyers were not allowed to take advantage of machine-sawn wood but instead were required to cut all the timber in the traditional way on site (saw-pits, 'top sawyer and bottom sawyer' and all).[19] And insofar as utopia can be realised in the suburbs, then it proved all too easy to adapt some of Morris's ideas to inform the design layouts and decorative trims of many garden suburbs.[20] But these distortions do not impinge on the fundamental utopian insight that demand for pleasure in labour has the most devastating implications for the system of labour relations that the utopian text seeks to supplant. Richard Sennett's suggestion that possibilities for self-directed meaningful labour of a craft kind are made available by digital open-course systems like Linux – while it has its own niche air when the predominant experience of interacting with the new digital technologies at work is via data-entry and call-centres – at least indicates that the principles of labour organisation rather the appearance suggested by design are what matters.[21]

Morris's utopian anticipations in the area of design have certainly been subject to some of the cruelties of hindsight. Pevsner's courageous inclusion of Morris among

[19]   See Peter Davey, *Arts and Crafts Architecture*. London: Phaidon, 1995. 164–5.

[20]   See Simon Dentith, 'From William Morris to the Morris Minor: An Alternative Suburban History', *Expanding Suburbia: Reviewing Suburban Narratives*. Ed. Roger Webster. New York: Berghahn Books, 2000. 15–30.

[21]   See Richard Sennett, *The Craftsman*. London: Penguin, 2008.

the pioneers of modern design has not prevented his various design commitments appearing definitively overtaken by the modern movement, to the extent that some aspects of Morrisian design now appear the very epitome of 'quaint'. The fate of Morris and Co is symptomatic of the wider history in this respect. It persisted as a separate entity well after Morris's death, finally going bankrupt in 1940 and being acquired by Sanderson and Co, who took over all the designs and indeed the original printing blocks for the fabrics and wallpapers. 'Morris and Co' still exists, but as a brand in part of a larger company, whose products branded in this way are produced internationally by methods which are the antithesis of those that Morris believed in. This aspect of the story – the conversion of Morris's design ideas into a version of kitsch – can be told in different ways: either as a sad falling-off from the true principles of his original designs, or as telling of a disjunction between superficial medievalist design in Morris's work and more fundamental design principles which are the grounds for Pevsner's surprising claim that he was one of the pioneers of modernism.[22]

The problem is one of divorcing the superficial aspects of design from the fundamental principles which inform them, though this is an unsatisfactory way of proceeding in Morrisian terms since design is not to be conceived as an optional add-on – the very problem that irritated Morris himself when considering the debased products of his own age. These fundamental principles are those of fitness for purpose, truth to materials, and use of vernacular styles where possible. These are excellent design principles, though they can lead to pastiche when the latter (vernacular materials) especially is applied too literally. In one inflection, however, they can clearly lead towards sustainable modes of building and production which, by a peculiar turn of the dialectical screw, now makes Morris's architectural modesty, his effort to run with the grain of the landscape ('this is the prettiest place for a house up and down these reaches'), enormously more appropriate and attractive than the utopianism of Le Corbusier and his 'Ville Radieuse'. In short, the complex history of twentieth-century design, and architectural design in particular, makes any full assessment of the episode of the 'obstinate refusers' especially ambivalent and suggestive of some surprising reversals: on the one hand the history of modernism in these design matters has taken one aspect of Morrisian principles and turned them against the designs of Morris himself; while on the other hand the architectural modesty and vernacular character of the house being built by Philippa and her work-mates stands as an implicit critique of the grandiose impositions on the landscape of some modernist projects.

Finally, the fact that the best carver among the obstinate refusers is a woman is obviously important. As so often in discussing nineteenth-century texts, difficult issues created by hindsight cluster around questions of gender relations. In the

---

[22] For an account of a twenty-first-century art project which sets in motion the disjunctions and ironies created by the history of the transformation of Morris's designs into kitsch, see David Mabb, 'Hijack: Morris Dialectically', with accompanying photographs. *William Morris in the Twenty-First Century.* 133–66.

case of *News from Nowhere*, there is a significant if not extensive discussion of these matters, resolved in what now seem contentious ways. It occurs in Chapter IX, 'Concerning Love', much of which deals with the relationship between Dick and Clara (they lived together for a while; she then went off with another man; now they are coming back together). So far so progressive, and this little narrative strand, along with Philippa the master-carver, certainly can make the basis for claims that Morris's utopianism here at least anticipates more liberal aspects of later modes of sexual and domestic relations.[23] It leads, however, to an explicit discussion of the 'woman question' already briefly signalled by an earlier scene in the romance, when William Guest is entertained at the Guest House by women 'waitresses' rather than by men. The discussion is between 'Guest' (Morris in one guise), the first-person visitor from the nineteenth century, and Hammond, the 'literary man' in Nowhere and the Guest's guide to its habits and mode of life:

> 'Very well,' I said, 'but about this woman question? I saw at the Guest House that the women were waiting on the men: that seems a little like reaction, doesn't it?'
>
> 'Does it?' said the old man; 'perhaps you think house-keeping an unimportant occupation, not deserving of respect. I believe that was the opinion of the "advanced" women of the nineteenth century, and their male backers. If it is yours, I recommend to your attention an old Norwegian folk-lore tale called How the Man minded the House, or some such title; the result of which minding was that, after various tribulations, the man and the family cow balanced each other at the end of a rope, the man hanging half-way up the chimney, the cow dangling from the roof, which, after the fashion of the country, was of turf and sloping down low to the ground. Hard on the cow, *I* think. Of course, no such mishap could happen to such a superior person as yourself,' he added, chuckling.[24]

We can notice the classic defamiliarising function of the utopian mode at work here, as the imagined voice from the future redescribes some custom or habit of

---

[23]   There is now an extensive literature on the question of gender, and especially the 'woman question', in relation to *News from Nowhere*. See especially, Florence Boos, 'An (Almost) Egalitarian Sage: William Morris and Nineteenth-Century Socialist-Feminism'. *Victorian Sages and Cultural Discourse*. Ed. Thaïs Morgan. New Brunswick: Rutgers University Press, 1990.187–206; Jan Marsh, 'William Morris and Victorian Manliness'. *William Morris, Centenary Essays*. Ed. Peter Faulkner and Peter Preston. Exeter: University of Exeter Press, 1999. 185–99; Jan Marsh, 'Concerning Love: *News from Nowhere* and Gender'. *William Morris and News from Nowhere: A Vision for Our Time*. Ed. Stephen Coleman and Paddy O'Sullivan. Bideford: Green Books, 1990. 107–25; Ady Mineo, 'Eros Unbound: Sexual Identities in *News from Nowhere*'. *Journal of the William Morris Society*. 9 (1992). 8–14; Ady Mineo, 'Beyond the Law of the Father: The "New Woman" in *News from Nowhere*', *Centenary Essays*. 200–206; Ruth Kinna, 'Socialist Fellowship and the Woman Question'. *Writing on the Image: Reading William Morris*. Ed. David Latham. Toronto: University of Toronto Press, 2007. 183–96.

[24]   William Morris. *News from Nowhere. The Collected Works of William Morris*. Vol 16. New York: Russell and Russell, 1966. 60.

thought from the present to make it appear strange: in this instance, the 'advanced' thought of one section at least of progressive opinion in the late nineteenth century. Hammond's recourse to an 'old Norwegian folk-lore tale' to reinforce his point is perhaps a minor instance of Morris's habitual recourse to cultural forms from the past in order to critique the present.[25] As such, it evokes a fund of traditional and partly comic 'wisdom' to cut down the pretensions of the present (the 1890s, not the presumed moment of this dialogue).

Up to this point it is hard not to disagree with William Guest's initial demurral: 'that seems a little like reaction, doesn't it?' But the dialogue does not rest there. After some further bantering from Hammond, he takes the discussion in another direction:

> 'Excuse me,' said he, after a while; 'I am not laughing at anything you could be thinking of, but at that silly nineteenth-century fashion, current amongst rich so-called cultivated people, of ignoring all the steps by which their daily dinner was reached, as matters too low for their lofty intelligence. Useless idiots! Come, now, I am a "literary man," as we queer animals used to be called, yet I am a pretty good cook myself.'
> 'So am I,' said I
> 'Well then,' said he, 'I really think you can understand me better than you would seem to do, judging by your words and your silence.' (60–61)

Now we are on rather different terrain, as the perspective of the future permits Hammond to assert a connection between the distorted class society of the nineteenth century and a disdain for the details of life. This is one of the aspects of *News from Nowhere* which Guest wishes to explore further; indeed it is one of the fundamental principles of the text, and its author's relish in the details of his imagined life (rooted, of course, in an actual campaigning and practical interest on Morris's part) is one of its principal features. But the admission on the part of both these men that they are 'pretty good' cooks themselves at once undermines the gender stereotyping that the archaic Norwegian folk-tale had reinforced.

This is not to say that something a 'little like reaction' does not remain the predominant impression that a reader would retain from his exchange. It suggests a real difficulty with the romantic critique of capitalism and class society with which I am associating *News from Nowhere*, in that its invocation of a notion of nature, including human nature, against the distortions created by the market, is what gives this tradition its force, yet by the same token it tends to assume some fixity in traditional gender relations. The recourse to the folk wisdom of a peasant society reinforces this effect. However, the text points in different directions (or is making a complex argument) at this point, and the explanation that it provides of

---

[25]   Morris alludes to the Norwegian tale 'The Husband Who Was to Mind the House'. *Popular Tales from the Norse: With an Introductory Essay on the Origin and Diffusion of Popular Tales.* Ed. George Webbe Dasent. Edinburgh: Edmonston and Douglas, 1859.

some of the distortions of Morris's contemporary feminism – distorted, that is, by its location in class society – is persuasive.[26]

This explanation is pursued in relation to the more difficult questions raised by child-bearing and maternity, as Guest continues:

> 'But I want to return to the position of women amongst you. You have studied the "emancipation of women" business of the nineteenth century: don't you remember that some of the "superior" women wanted to emancipate the more intelligent part of their sex from the bearing of children?'
>
> The old man grew quite serious again. Said he: 'I *do* remember about that strange piece of baseless folly, the result, like all other follies of the period, of the hideous class tyranny which then obtained. What do we think of it now? you would say. My friend, that is a question easy to answer. How could it possibly be but that maternity should be highly honoured amongst us? Surely it is a matter of course that the natural and necessary pains which the mother must go through form a bond of union between man and woman, an extra stimulus to love and affection between them, and that this is universally recognised.' (61)

'Nature' has now returned with a vengeance, as a justification it seems for the pains of childbirth. Several distinct strands of argument need disentangling here, involving their own different modes of anticipation and retrospection. The 'superior' women themselves are looking forward to a future in which some women at least will be emancipated from childbearing – a proposal which, eighty years later, will feature in some utopian texts, most notably Marge Piercy's *Woman on the Edge of Time* (1976). Morris's critique of the class-distorted basis of the proposal remains powerful however, and suggests its own anachronistic parallel in the contemporary phrase 'too posh to push'. But while there is some force to the analysis, made formally possible by the perspective of the future, that there is a relationship between disdain for the labouring classes and disdain for the body itself, medical advances no longer mean that this analysis need rest in the queasy celebration of maternal suffering itself. The ambivalence of that recourse to nature reappears here, as it at once measures the 'hideous class tyranny' which seeks to repudiate the natural facts of the body, and ends up sentimentalising those sometimes brutal facts themselves.

Morris continues the critique of contemporary class relations and their impact on sexual and maternal feelings with this concluding flourish, as Hammond ends with a paean of praise to women in utopia:

---

[26] Morris was immersed in debates about the 'woman question' in the 1880s and 1890s, if only by virtue of his leadership of the Socialist League and his friendships with Eleanor Marx and Belfort Bax. The latter's virulent anti-feminism explains some of the failings of *Commonweal*. For Morris's multiple socialist alliances in the 1880s, see E.P. Thompson, *William Morris: Romantic to Revolutionary*. 2nd ed. London: Merlin Press, 1977; and for the potentially baleful influence of Bax, see Boos, 'An (Almost) Egalitarian Sage', 1990.

'So that, you see, the ordinary healthy woman (and almost all our women are healthy and at least comely), respected as a child-bearer and rearer of children, desired as a woman, loved as a companion, unanxious for the future of her children, has far more instinct for maternity than the poor drudge and mother of drudges of past days could ever have had; or than her sister of the upper classes, brought up in affected ignorance of natural facts, reared in an atmosphere of mingled prudery and ignorance.' (62)

The function of utopia to act as critique of the present is especially apparent here, though it is also true that its corollary danger – that its projection of an alternative will only repeat the terms of the problem – is also in evidence. Nevertheless, the conclusion, which indicates the differential relation to their own bodies of the different social classes, has a real power and animus that introduces the next phase of the argument.

That phrase 'at least comely' in Hammond's speech introduces the final section of the chapter, in which he rather astonishingly claims that the people in Nowhere are especially beautiful because of the unforced sexual relations between their parents:

'Well, as to our looks, the English and Jutish blood, which on the whole is predominant here, used not to produce much beauty. But I think we have improved it. I know a man who has a large collection of portraits printed from photographs of the nineteenth century, and going over those and comparing them with the everyday faces in these times, puts the improvement in our good looks beyond a doubt. Now, there are some people who think it not too fantastic to connect this increase of beauty directly with our freedom and good sense in the matters we have been speaking of: they believe that a child born from the natural and healthy love between a man and a woman, even if that be transient, is likely to turn out better in all ways, and especially in bodily beauty, than the birth of the respectable commercial marriage bed, or of the dull despair of the drudge of that system. They say, Pleasure begets pleasure. What do you think?'
'I am much of that mind,' said I. (62–3)

This is an extraordinary passage, and its strangeness is certainly not wholly created by hindsight. Its frankness is firstly noticeable: the assertion that 'Pleasure begets pleasure'. But it is also the nearest that Morris's writings ever come to eugenics, from which, you would think, his earlier invocation of 'nature' would save him. It is also, of course, the late nineteenth-century belief most discredited by the passage of subsequent history, the traces of which in any writing seems most likely to consign it to the archive – were it not for the contemporary recrudescence of the belief under various medical guises. But this is eugenics with a difference, aestheticist eugenics if you wish, where the criterion for racial improvement is not health but beauty. Hindsight scarcely operates here, other perhaps than to suggest different criteria for beauty than Burne-Jones and John William Waterhouse. Whatever theories of heredity characterised the nineteenth century – and the Mendelian revolution was imminent when Morris wrote this passage, leaving space for all sorts of misunderstandings – none, I believe, proposed that the quality of people's sex lives affected the beauty of their children.

The ground even of this remarkable fantasy is Morris's insistence on the creaturely, or, if you prefer, biological condition of human pleasure, happiness, and potential for fulfilment. In this he recalls Ruskin at least as I argued in the previous chapter; Morris implicitly follows Ruskin's motto from *Unto This Last*, 'There is no Wealth but Life', and this creaturely understanding of humankind underlies as much his discussion of pleasure in labour, in the 'face of the earth' in all the innumerable details of life, as it does his discussion of the 'woman question'. One last contemporary (i.e., twenty-first century) context lends a particular salience to this insistence, namely arguments about the 'posthuman', in turn underlain by the remarkable advances in the life sciences, genetics, and bio-engineering. But it is possible to distinguish two different versions of the notion of the posthuman. Jed Mayer, following Cary Wolfe, tentatively aligns Morris with the first of these alternatives, which might perhaps more properly be categorised as 'posthumanist': it recurs to pre-Renaissance models of the human to provide a critique of the individualist or Cartesian ego, and to insist on the embodiment of the individual human subject and its immersion in multiple social and biological networks.[27] The second alternative, following the characteristic ambivalence that attaches to all 'post-' formulations (continuation or repudiation?), in effect repeats and exaggerates the logic of Cartesian humanism into a fantasy of technological transcendence of human embodiment altogether. Morris offers an emphatic repudiation of this fantasy and locates it in the distortions of class society and the division of labour. In doing so he provides a further example of how the illumination provided by hindsight reveals hitherto overlooked features of a text and at the same time can recognise their resistance to the history which initiated the backward look in the first place.

Morris's various anticipations of a utopian future, then, have inevitably now accreted multiple complexities as the history of the twentieth century unfolded both to confirm and deny his best hopes. In the specific areas discussed in this section – pleasure in labour, design, and gender relations - his various projections and commitments, springing as they do from the various social forms of his own period, have inevitably fared differently as the social forms from which they emerge and to which they were addressed have themselves evolved, mutated or become superseded. But this is not a story of simple supersession, like the passing of the land of Cockaigne now that most of Europe has – for the moment at least – moved beyond the society of scarcity that generated it. Two large historical continuities and developments above all give *News from Nowhere* its particular complex force in our present. Still more than in the late nineteenth century, we live in a world of divided labour, and Morris's capacity to speak to that condition is a voice that we still can hear. But perhaps most importantly, and in a way that was much more latent at the time that Morris was writing, we live in a world of imminent ecological catastrophe, and it is a particular capacity of the romantic critique of capitalism to speak to it.

---

[27] Jed Mayer. 'A Darker Shade of Green: William Morris, Richard Jefferies, and Posthumanist Ecologies'. *Journal of the William Morris Society.* 19.3 (2011). 79–92.

III

The discovery of Morris the Green is not of course simply a recent matter; in fact, interpretations and assimilations of Morris's writings, especially *News from Nowhere*, reached a crescendo in the early 1990s and especially around the centenary celebrations in 1996.[28] However, the urgency of the debates about Morris has intensified as the urgency of our current ecological crisis has become apparent, and as the priority awarded to this matter has altered. A simple indication of how things have changed can be gauged from E.P. Thompson's order of priorities in his 1976 'Postscript' to *William Morris: Romantic to Revolutionary*. In struggling to anticipate the legacy of Morris, he concludes that he is 'a pioneer of responsible "ecological" consciousness', but sees this as only a minor theme to be taken out of his writings.[29] If the nature of Morris's green position in his utopia now appears central to our sense of the work, then it is a reflection of the way that 'ecological consciousness' can no longer be seen as a mere subsidiary element in a wider political assessment.

Clearly, the attractiveness of Morris's utopia, in the context of environmental degradation and multiple threats to a sustainable human ecology, is readily understood: he offers a vision of a world where the ravages of industrial capitalism have been repaired, and where people's labour works with the grain of nature rather than against it. Much contemporary scholarship on Morris the Green consists of expositions of the many ways in which *News from Nowhere* envisages an environmentally sustainable mode of life, and, in doing so, how it anticipates current concerns; it often thus recasts Morris's text into contemporary language. This is an inevitable effect of hindsight, as the backward glance, informed by contemporary concerns, recasts old material into the terms of the present.

Such scholarly procedures have nevertheless provoked a backlash, which, in a way characteristic of the resistance to hindsight, has sought to re-emphasise the original terms and contexts in which Morris's arguments were made and in which his vision of the future was elaborated. Sara Wills, in *The Greening of William Morris: A Reasonable Share in the Beauty of the Earth*, has offered a bracing re-statement of Morris's thinking in relation to the question of 'nature', emphasising throughout how his characteristic stress is placed upon a human-centred politics and vision.[30] Taking issue with what she describes as 'presentist' readings of Morris

---

[28]   For a review of the scholarship in this area, see Patrick O'Sullivan, 'Morris the Red, Morris the Green – A Partial Review'. *Journal of the William Morris Society*. 19.3 (2011): 22–38. This article features in a special issue of the journal devoted to 'Morris the Green'.

[29]   E.P. Thompson 1977, 801. It seems to me that O'Sullivan misreads Thompson's irony here, when Thompson asserts that the renewed attention to Morris as an ecological thinker is a 'remarkable discovery!'. Far from being a denial of this discovery, as O'Sullivan asserts, this surprise registers Thompson's amazement that people should have for so long missed what should have been obvious.

[30]   Sara Wills. *The Greening of William Morris: A Reasonable Share in the Beauty of the Earth*. Beaconsfield: Circa, 2006.

which recast his writings into an alien contemporary vocabulary, she writes: 'Such "presentist" interpretations fail to consider that words such as 'ecology' and 'eco-centrism' were not Morris's words, and that the historical context of Morris's work was more properly humanism, materialism and a livelihood within nature and culture, rather than "eco-centrism", ecology and nature on its own' (12). This is not a mere debunking of contemporary scholarship, but rather an attempt to return to the original arguments and contexts of Morris's works, to recognise their difference from the eco-centred arguments of the present, and nevertheless to put them to work in the here and now – above all by stressing the priority given by Morris to human justice in access to the bounty of nature as worked upon by humanity. The phrase of Morris to which Wills recurs, and which forms the sub-title of her book, is 'a reasonable share in the beauty of the earth', the guiding principle, as she sees it, of his various and multiple writings on these matters.

Reading *News from Nowhere* in this light leads Wills to emphasise the human-centred nature of this utopia: 'It is therefore clear that the 'lovely nature' presented in *News from Nowhere* is not a timeless essence or 'ecotopia', but has history linked to the human activities and cultural practices which had sought to know, enjoy, control and exploit it.' (179). Furthermore, 'in Morris's "garden of England", the people have not gone "back to nature", but have further acculturated nature, forcing it back to them' (190). These are important emphases, and they enable us to take the measure and importance of Morris's text in our present moment more clearly. But the complexity of the situation needs to be acknowledged: the increasing intensity of our current ecological concerns leads us to re-evaluate Morris's writing, and in some instances to re-write it as anticipating our very present vocabularies; the effort to correct this involves resistance to the 'bad hindsight' it is premised on, and makes a claim to seeing Morris's writing more thoroughly in its own terms and in its original context. But this gesture also is finally valuable not as a mere scholarly correction but as in itself being capable of making Morris speak, partly in terms which are historically other to our own, to the very matter of ecological crisis which set the whole process off in the first place.

At all events, there is a salience given to the greenness of Nowhere by the range and depth of current ecological emergencies. This is compounded by the distinctiveness of Morris's utopia, which, we have seen in our earlier discussion of Susan Buck-Morss's *Dreamworld and Catastrophe*, represents a radically different tradition than the predominant twentieth-century investment in the future, which has been overwhelmingly technological, scientific, and premised upon the mastery of nature. There is nevertheless an alternative tradition of ecologically-based utopias in the twentieth century, of which Ernest Callenbach's *Ecotopia* (1978) is perhaps the best-known example; this springs from the upsurge of utopian thought that accompanied the great social movements of the 1960s and 1970s, and it is doubtless happy to recruit *News from Nowhere* as a predecessor.[31]

----

[31] For a brilliant account of this twentieth-century ecotopian tradition, and how News from Nowhere can appear transformed in the light of it, see Tony Pinkney, 'Versions of

Indeed, Morris's text becomes a necessary resource, an alternative model of a future socialist society only partly hampered by visions of mastery over nature – but one which can only play this function due to its own specific insertion in the complex dynamics of its own historical moment.[32] By an extraordinary dialectical turn, it is *because* Morris starts from Ruskin and Pre-Raphaelitism that he can now be invoked in our current emergency, when the aesthetics of this critic and this movement can never have the same currency.

We need finally to recur to Jameson's gloomy contention that no utopia can now be persuasive which relies upon the category of 'nature' as the measure of the inadequacies of the world we actually inhabit, in view of the extension of commodified forms to all corners of the globe – wall-to-wall capitalism as he put it in his earlier seminal essay on postmodernism. As we earlier observed, this is a classic instance of the way that hindsight can disrupt the rhetorical economy of a text. The corollary of his contention is that 'nature' only figures in contemporary ecological discourse as catastrophe, as the resurgent power of damaged eco-systems to bite back. If this were true it would make the appeal of *News from Nowhere* a matter of nostalgia, truly a road not taken, and one to which we are now definitively denied access. Contemporary scholars of Morris's work who are engaged in loving reconstructions of its ecological implications would thus be engaged in an elaborate exercise in self-delusion.

But perhaps Jameson is too quick to assign all utopias based on notions of nature – *News from* Nowhere is pre-eminent among them – to the file marked 'superseded by events'. Morris's text certainly retains the defamiliarising power of the genre, in the complex ways that we have seen, and which have been multiplied and complicated in various ways by the terrible history that has succeeded its publication. And certainly those many contemporary scholars who find in *News from Nowhere* a resource in our contemporary emergencies are responding to the historically-created possibilities in the text – perhaps this is another way of conceding to Jameson that 'nature' can now only be invoked in the key of catastrophe. But ultimately the persuasive power of *News from Nowhere* will depend in the largest sense on what happens to the world in the future – above all on whether the ravages of industrial capitalism can be repaired in the manner that Morris envisaged. That, of course, remains an open question.

Ecotopia in News from Nowhere'. William Morris in the Twenty-first Century. Ed. Phillippa Bennett and Rosie Miles. Oxford: Peter Lang, 2010. 93–106.

[32] For a characteristic example of contemporary recruiting of Morris for ecosocialism, see Bradley MacDonald, 'William Morris and the Vision of Ecosocialism'. Contemporary Justice Review. 7 (2004): 287–304. MacDonald helpfully sets out some of the differences among radical ecological positions, and provides an account of the correction to socialism required by ecology that is potentially cognate with the analysis of modernist utopias provided by Susan Buck-Morss.

Chapter 8
Writing with Hindsight:
The Victorian Novel in
Succeeding Centuries

I

In this final chapter I switch my topic from '*reading* with hindsight' to '*writing* with hindsight', as I address the problematic of hindsight as it works itself out in twentieth- and twenty-first-century novels set in the nineteenth century. This flatness of definition is deliberate, since it seeks to avoid the contentious issues surrounding such terms as 'historical novel', 'costume drama', and 'neo-Victorian novel'; I address some of these categorical distinctions below. In the meantime I simply observe that the formal variety and flexibility of the novel form as it is now available – a repertoire of possible ways of writing novels that is the legacy of several hundred years of formal experimentation and contention – permits the action of hindsight to be realised or kept at bay by a wide variety of formal means, which turn especially on the multiple ways in which the distance between past and present is realised in the narration. From the simplest-seeming first- or third-person narratives, through all the complications of multiple narration, double-time stories, 'found' narratives involving extensive pastiche, to the complexities of historiographic metafiction, novels set in the past, to revert to my initial deadpan formulation, inevitably realise hindsight, or seek to resist it, one way or another.

One contemporary historical novelist has forcefully expressed a view on these matters, in formulating a distinction between the practices of the novelist and the historian. In 'The Novelist's Arithmetic', a brief essay appended to *Wolf Hall*, Hilary Mantel writes as follows:

> Unlike the historian, the novelist doesn't operate through hindsight. She lives inside the consciousness of her characters, for whom the future is a blank. Acting always on imperfect information, only half-conscious of their own motivations, they have to hazard the unknown. It is up to the historian to analyse their actions and pass judgement in retrospect. The novelist agrees just to move forward with her characters, walking into the dark.[1]

The distinction between the practices of novelist and historian is especially relevant to *Wolf Hall* since its protagonist is the historically significant figure

---

[1] Hilary Mantel. 'The Novelist's Arithmetic'. *Wolf Hall*. London: Fourth Estate, 2010. 14 of P.S. section.

Thomas Cromwell, and Mantel is protecting her flank against potential assaults from historians guarding their turf. However, the claim that she makes should properly be seen as normative rather than descriptive, since it expresses a strong aesthetic preference for a certain kind of novel, and certainly does not describe the generality of historical novels, some of which depend upon hindsight and deploy it forcefully in the service of their aesthetic effects. Mantel's assertion is surely, for all that, an honourable one: it seeks to protect the legitimacy or validity of people's knowledge *at the time* from the potentially destructive retrospective view, and the formal challenge of realising this aesthetic in actual novelistic practice is formidable. However, her acknowledgement that the novelist's characters always act 'on imperfect information', and that they are 'only half-conscious of their own motivations', while providing classically fertile ground for the novelist, also permits, in other hands, writers to round out the imperfections of this knowledge, and this half-consciousness of motive, with the benefit of hindsight.

I begin with a discussion of two of the formative modern novels set in the nineteenth century, J.G. Farrell's *The Siege of Krishnapur* (1973) and John Fowles's *The French Lieutenant's Woman* (1969). These novels are formally very dissimilar, a difference most obvious in the self-referential or metafictional pyrotechnics of the latter – the famous garrulous narrator, the author who appears in his own novel to accompany its hero on a train journey, the alternative endings between which the reader can choose or, if sufficiently nimble-witted, hold both in mind simultaneously. Farrell's novel, by contrast, is for the most part formally severe, sticking to a rigorous third-person narration with only the occasional acknowledgement of its twentieth-century moment of narration. Both novels are now sufficiently ancient themselves to require reading with hindsight – both can be seen as emerging from the euphoric moment of modernisation in Britain known as 'the Sixties', a moment which required yet another renegotiation of the country's 'Victorian' inheritance. And both novels are themselves suffused with hindsight, in a way that contradicts Hilary Mantel's prescription, since in the two cases the novels' characters, their actions and their motives, are subject to forensic retrospective judgement. Farrell and Fowles realise this judgement in different formal ways, but in both cases the novels exemplify the characteristic aesthetic equivalent of one kind of hindsight, namely subjecting their characters to ferocious irony.

Irony is the predominant aesthetic effect especially of *The Siege of Krishnapur*, and at times readers may feel that it is too insistent and pervasive. It focuses especially around the notion of progress, in particular as it is materialised in the all too risible objects of the Great Exhibition – indeed the novel is a prime instance of the historiography of the Exhibition, whose Catalogue provides endless and seemingly irresistible opportunities for laughter. The novel's central character, the Collector, is speaking:

> 'Let me just quote at random from this catalogue of the Exhibition to which the Padre referred a moment ago, that Exhibition which I beg you to consider as a collective prayer of all the civilized nations ... Let me see, Number 382:

Instrument to teach the blind to write. Model of an aerial machine and of a navigable balloon. A fire annihilator by R. Weare of Plumstead Common. A domestic telegraph requiring only one bell for any number of rooms. An expanding pianoforte for yachts etc. Artificial teeth carved in hippopotamus ivory by Sinclair and Hockley of Soho. A universal drill for removing decay from teeth. A jaw lever for keeping animals' mouths open. Improved double truss for hernia, invented by a labouring man ... There seems to be no end to the ingenuity of mankind and I could continue indefinitely quoting examples of it. But I ask you only to consider these humble artefacts of man's God-given ability to observe and calculate as minute steps in the progress of mankind towards union with that Supreme Being in whom all knowledge *is*, and ever shall be.'[2]

There is another chapter to be written about the fate of the things collected by the Collector in this novel, as the objects he has painstakingly accumulated as symbols of mankind's progress are progressively destroyed, pressed into service as part of the city's defences, or otherwise gleefully smashed to pieces by the novelist. But the point here is precisely this notion of progress which the novel sets out to subject to irony; at the end of the novel the Collector will come to realise how frivolous and inadequate all his cherished notions of progress were: 'Perhaps, by the very end of his life, in 1880, he had come to believe that a people, a nation, does not create itself according to its own best ideas, but is shaped by other forces, of which it has little knowledge' (345). These are the concluding words of the book and even though they are hedged around by a 'perhaps' they nevertheless explain the fundamental ironic strategy of the whole novel.

This transition, it might nevertheless be felt, is no more than the characteristic movement of the realist novel, as its protagonist is led from ignorance to knowledge, or from innocence to maturity, or through any other such charged ideological pairing. The relevance of this transition here is that the position of greater knowledge is occupied by the contemporary, twentieth-century writer or reader, while the ignorance is a specific historical ignorance, which is presumed to be characteristic of a whole phase or moment of the past. Hence the relentless ironies of the novel are inextricable from the moment which we now occupy and which permits the hindsight on which the novel depends. The irony insists that the characters can never know the truths of their own situation, since these are dependent on the superior knowledge which is now available to us. As in many cases of novels set in the past, improved medical knowledge most clearly exemplifies this position of knowledgeable hindsight. Accordingly, one of the highlights of *The Siege of Krishnapur* is a public debate, at the very climax of the siege which the novel recounts, between two doctors on the aetiology of cholera. One of the doctors is clearly undergoing a breakdown, and is convinced of the miasma theory; the other, the rational, sardonic voice in this scene, is persuaded of the water-borne theory – which we now know to be true. In a particularly disgusting episode, the mistaken doctor drinks the fluid excreta of one of his patients to disprove

---

[2]   J.G. Farrell. *The Siege of Krishnapur*. Harmondsworth: Penguin Books, 1980. 59.

his opponent's theory: he duly dies. But the point of the scene is not this visible demonstration of cause and effect, but rather that the witnesses of the debate are if anything persuaded by the mistaken belief. The truth of the matter, it seems, is perhaps available to those who would see it, but in general remains unavailable to the majority – human beings are constituted to remain wedded to error and mistake, and this is especially visible when looking back. In this respect the novel embodies a committed but frustrated rationalism, ironically not dissimilar from some nineteenth-century beliefs, such as that indicated by the title of a book published contemporaneously with the Great Exhibition, *Extraordinary Popular Delusions and the Madness of Crowds*, by Charles Mackay.[3]

The Siege of Krishnapur, as we have seen, follows the classic trajectory of the realist novel in taking its protagonist from a state of ideological befuddlement to something like enlightenment, though the novelist is careful not to make this explicit in his own voice (or that of a 'narrator') and much of the novel consists of the free indirect discourse, and indeed the direct discourse, of its characters. Hence the irony, though broad, is always implicit, by strong contrast with that in *The French Lieutenant's Woman*. It can be seen at its most flagrant in a passage like the following, where the Collector is again expatiating on the topic of progress:

> 'There are rules of morality to be followed if we are to advance, just as there are rules of scientific investigation ... Mrs Lang, we are raising ourselves, however painfully, so that mankind may enjoy in the future a superior life now which we can hardly conceive! The foundations on which the new men will build their lives are Faith, Science, Respectability, Geology, Mechanical Invention, Ventilation and Rotation of Crops! ... '
>
> The Collector talked on and on but Miriam, soothed by the heat and the poppy fumes, cradled by the worn leather upholstery of the landau, found that her eyelids kept creeping down in spite of herself. Even when the Collector began to shout, as he presently did, about the progress of mankind, about the ventilation of populous quarters of cities, about the conquest of ignorance and prejudice by the glistening sabre of man's intelligence, she could not manage to keep her eyes properly open.
>
> And so, as the landau creaked away into the distance, dust pouring back from the chimneys of its wheels, the Collector's shouts ran emptily over the Indian plain which stretched for hundreds of miles in every direction, and Miriam fell at last into a deep sleep. (90)

Here the ground of the irony differs from the defeated rationalism that elsewhere underlies the text. It has two dimensions, feminist and postcolonial. The Collector's monologue, in the first perspective, seems simply to be that of yet another authoritative man droning on, and driving his captive female audience not to revolt so much as to sleep. In the second perspective, his ironised words simply disappear in the vastness of an indifferent India, where notions of progress,

³   Charles Mackay. *Extraordinary Popular Delusions and the Madness of Crowds*. London: National Illustrated Library, 1852.

especially as constituted here, appear simply inadequate and foolish when faced with this geographical and historical immensity.

Farrell's ironic method, moreover, points us towards another aspect of historical novels of the nineteenth century, their extensive use of parody and pastiche. The strongly ironic accent under which the Collector's speech appears in this passage certainly suggests parody; while there is no hard and fast distinction to be drawn between the two, pastiche is also characteristic of many such fictions. Simon Joyce has pointed out, in a comparable context, how the dominance of subjective forms of narration in contemporary fiction makes such fiction unlikely to be hospitable to the classical Lukacsian form of the historical novel which, taking Scott as its exemplar, has used a powerful narrator to encompass and seek to comprehend moments of historical transition.[4] A comparable point can perhaps be made with respect to the strongly ironised or parodied speech of the Collector in *The Siege of Krishnapur*; the aesthetic preference that it betrays – in modernist parlance, for showing over telling – leads to the directly ironic effects that we have observed but cannot generate any explanatory vocabulary for situating the behaviour and beliefs that are subject to this irony. At all events, in the novels that follow Farrell's and Fowles's texts discussed here, parody and pastiche will be central aesthetic strategies, even dominant ones, especially in those novels now dubbed 'neo-Victorian'.

The French Lieutenant's Woman does deploy pastiche, but in general poses a striking formal contrast to *The Siege of Krishnapur* insofar as the ironic effects to which it is drawn are explicitly signalled as effects of hindsight; that is, we are straightforwardly told that the characters could not understand their own motives because they lacked the knowledge that we now possess. Overwhelmingly this is sexual knowledge; the novel is a primary instance of what Foucault called the 'repressive hypothesis', the notion that the 'Victorians' actively repressed knowledge and consciousness of sexuality as far as they were able.[5] Accompanying this apparently simple corrective to Victorian self-understanding in Fowles's text is an emphasis on freedom understood in existentialist terms; this too needs to be deployed in order for the characters' behaviour to be explicable to us as readers, though it will always remain inexplicable to themselves. This is the characteristic aesthetic manifestation of these attitudes; here, the novel's hero has just met its heroine and, as usual, is baffled by her:

There was a wildness about her. Not the wildness of lunacy or hysteria – but that same wildness Charles had sensed in the wren's singing ... a wildness of

    [4]   Simon Joyce. *The Victorians in the Rearview Mirror*. Athens: Ohio University Press, 2007. 145.
    [5]   The bibliography on Foucault and Victorian sexuality is now immense. For an authoritative correction to the 'repressive hypothesis', though delivered in explicitly non-Foucauldian terms, see especially Michael Mason, *The Making of Victorian Sexuality*. Oxford: Oxford University Press, 1994; and *The Making of Victorian Sexual Attitudes*. Oxford: Oxford University Press, 1994.

innocence, almost an eagerness. And just as the sharp declension of that dawn walk has so confounded – and compounded – his earnest autobiographical gloom, so did that intensely immediate face confound and compound all the clinical horrors bred in Charles's mind by the worthy doctors Mathaei and Grogan. In spite of Hegel, the Victorians were not a dialectically minded age: they did not think in opposites, of positives and negatives as aspects of the same whole. Paradoxes troubled rather than pleased them. They were not the people for existentialist moments, but for chains of cause and effect: for positive all-explaining theories, carefully studied and studiously applied. They were busy erecting, of course: and we have been busy demolishing for so long now that erection seems as ephemeral an activity as bubble-blowing. So Charles was inexplicable to himself. He managed a very unconvincing smile.[6]

Examples of writing of this kind can be found throughout the novel – they are indeed its basic assertion. Charles, an exemplary Victorian, was therefore and by virtue of this situation 'inexplicable to himself'. Looking back now, from the position of this prominent narrator, we can see the nature of his problem (no dialectical thought; systematic thinking of a necessarily precarious kind) and understand him better than he could himself.

The novel is extraordinarily insistent on this contemporary perspective (already, in the twenty-first century, subject to hindsight, as we have noted); this insistence marks it off from Farrell's novel, as, in the opening chapters especially, readers get a series of little essays on aspects of Victorian life. In short the novel reproduces the discursive hierarchy of the classic nineteenth-century realist novel, though now the distance between 'narrator' and characters is historically greater than in, say, *The Mill on the Floss*, and does not permit any of the reverse ironies that characterise that novel: the possibility that the knowledge available in the past has the capacity to undermine our own safe cultural assumptions. Rather, Fowles deploys Victorian ignorance to underline our own greater sophistication.

As I have suggested, this is part of a cultural battle being fought out in his own historical moment, and repeats a frequent manoeuvre in English cultural life in which each generation's modernity has to be proved by its repudiation of the Victorian.[7] As I have insisted, the particular ignorance which the twentieth century has been keen to impute to the Victorians has been ignorance of sexuality, and there is indeed an almost pantomimic element to Charles Smithson's failure to recognise the nature of his own attraction to Sara Woodruff, with the knowing late twentieth-century reader shouting 'look behind you' from the first. In this respect, *The French Lieutenant's Woman* is no more than the respectable high-cultural version of its contemporary Flashman series, the first of which was published in the same year as Fowles's novel. George Macdonald Fraser's books are a different kind of 'writing back' than that usually applauded by the academy, where, in

---

[6]   John Fowles. *The French Lieutenant's Woman*. London: Triad Panther, 1984. 215.

[7]   Simon Joyce, *The Victorians in the Rearview Mirror*, gives an excellent account of this.

exemplary instances like Jean Rhys's *Wide Sargasso Sea* (1966) or Peter Carey's *Jack Maggs* (1997) the colonial other is reimagined to challenge the hegemony of nineteenth-century narratives; in the Flashman novels the Victorian cad, the villain in Thomas Hughes's *Tom Brown's Schooldays* (1857), is called upon to reimagine multiple episodes in nineteenth-century history – a reimagination which turns out to involve the most conservative versions of these stories, with lots of fantasy sex added in. The ambivalence of that Sixties moment of sexual 'liberation' is apparent when it is conducted by this kind of writing back to the Victorians.

George Macdonald Fraser's books aspire to be no more than entertainments, though their conservative agenda is explicit and their repudiation of the high-minded Arnoldianism and Christian Socialism of Thomas Hughes is indeed their starting point. I invoke them here to register the way in which they contributed to a 'Sixties' advance to modernity via a renegotiation with a perceived cultural inheritance from the nineteenth century. *The French Lieutenant's Woman* and *The Siege of Krishnapur* have more serious aspirations towards being historical novels, but their very different formal characteristics point in different directions for the ways in which historical novels set in the nineteenth century will be written. Fowles's text, with its metafictional display, points towards 'historiographical metafiction', to use Linda Hutcheon's term: fiction which engages with the historical past but dramatises its own moment of narration, and foregrounds the constructedness of its narrative and repudiates grand narratives of historical progression.[8] Farrell's, intent on displaying the mentality of its characters, points towards the large reliance on forms of parody and pastiche in later novels set in the Victorian period. Both novels are strongly narrated, though in contrasting ways, and to that extent can be assimilated to a generally Lukacsian kind of historical novel in which the underlying narrative is that of the transition from past to present, identifying the world-historical forces which power all such transitions. Both novels, as we have seen, rely heavily on hindsight to create their characteristically ironic effects, and to that extent belie Hilary Mantel's conscientious assertion that the novelist eschews hindsight in order to honour the being-in-the-moment of her characters. Both novels could be described as deriving from a debunking impulse, for which I have found a popular-cultural equivalent in the novels of George MacDonald Fraser, but Tony Richardson's film *The Charge of the Light Brigade* (1968) would be equally apposite. But neither novel is an act of recovery, an attempt to find other alternative voices to those excluded by the dominant narratives which both subject to hindsight's withering stare. Nor does either novel follow out the aesthetic impulse suggested by Hilary Mantel, and seek to protect the forms of self-understanding of historical actors from that stare.

---

[8] See Linda Hutcheon, *A Poetics of Postmodernism: History, Theory, Fiction.* London: Routledge, 1988.

II: Resisting 'the enormous condescension of posterity'

In this section I shall discuss a couple of early twenty-first-century novels which, in contrasting ways, are yet both acts of recovery, are both attempts, that is to say, to recover voices and experiences counter to the dominant narratives of the nineteenth century – though even that judgement will need reconsideration, as we shall see. But to the extent that this is the case, these novels appear to be cognate with earlier acts of recovery in historiography, memorably captured in the title of Sheila Rowbotham's 1973 book on women's history, *Hidden from History.* Indeed, the historiographical debates of that earlier generation, including especially the work of Rowbotham's intellectual mentor, E.P. Thompson, provide a significant context for the forthcoming discussion, as well as providing an instructive parallel to the forensic irony, born of the hindsight that we saw directed at the dominant voices of nineteenth-century culture in *The French Lieutenant's Woman* and *The Siege of Krishnapur.*

So it is worth recalling E.P. Thompson's famous words in the Preface to *The Making of the English Working Class* (1963), words which have resonated through the historiography of the nineteenth century in the fifty years or so since they were written:

> I am seeking to rescue the poor stockinger, the Luddite cropper, the 'obsolete' hand-loom weaver, the 'utopian' artisan, even the deluded follower of Joanna Southcott, from the enormous condescension of posterity. Their crafts and traditions may have been dying. Their hostility to the new industrialism may have been backward-looking. Their communitarian ideals may have been fantasies. Their insurrectionary conspiracies may have been foolhardy. But they lived through these times of acute social disturbances, and we did not. Their aspirations were valid in terms of their own experience; and, if they were casualties of history, they remain, condemned in their own lives, as casualties.[9]

It may well be that the Thompsonian revolution in nineteenth-century historiography is over in the narrow sense of the social history that it inspired, and in two respects: in the first instance, because it has produced its own revisionist challenge to the dominance that it attained, and secondly because of the occlusion of class as one of the central concerns of our culture since the onset of neoliberal orthodoxies. Indeed, Thompson's own occlusions can be seen in this very paragraph, where history's losers seem to be exclusively male, though doubtless some of those deluded followers of Joanna Southcott were women. Nevertheless, the impulse represented by Thompson's resonant paragraph, to seek to rescue the voices shut out by a history of the winners, has been enormously powerful in the novel-writing of the last thirty years, though history's casualties have been overwhelmingly seen in terms of gender and race as much as class.

---

[9]   E.P. Thompson. *The Making of the English Working Class*. London: Penguin Books, 1991. 12.

Thompson's words repeat one of the principal ways in which people have understood the problematic of hindsight, and sought to resist it. In the preceding paragraph to the one I have quoted, he states his objection to what he calls a 'Pilgrim's Progress' historiography, in which 'the period is ransacked for forerunners – pioneers of the Welfare State, progenitors of a Socialist Commonwealth, or (more recently) early exemplars of rational industrial relations' (11). Thompson objects to this 'because it reads history in the light of subsequent preoccupations, and not in fact as it occurred' (12). It is in this light that we should respect people's aspirations which were 'valid in terms of their own experience'. This is not just an invitation to a certain way of doing history, though it does enjoin immersion in the actual language and ideas of history's casualties, insofar as these can be recovered. Thompson's famous declaration also entails an attitude towards history, to contrast with Benjamin's famous *Theses on the Philosophy of History*, or Bakhtin's utopian assertion that 'every meaning shall have its homecoming festival' (quoted in the first chapter), or indeed Hilary Mantel's soberer assertion that it is the task of the novelist, and not the historian, to defend historical actors from the depredations of hindsight. Nevertheless, this does pose a significant formal problem for the novelist, as opposed to the historian famously confined to her sources; and hence the multiple ways in which novelists have sought to reproduce the language of the past, to find some way around the destructive backward knowledge and reproduce some version of people's aspirations 'valid in terms of their own experience'.

I wish to pursue the contrast between Thompson and Benjamin further, as a prelude to a discussion of novels set in the nineteenth century which can be seen as acts of recovery or, as Thompson phrases it, of 'rescue'. At first glance it seems as though there is a significant opposition between their two historiographical manifestoes: Benjamin precisely figures the angel of history as fixated by hindsight, advancing backwards into the future as the rubble of history piles up before his horrified gaze. If it wasn't for intimations of the transformative possibilities of revolution in the present moment, the backward glance would be overwhelmingly sad:

> To historians who wish to relive an era, Fustel de Coulanges recommends that they blot out everything they know about the later course of history. There is no better way of characterizing the method with which historical materialism has broken. It is a process of empathy whose origin is the indolence of the heart, *acedia*, which despairs of grasping and holding the genuine historical image as it flares up briefly. Among medieval theologians it was regarded as the root cause of sadness. Flaubert, who was familiar with it, wrote: '*Peu de gens devineront combien il a fallu être triste pour ressusciter Carthage*' ['Few people will guess how sad one had to be to resuscitate Carthage'].[10]

---

[10] Walter Benjamin. 'Theses on the Philosophy of History'. *Illuminations*. Ed. Hannah Arendt. New York: Shocken Books, 1968. 256.

It is surely significant that Benjamin should use the example of a novelist to provide the most extreme form of the *acedia* which he feels threatens a pure historicism, understood here as the exhaustive attempt to relive the past in its own terms. Flaubert's novel *Salammbô* (1862) is an extreme example of an attempt at historical reconstruction where there is no connection to a living stream of history; Benjamin repudiates it. It would nevertheless be a mistake to place Thompson's effort to respect the 'experience' of his historical figures, and their attempts to act on their experience, on the same side of the equation as Flaubert appears in Benjamin's damning assessment. On the contrary, while he could not be said to hold 'the genuine historical image as it flares up briefly' – Thompson's method is far too painstakingly immersed in the details of the historical past for that characterisation to be appropriate – Thompson does seek to make his act of rescue or resuscitation serve in a contemporary class politics, just as later acts of historical recovery have served other agendas in the present. *Pace* Benjamin, resistance to hindsight need not mean acceding to *acedia*.

Using Thompson as our starting-point for this section leads us then to two questions: the issue of whose experience exactly the writer seeks to recover; and the formal means that the novelist has available to make that act of recovery. These issues can be approached via two novels from the beginning of the twenty-first century, Peter Carey's *True History of the Kelly Gang* (2000), and Michael Faber's *The Crimson Petal and the White* (2002). The first of these, in fact, is quoted by Simon Joyce as one of those subjectivist novels which by their very form – an extended pastiche of the written language of nineteenth-century Australian poor farmers – disqualifies it from consideration as a genuinely Lukacsian historical novel. However, its attempted act of recovery is absolutely emblazoned on every page, for this is the great Australian historical novel, Lukacsian or not, which seeks to tell the national story as one of dispossession, violence and ultimately unsuccessful outlawry.

It might be felt that Ned Kelly's story is scarcely equivalent to that of a poor stockinger, or a Luddite cropper, since he had already passed into the national mythology when Carey wrote the novel, and had museums and films devoted to him. Nevertheless Carey tells the story in a way which insists not so much on the acts of individual bravery or the famous final gunfight with homemade armour, but as a collective story of rural poverty and dispossession, given a strongly Irish colouring as the struggles of dispossessed rural farmers and labourers are portrayed as a direct continuation of the anti-colonial struggles in Ireland itself. Insofar as this is a national story, therefore, it emerges as one founded on the violent suppression of a class of impoverished rural workers and farmers ('selectors'), in which the organs of the state are deployed directly on behalf of a prosperous squatter class. The novel achieves this act of collective recovery, despite Simon Joyce's caveat, via aesthetic means which are resolutely subjectivist – indeed, the whole novel is narrated in the voice of Ned Kelly himself, as found in the (fictitious) account he has left of his life.

'To articulate the past historically does not mean to recognize it "the way it really was" (Ranke). It means to seize hold of a memory as it flashes up at a moment of danger.' (Benjamin, *Illuminations*, 255). Benjamin's famous words provide a justification, perhaps, for the present politics of *True History of the Kelly Gang*, though it should be said that the dangers faced by Benjamin and Europe in the late 1930s were of a different order from those faced by Australia at the beginning of the twenty-first century. At all events the novel gives a strongly partial account of nineteenth-century Australian history as a way of redirecting the national story and insisting on the class injustice and violence at its root.

This is partly a matter of the story that the novel tells – one that might have been written with a copy of Eric Hobsbawm's *Bandits* (1969) constantly to hand, so perfectly does the novel fit the thesis of that book, in which indeed Kelly features.[11] But the novel's success also depends on its remarkable and extended pastiche of the language of a poor farmer in the 1870s. While it is of course important to remember that this is a construction, nevertheless this language does carry a whole social history which the reader gets a sense of in the act of reading. To that extent it is appropriate to invoke Bakhtin rather than Lukács as a guide to the novel; the density of the language itself, even though realised in an act of retrospective and fictional reproduction, carries intimations of a social whole in a way which is different, to be sure, from the strongly narrated historical novel of Walter Scott, Lukács's exemplary instance, but is nevertheless visible.

In the following paragraphs, for example, a particular social and ideological mentality is evident:

> One morning in the summer of 1872 my mother were 42 yr. old she had 2 sons in prison also 1 brother & 1 uncle & 1 brother in law. 2 of her beloved daughters was buried beneath the willow tree and God knows what worse were on the way. On this bleached and dusty morning she and Maggie was staking tomatoes when a stranger come and asks her for a jar of brandy. This one were an American tall and wiry with a small beard hooded eyes and a little smile working behind the cover of his mouth as though he found the world so very droll but were not were not permitted to tell you exactly what the joke might be. Like the stinky man he claimed to have no money only a cheque he couldnt cash until Benalla.
>
> Maggie began to act sarcastic towards him but my mother suddenly turned v. passionate against her. Listen to you girl said she anyone would think we had no adjectival charity. Go on said she and bring the gentleman his drop.
>
> I am to serve him asked Maggie astonished her muddy hands upon her strong broad hips.
>
> What would prevent you?
>
> Well said Maggie do you mind that? But she done as she were told and my mother went back to staking the tomatoes. For a long time she believed the rats didn't depart until Maggie donated George King that glass of grog.[12]

---

[11]   Eric Hobsbawm. *Bandits*. London: Abacus, 2000.

[12]   Peter Carey. *True History of the Kelly Gang*. London: Faber and Faber, 2000. 167.

Although this can still be described as pastiche, it is very different from the kind of pastiche in the novels by Fowles and Farrell, where the reproduction of a 'Victorian' mentality was designed to show its evident insufficiency: indeed, in the case of the Collector's enthusiasm for 'progress', its absurdity. The pastiche in Carey's text comes if anything from an opposite impulse, to rescue this language and use it for powerful literary effects. There is no doubt that it is an invented language; as twenty-first-century readers we are asked to recognise its distinctiveness, heavily marked as it is by non-standard written forms. To use a Bakhtinian vocabulary, this is 'double-voiced' discourse, in which we are conscious both of the language of the ostensible narrator, Kelly himself, and of the author who is presenting this distinctive language as worthy of respect.

This fundamental aesthetic strategy, which marks the whole novel, is perhaps more important than the intimations that a passage like this gives us ('showing' not 'telling') of the life and mentality of its characters, marked by unrelenting agricultural work, and by traditional notions of hospitality – indeed, there is some suggestion here of the superstitious belief that to flout these notions is to invite disaster, for the 'stinky man' referred to had brought a plague of rats on the household when he had been refused charity. Carey's *tour de force* in maintaining this language is the most striking aspect of the act of recovery that the book enacts, and indeed the politics of this linguistic practice seems to me to be far more challenging than the retelling of the national story of Ned Kelly itself. What this means for the politics of recovery – rescuing this story from 'the enormous condescension of history' – is that the novel's challenge is not in retelling the twice-told tale of Ned Kelly, but in seeking to recover the whole distinctive class history of which he was the victim and against which, in the manner of Hobsbawm's 'social bandits', he rebelled. This complex act of recovery is achieved by the sustained act of linguistic inventiveness that the whole novel represents.

The contrast with the contemporaneous Michel Faber's *The Crimson Petal and the White* (2002), also by a novelist with Australian connections, is clear; this novel too can be seen as an act of recovery, but its discursive organisation is more similar to *The French Lieutenant's Woman* than the apparent subjectivism of Peter Carey's text. Hindsight is therefore built into the structure of the text, as a confident narratorial voice guides the twenty-first-century reader around unfamiliar parts of nineteenth-century London. In this respect the discursive organisation of the text – along with many of its narrative tropes – reproduces the organisation of those nineteenth-century novels of London, most obviously by Dickens but not only by him – which sought to introduce the presumed middle-class reader to unknown and degraded parts of the city, and to bring its disparate parts into connection. The novel could therefore be described more narrowly as 'neo-Dickensian' than 'neo-Victorian'. Some of its tropes are familiar to readers of *Oliver Twist* or *Bleak House* – though of course this is a historical novel, and the ignorance that it takes upon itself to correct is not the culpable social ignorance that Dickens addressed, but a historical ignorance that Faber's novel can rectify.

Consider, for example, the introductory pages of the book, where a confident narrator takes it upon himself to guide the reader through one of the most degraded rookeries in London; at this point the reader is positioned both as the contemporary twenty-first-century reader and as a potential customer for the prostitute to whom we are about to be introduced:

> You may wonder, then: why did I bring you here? Why this delay in meeting the people you thought you were going to meet? The answer is simple: their servants wouldn't let you in the door.
>
> What you lack is the right connections, and this is what I've brought you here to make: connections. A person who is worth nothing must introduce to a person who is worth next-to-nothing, and that person to another, and so on and so forth until finally you can step across the threshold, almost one of the family.
>
> That is why I've brought you here to Church Lane, St Giles: I've found just the right person for you.[13]

For readers of Dickens, this immediately recalls the famous section in *Bleak House* when the narrator asks 'what connection can there be, between the place in Lincolnshire, the house in town, the Mercury in powder, and the whereabout of Jo the outlaw with the broom … ? What connection can there have been between many people in the innumerable histories of this world, who, from opposite sides of great gulfs, have, nevertheless, been very curiously brought together!'[14] For Dickens, the connections to be established are those of class and political exclusion, though there will be a sexual secret at their heart also: the closest connection between the highly aristocratic 'place in Lincolnshire' and Jo the crossing-sweeper is that the latter has been befriended by the old lover of Lady Dedlock, mistress of this very place. Nevertheless, overwhelmingly Dickens wishes to assert the moral and political responsibility of the governing class for the misery and degradation of Jo's environment, summed up in the place called 'Tom-All-Alones', a rookery just like St Giles. Michel Faber's set of connections, by contrast, will prove to be predominantly sexual ones: the six degrees of separation (hardly so many) will all be linked by a chain of sexual liaisons. We start with the prostitutes and work our way up the social ladder to respectable society. What Faber's privileged position of hindsight allows him is explicitly to fill in the details of those sexual connections in ways that were impossible in the respectable literature of the nineteenth century, though of course pornography and unrespectable writing like *My Secret Life* managed to be sufficiently explicit in their own terms.

Indeed, while it is often claimed that neo-Victorian novels write the books that the Victorians themselves dared not or could not write, the trope of hidden connections across the classes betrayed by an illicit sexual connection is absolutely a nineteenth-century one. If anything, it goes back to the eighteenth century: Blake's

---

[13]   Michel Faber. *The Crimson Petal and the White*. Edinburgh: Canongate, 2002. 4.

[14]   Charles Dickens. *Bleak House*. Ed. Nicola Bradbury. London: Penguin Books, 2003. 256.

'youthful harlot's curse ... smites with plagues the marriage hearse' in 'London' in 1794.[15] It is fair to say however that it particularly gained traction at the end of the century, when Ibsen and the New Woman novelists, like Blake, made syphilis the evident consequence and marker or sign of these connections. Even Faber's notion of one character leading to another by a train of sexual friendships and connections was anticipated in the late nineteenth century with Arthur Schnitzler's play *Reigen* (1899). Equally, the notion of introducing readers to unknown and degraded parts of London is absolutely central to nineteenth-century writing about the city, with *Oliver Twist* providing only the most famous example, when Dickens takes the 'visitor' on a tour of Jacob's Island: 'he walks beneath tottering house-fronts projecting over the pavement, dismantled walls that seem to totter as he passes, chimneys half crushed half hesitating to fall, windows guarded by rusty iron bars that time and dirt have almost eaten away, and every imaginable sign of desolation and neglect'.[16] All of these aspects make *The Crimson Petal and the White* perhaps the most Victorian of the 'neo-Victorian' novels.

Nevertheless, it is fair to describe the novel as performing an act of recovery, as it seeks to place the experience of the prostitute at the centre of the story of nineteenth-century London. This is predominantly the story of a very exceptional prostitute, the novel's heroine Sugar; but the book is insistent also on the milieu from which she emerges, in which her atypicality is absolutely evident. If there is an act of linguistic recovery – an attempt to give a voice to the prostitute – it is made through the novel that she is imagined to be writing, and through the angry annotations that she makes to her reading. Thus Sugar is shown reading and annotating a medical journal article, and responding to it:

> *No woman can be a serious thinker, without injury to her function as the conceiver and mother of children. Too often, the female 'intellectual' is a youthful invalid or virtual hermaphrodite, who might otherwise have been a healthy wife.*
>
> *Let us close our ears, then, to siren voices offering us a quantity of female intellectual work at the price of a puny, enfeebled and sulky race. Healthy serviceable wombs are of more use to the Future than any amount of feminine scribbling.*
>
> No, it's not the text, but Sugar's handwritten comments in the margins that her new benefactor must at all costs not see: *Pompous oaf!* here; *Tyranny!* there; *Wrong, wrong, wrong!* over there and, scrawled under the conclusion in angry blotted ink: *We'll see about that, you poxy old fool! There's a new century coming soon, and you and your kind will be DEAD!* (171–2)

Since we now inhabit a new century (admittedly the one after that envisaged by Sugar) these annotations are particularly gratifying to our ears, hindsight having

---

[15]   William Blake, 'London'. *The Poems of William Blake*. Ed. W.H. Stevenson. London: Longman, 1980. 213.

[16]   Charles Dickens. *Oliver Twist*. Ed Philip Horne. London: Penguin Books, 2002. 417.

conferred on them the stamp of justified outrage, and hindsight having conceived them in the first place.

Similarly, Sugar's novel is presented as a sustained act of imaginative revenge and retribution, in the manner of Jenny's song in *The Threepenny Opera*:

> Sugar leans her chin against the knuckles of the hand that holds the pen. Glistening on the page between her silk-shrouded elbows lies an unfinished sentence. The heroine of her novel has just slashed the throat of a man. The problem is how, precisely, the blood will flow. *Flow* is too gentle a word; spill implies carelessness; *spurt* is out of the question because she has used the word already, in another context, a few lines earlier. *Pour out* implies that the man has some control over the matter, which he most emphatically doesn't; *leak* is too feeble for the savagery of the injury she has inflicted upon him. Sugar closes her eyes and watches, in the theatre of her mind, the blood issue from the slit neck. When Mrs Castaway's warning bell sounds, she jerks in surprise.
>
> Hastily, she scrutinises her bedroom. Everything is neat and tidy. All her papers are hidden away, except for this single sheet on her writing desk.
>
> *Spew*, she writes, having finally been given, by tardy Providence, the needful word. (197)

Given the basic premise of a highly intelligent and self-educated prostitute, this seems to be to be altogether more plausible than the subsequent path of class transition and motherly responsibility that the novel goes on to trace for its heroine. At all events, the novel dramatises current historiography of the nineteenth century, and gives a voice to one of the nineteenth century's most notorious victims – though in doing so it is always in danger of confirming what we already know.

And this kind of benign hindsight is especially visible, as so often, in the area of medical knowledge. Sugar's female counterpart or alter ego in the novel is her lover's wife, explicitly offered as a characterisation of mid-Victorian female perfection and in effect the sexless angel in the house – but who is also neurotic, even mad. For much of the novel we are encouraged to read her behaviour as brought on by her situation – the demands of her social and gender position, the stupidity of her husband, the regular sexually invasive examinations by her doctor. But then this:

> In Agnes's head, inside her skull, an inch or two behind her left eye, nestles a tumour the size of a quail's egg. She has no inkling it's there. It nestles innocently; her hospitable head makes room for it without demur, as if such a diminutive guest could not possibly cause any trouble. No one will ever find it. Roentgen photography is twenty years in the future, and Doctor Curlew, whatever parts of Agnes Rackham he may examine, is not about to go digging in her eye-socket with a scalpel. Only you and I know of this tumour's existence. It is our little secret. (218–19)

Once again the contemporary twenty-first century reader is granted an explanation of human behaviour explicitly beyond what is available to the human actors about whom the novel writes. In this case it seems to me to be destructive of the fabric of the novel, and certainly to work against the ideal of the historical novel as set out by Hilary Mantel. The passage reiterates the position of narrative knowingness with respect to the nineteenth century that we first encountered in *The French Lieutenant's Woman.*

The ideological gestures made by these novels by Peter Carey and Michael Faber might therefore appear to be similar, and to be the novelistic equivalents of the acts of rescue proposed in historiography by E.P. Thompson, and, in different terms, by Walter Benjamin. But what these two brief accounts of the novels suggest is, perhaps surprisingly, the remarkable implications of the differing formal organisations of the novels, so that the discursive hierarchy of *The Crimson Petal and the White* can entail debilitating effects of hindsight which *The True History of the Kelly Gang* in part evades – despite the fact that both novels start from acts of reconstruction which are necessarily created out of hindsight. In the last resort, perhaps, Benjamin's invocation of a redemptive angel of history was only ever a mystical hope, just as Bakhtin's notion that 'every meaning shall have its homecoming festival' offers small comfort to those whose meanings come home in the ignorance of their originators. Nevertheless these two novels suggest different ways for us to persuade ourselves, however briefly, that some of those occluded nineteenth-century meanings have been rescued.

III: Neo-Victorian: Parody or Pastiche?

Two final novels set in the nineteenth century can conclude this brief account of what has been called, contentiously, 'neo-Victorian' fiction.[17] The first is A.S. Byatt's *The Children's Book* (2009), which sets out to recreate the lives and milieu of a particular social fraction at the end of the nineteenth century, that of the Fabian, Arts and Crafts, mildly progressive upper middle class and their children born in the 1880s, 1890s, and 1900s. These are in part the children alluded to in the title, and the hindsight which overhangs them is of course our knowledge of the First World War and the destiny to which they are headed. The second is Jane Harris's *The Observations* (2007), a more familiar act of recovery and tale of female alienation and solidarity.

Byatt in fact eschews all the heavy-handed ironies made possible by a story which concentrates on the lives of a generation of children born of an age to fight, we now know, in the Great War – a heavy-handedness that hardly escaped Thomas Gray in the eighteenth century when contemplating the adulthood that awaited the children of Eton College: 'Alas, regardless of their doom,/The little victims play'. On the contrary, the whole point of the novel could be said to resist such ready-to-hand ironies, as it is a novel determined to enter into the life-worlds of

---

[17]   See, for the definitive account of the range of twenty-first-century novelistic work gathered together under this heading, Ann Heilmann and Mark Llewellyn, *Neo-Victorianism: The Victorians in the Twenty-First Century*. Basingstoke: Palgrave Macmillan, 2010.

its characters, to take their lives at the valuations which they set on them, and to set out the happinesses, frustrations, tragedies and possibilities open to them. In that sense the novel is strongly anti-teleological, determined not to measure lives by their end-point, and thus conforming in its own way with Mantel's honourable aesthetic manifesto. The conclusion to the novel – in which a shattered fragment of the war-damaged generation remains, providing a possible tableau of national reconciliation on a very muted scale, suggests an end-point indeed for the novel but does not devalue the intensity of the lives lived up to that point and in inevitable ignorance of it.

Which is not to say that the novel pretends to be anything other than written in the early twenty-first century, for all that A.S. Byatt is the acknowledged mistress of pastiche, and puts her talents in this direction to good use, though not to the extent that characterises her earlier 'neo-Victorian' novels *Possession* (1990) and *Angels and Insects* (1992). But it does not reproduce that worrying discursive hierarchy by which the narrator occupies the space of knowledgeable hindsight with respect to the characters. In this context some of the critical controversy which greeted the novel on its first appearance, as in a review by James Wood in *The London Review of Books,* is beside the point. Wood argued that there is something essentially wooden about the characterisations in the novel because Byatt too persistently signals her own knowledge – that is to say invention – of the characters' inner lives.[18] The point here is that this authorial knowledge, however intimated, is not claimed as a superior knowledge legitimised by the passage of time. The book can therefore legitimately claim to be an act of historical recovery without subjecting its characters to the destructive backward gaze as practised, in their different ways, by Fowles and Farrell.

Which is not to say that the characters aren't in many ways offered as historically typical – throughout the novel Byatt insists on the representativeness of their beliefs and behaviour, and indeed the book is as marked by mini-lectures on the late Victorian and Edwardian period as Fowles's earlier novel. But the realist novel at its best is capable of holding together two opposing poles: both the social typicality of its characters, the knowledge that people are historically and socially formed and emerge from particular places and times – and its characters' individuality and specificity, which, by virtue of the uniqueness of any individual's combination of personal and historical circumstances, burst the bounds of that formation. Byatt's fiction, it can be said, effectively achieves this synthesis, and by doing so gives a plausible immediacy and richness to her act of historical reconstruction. We will revert to the ultimate value of such a reconstruction in a moment.

Before doing so, however, it is worth considering one final novel in this group of novels which engage with what is now the century before last. Jane Harris's *The Observations* (2007) is concerned with the relations of servant to mistress, telling the story, narrated in the first person, of a servant who develops from a life of prostitution to one of devoted service to her mistress – though the 'observations'

---

[18]   James Wood. 'Bristling with Diligence'. *London Review of Books.* 8 October 2009: 6–8.

of the title are both her own account of her life, and the observations made by her mistress on her servants' behaviour, conceived in a falsely scientific mode. The novel thus provides a classic instance of historical recovery, in the first instance of the servant herself, and secondly of the highly intelligent mistress forced by her circumstances to misdirect her intellectual energies into this oppressive mode. While the novel avoids the sensational and the Gothic, which haunt neo-Victorian writing, it does conclude with the mistress in a lunatic asylum and her servant faithfully attending her as one of its respectable employees.

The novel thus manages to combine an act of recovery – of the servant's perspective – with an ironic reading of the misplaced scientism and class condescension of the mistress's language, which provides the most extensive exercise in pastiche in the novel:

> *For the past week or so, I have been anxious that the subject may have formed too great an attachment to me and I am sorry to recount that my fears have not been without foundation. This has become inescapable over the last few days. Yesterday, while we happened to be tidying my press in preparation for my husband's return, the girl blurted out something that seems to go beyond the bounds of what might be viewed as appropriate, professing a love for me and stating that she would do anything for me, including laying down her own life to ensure my happiness. Needless to say I had to bring our little rendezvous to an abrupt end and have tried to avoid her company ever since.*[19]

The irony that surrounds this writing is in part created by the formal structure of the novel itself: the servant (the 'subject' of this discourse) discovers the notebook and is duly hurt and humiliated by it. But it is also an irony created by hindsight: the writer presumes that her reader will be as shocked by the cold-hearted calculation of this as Bessy herself, an expectation borne of historical distance by virtue of which we are now expected to be shocked that a mistress's life can be valued more highly than that of her servant. Harris also manages to suggest an affection felt for the maid by the mistress despite her efforts at scientific detachment.

The contrast with the servant's own language is striking, and indicates the dual thrust of the novel at once to rescue the language of the servant and to ironise that of her mistress:

> I had reason to leave Glasgow, this would have been about three four years ago, and I had been on the Great Road about five hours when I seen a track to the left that said 'Castle Haivers'. Now there's a coincidence I thought to myself, because here was I on my way across Scratchland to have a look at the Edinburgh castle and perhaps get a job there and who knows marry a young nobleman or prince. I was only 15 with a head full of sugar and I had a notion to work in a grand establishment. (Chapter 1)

---

[19]   Jane Harris. *The Observations*. London: Faber and Faber, ebook edition, 2010. Chapter 7. Italics in the original.

This is taken from the beginning of the book when Bessy's language is furthest from the Standard English to which it tends in the course of the book. There is nevertheless an act of recovery here, and the book lays claim to some of the idiomatic jauntiness of this language. While it does not attempt the sustained act of literary recovery we saw at work in *The True History of the Kelly Gang*, this aspect of the book emerges from a similar aesthetic impulse, which is of course an ethical impulse also. Pastiche thus moves in two directions in the novel, in part because of the transformed situation in relation to the external markers of class that characterise the twenty-first century compared to the nineteenth.

Which takes us back to the position of hindsight which all of these novels adopt, by necessity, in relation to the century in which they are set. We have seen how early examples of 'neo-Victorian' novels exploit fully the possibilities for irony that hindsight makes abundantly available, though that irony can be realised in differing formal ways. A differing aesthetic, social and historical impulse, cognate with E.P. Thompson's famous claim to rescue some of history's victims from the 'enormous condescension of posterity', has sought various means of rescuing, in novelistic terms, the evident victims of nineteenth-century society, a project often requiring a linguistic recovery also and therefore forms of positively-coded pastiche, the opposite of that practised by Farrell and Fowles. In all these novels, the actual formal organisation of the text is crucial in determining how the particular modes of hindsight, and resistance to it, are played out. Many of them spring from wholly honourable cultural impulses, and of course are addressed to the cultural politics of the moment, which, by a familiar logic, appears to require routing through an intervention in the way we think about the nineteenth century and in particular the Victorians. Perhaps none could live up to the millenarian requirements of Benjamin's *Theses on the Philosophy of History*, with their injunction to hold 'the genuine historical image as it flares up briefly'. Perhaps some even – and I am thinking especially of A.S. Byatt's *The Children's Book* – fall prey to the *acedia* which Benjamin claims stalks all efforts at historical reconstruction without such a redemptive possibility. The logic of this position would force you to abandon the historical novel altogether, quoting Marx or perhaps Christ to 'let the dead bury the dead'. The ambivalent logic of hindsight is more forgiving, allowing us to recognise alternative historical eventualities even as it insists that one and one only path from the past into the present occurred. Those novels which allow us to recognise those alternative possibilities do something at least to keep Benjamin's *acedia* at bay.

Afterword:
With the Benefit of Hindsight

People sometimes wonder, when considering the evident insufficiencies of the attitudes, beliefs and feelings of those in the past (insufficiencies to be rounded out by hindsight), what comparable shortcomings or shocking violations of common sense will be perceived by people in the future as they look back on the present. Indeed, partly following Matthew Beaumont, I have argued in the chapter on William Morris's *News from Nowhere* that part of the point of utopian texts is to provide just this defamiliarising function, to reveal the essential oddity of our present moment in the light of a putative future one. The peculiarity of *News from Nowhere*, however, is that this future utopia can only be conceived by virtue of Morris's massive imaginative investment in past social and artistic forms.

Something similar, I claim – a comparable defamiliarising function – can be mobilised by texts from the past as they are put to work in the present. I hope this does not sound like another version of the 'wisdom of the ages', or another version of the humanist pieties that are often mobilised in support of reading 'great literature'. What distinguishes my claim from these familiar homilies, I hope, is the insistence on the historical provenance of all acts of writing, and that it is precisely this embeddedness in past social forms that gives power to writing in its unimagined futures. Hindsight's capacity to explain and situate those past texts is the condition for their salience but need not provide an exhaustive explanation of them.

I also claim, scarcely contentiously, that no past historical moment is homogenous, any more than the present. But I draw from this the conclusion that the writing of the past emerges from its complex and conflict-ridden social and cultural milieu, and its capacity to speak to the equally complex present depends on the multiple survivals and continuities between then and now, a process that is carnivalesque and contentious and which involves extraordinary transvaluations as much as direct lineations. These general reflections bear particular weight in relation to the relatively recent nineteenth-century past; I have attempted to trace the complex ways in which some nineteenth-century canonical texts have been transformed as subsequent history has unrolled, yet can continue to have a defamiliarising force in the present.

This book has been an exercise in method as much as an effort towards a substantive cultural history. As such, there is indeed something arbitrary about the canonical texts that I have chosen. Yet if there is a logic that connects them, which connects, that is to say, novels by Dickens and George Eliot with tracts by Ruskin and Morris, it is a historical logic that has placed these cultural monuments on the opposite side of a transformation that has led from the liberal state in which they wrote, through the partial reining in of the capitalist economy that underlay that liberal state, to its more recent unleashing under neoliberalism. This extraordinary story underlies the valuations and transvaluations that confront us as we read this material, turning notions of progress on their head, giving Ruskin's reactionary commitments a progressive air, and making George Eliot's moral commitments apparently inaccessible to the liberals trained up by neoliberalism. Gadamer, in a passage to which I have repeatedly returned, argued that 'Time is no longer primarily a gulf to be bridged because it separates; it is actually the supportive ground of the course of events in which the present is rooted'. This is surely true; if it were not for the supportive ground we would not be able to perceive historical difference. But there is a danger that Gadamer's appropriate caveat, aimed at a romantic historicism which sought to think itself out of its own historical moment in the effort to see the past as it really was, has the effect of obscuring historical difference altogether. There is a gulf which separates us from the nineteenth century, and it can be described; we are nevertheless joined to that century by innumerable traditions which are more or less active at the present moment. Those nineteenth-century texts, with their particular commitments and investments in their own present, turn out to have a wholly different purchase on the present according to the twists and turns of the social and cultural history which subtends them.

The benefit of hindsight is real; at the very least it makes salient that which, to an observer caught up in all the cacophony of the moment, can appear insignificant. The dangers of hindsight are real also, and I have sufficiently dwelt on them both in discussing nineteenth-century writing and contemporary twentieth- and twenty-first-century writing about the nineteenth century. These complementary limitations are also the conditions by which texts from the past do and do not have force for us in the present.

Bibliography

Anderson, Perry. 'The River of Time.' *New Left Review* 26 (Mar/Apr 2004): 67–77.

Arnold, Matthew. 'Stanzas from the Grande Chartreuse.' *Poetical Works*. Ed. C.B. Tinker and H.F. Lowry. London: Oxford University Press, 1969.

Bakhtin, M.M. 'Discourse in the Novel.' *The Dialogic Imagination*. Trans. Caryl Emerson. Ed. Michael Holquist. Austin: University of Texas Press, 1981.

———. 'Towards a Methodology of the Human Sciences.' *Speech Genres and other Late Essays*. Trans. Vern W. McGee. Ed. Caryl Emerson and Michael Holquist. Austin, Texas: University of Texas Press, 1986.

Bate, Jonathan. *Romantic Ecology: Wordsworth and the Environmental Tradition*. London: Routledge, 1991.

———. *The Song of the Earth*. London: Picador, 2000.

Beaumont, Matthew. 'To Live in the Present: *News from Nowhere* and the Representation of the Present in Late Victorian Fiction.' *Writing on the Image: Reading William Morris*. Ed. David Latham. Toronto: University of Toronto Press, 2007.

———. *Utopia Ltd: Ideologies of Social Dreaming 1870-1910*. Leiden: Brill, 2005.

Beningfield, Gordon. *Hardy Country*. London: Allen Lane, 1983.

Benjamin, Walter. 'Theses on the Philosophy of History.' *Illuminations*. Ed. Hannah Arendt. New York: Shocken Books, 1968.

Birch, Dinah. *Our Victorian Education*. Oxford: Blackwell, 2008.

Blake, William. 'London.' *The Poems of William Blake*. Ed. W.H. Stevenson. London: Longman, 1980.

Blakesley, Rosalind P. *The Arts and Crafts Movement*. London: Phaidon, 2006.

Blond, Philip. *Red Tory: How the Left and Right Have Broken Britain and How We Can Fix It*. London: Faber and Faber, 2010.

Boos, Florence. 'An (Almost) Egalitarian Sage: William Morris and Nineteenth-Century Socialist-Feminism.' *Victorian Sages and Cultural Discourse*. Ed. Thaïs Morgan. New Brunswick: Rutgers University Press, 1990.

Bowen, John and Robert L.Patten. *Palgrave Advances in Charles Dickens Studies*. Basingstoke: Palgrave, 2006.

Bronk, Richard. *The Romantic Economist: Imagination in Economics*. Cambridge: Cambridge University Press, 2009.

Brontë, Charlotte. *Jane Eyre*. Ed. Q.D. Leavis. Harmondsworth: Penguin Books, 1966.

———. *Villette*. Ed. Mark Lilly. London: Penguin Books, 1985.

Buck-Morss, Susan. *Dreamworld and Catastrophe: The Passing of Mass Utopia in East and West*. Cambridge, MA: MIT Press, 2000.

Buckton, Oliver S. "'The Reader whom I love": Homoerotic Secrets in *David Copperfield*.' *English Literary History* 64 (1997): 189–222.
Burnett, John. *Useful Toil*. Harmondsworth: Penguin Books, 1984.
———. *Destiny Obscure*. Harmondsworth: Penguin Books, 1984.
Byatt, A.S. *The Children's Book*. London: Chatto and Windus, 2009.
Carey, Peter. *True History of the Kelly Gang*. London: Faber and Faber, 2000.
Carlyle, Thomas. 'Shooting Niagara – and After?' *Critical and Miscellaneous Essays*. Vol 5. London: Chapman and Hall, 1899.
———. *Past and Present*. London: Dent, Everyman's Library, 1978.
Clarke, I.F., ed. *The Tale of the Next Great War, 1871-1914*. Liverpool: Liverpool University Press, 1995.
———, ed. *The Great War with Germany, 1890-1914*. Liverpool: Liverpool University Press, 1997.
Cowling, Maurice. *1867: Disraeli, Gladstone and Revolution: The Passing of the Second Reform Bill*. Cambridge: Cambridge University Press, 1967.
Dante Alighieri. *The Inferno*. Trans. John D. Sinclair. Oxford: Oxford University Press, 1961.
Davey, Peter. *Arts and Crafts Architecture*. London: Phaidon, 1995.
Davis, Mike. *Planet of Slums*. London: Verso, 2006.
Dawkins, Richard. *Climbing Mount Improbable*. London: Viking, 1996.
de Beauvoir, Simone. *Memoirs of a Dutiful Daughter*. Trans. James Kirkup. Harmondsworth: Penguin Books, 1963.
Dentith, Simon. 'From William Morris to the Morris Minor: An Alternative Suburban History.' *Expanding Suburbia: Reviewing Suburban Narratives*. Ed. Roger Webster. New York: Berghahn Books, 2000. 15-30.
———. 'Realist Synthesis in the Nineteenth-Century Novel: "That unity which lies in the selection of our keenest consciousness".' *Adventures in Realism*. Ed. Matthew Beaumont. Oxford: Blackwell, 2007. 33–49.
———. '"The Shadow of the Workhouse": The Afterlife of a Victorian Institution.' *Literature, Interpretation, Theory* 20 (2009): 79–91.
Dickens, Charles. *Bleak House*. Ed. Nicola Bradbury. London: Penguin Books, 2003.
———. *David Copperfield*. Ed. Jeremy Tambling. London: Penguin Books, 2004.
———. *Oliver Twist*. Ed Philip Horne. London: Penguin Books, 2002.
———. *Pickwick Papers*. Ed. James Kinsley. Oxford: Clarendon Press, 1986.
Dowling, Andrew. *Manliness and the Male Novelist in Victorian Literature*. Aldershot: Ashgate, 2001.
Eliot, George. 'The Natural History of German Life.' *Selected Essays, Poems and Other Writings*. Ed. A.S. Byatt and Nicholas Warren. London: Penguin, 1990.
———. *The Mill on the Floss*. Ed.A.S. Byatt. Harmondsworth: Penguin Books, 1982.
Ermarth, Elizabeth. 'Maggie Tulliver's Long Suicide.' *Studies in English Literature* 14 (1974): 587–601.
Faber, Michel. *The Crimson Petal and the White*. Edinburgh: Canongate, 2002.

Farrell, J.G. *The Siege of Krishnapur*. Harmondsworth: Penguin Books, 1980.

Fowles, John. *The French Lieutenant's Woman*. London: Triad Panther, 1984.

Fraiman, Susan. *Unbecoming Women: British Women Writers and the Novel of Development*. New York: Columbia University Press, 1993.

Frost, Robert. 'The Road Not Taken.' *The Poetry of Robert Frost: The Collected Poems*. Ed. Edward Connery Lathem. New York: Henry Holt, 1975.

Furneaux, Holly. *Queer Dickens: Erotics, Families, Masculinities*. Oxford: Oxford University Press, 2009.

Gadamer, Hans-Georg. *Truth and Method*. Rev. ed. Translation revised by Joel Weinsheimer and Donald G. Marshall. Continuum: New York and London, 1989.

Gagnier, Regenia. *The Insatiability of Human Wants: Economics and Aesthetics in Market Society*. Chicago: University of Chicago Press, 2000.

García Landa, José Angel. 'The Chains of Semiosis: Semiotics, Marxism, and the Female Stereotypes in *The Mill on the Floss*.' *Papers in Language and Literature* 27:1 (1991): 41–50.

García Márquez, Gabriel. *One Hundred Years of Solitude*. Trans. Gregory Rabassa. London: Picador, 1983.

Garrett, Peter K. *The Victorian Multiplot Novel: Studies in Dialogical Form*. New Haven: Yale University Press, 1980.

Gaskell, Elizabeth. *North and South*. Ed. Dorothy Collin. Harmondsworth: Penguin Books, 1970.

Geddes, Patrick. *John Ruskin, Economist*. The Round Table Series, 3. Edinburgh: William Brown, 1884.

Godwin, William. *Inquiry Concerning Political Justice*. Ed. Isaac Kramnick. Harmondsworth: Penguin Books, 1976.

Golby J.M., and A.W. Purdue. *The Civilisation of the Crowd: Popular Culture in England 1750-1900*. London: Batsford, 1984.

Gray, Alasdair. *The Book of Prefaces*. London: Bloomsbury Publishing, 2000.

Hagan, John. 'A Reinterpretation of *The Mill on the Floss*.' PMLA 87:1 (1972): 53–63.

Hardy, Thomas. *The Return of the Native*. Ed. George Woodcock. London: Penguin, 1978.

Harris, Jane. *The Observations*. London: Faber and Faber, 2010. e-book.

Hart, Herbert W. *How to Return Members of Parliament without the Corruption, Bribery, Intimidation, Turmoil and Disorder at present Attendant on General Elections*. London: Simpkin, Marshall and Co, 1868.

Harvey, David. *Spaces of Hope*. Edinburgh: Edinburgh University Press, 2000.

Heilmann, Ann and Mark Llewelyn. *Neo-Victorianism: The Victorians in the Twenty-First Century*. Basingstoke: Palgrave Macmillan, 2010.

Hobsbawm, Eric. *Bandits*. London: Abacus, 2000.

Hobson, J.A. *John Ruskin, Social Reformer*. London: James Nisbet, 1898.

Howard, Ebenezer. *Garden Cities of Tomorrow*. Builth Wells: Attic Books, 1993.

Hutcheon, Linda. *A Poetics of Postmodernism: History, Theory, Fiction*. London: Routledge, 1988.

Jacobus, Mary. 'Men of Maxims and *The Mill on the Floss.*' *Reading Woman: Essays in Feminist Criticism*. London: Methuen, 1986.

Jacoby, Russell. *Future Imperfect: Utopian Thought for an Anti-Utopian Age.* New York: Columbia University Press, 2005.

Jameson, Fredric. 'The Politics of Utopia.' *New Left Review* 25 (Jan/Feb 2004): 35–54.

Johnson, Edgar , *Charles Dickens: His Tragedy and Triumph*. Harmondsworth: Penguin Books, 1977

Joyce, Simon. *The Victorians in the Rearview Mirror*. Athens: Ohio University Press, 2007.

Kaplan, Cora. *Victoriana: Histories, Fictions, Criticism*. Edinburgh: Edinburgh University Press, 2007.

Kinna, Ruth. 'Socialist Fellowship and the Woman Question.' *Writing on the Image: Reading William Morris*. Ed. David Latham. Toronto: University of Toronto Press, 2007. 183–96.

Le Queux, William. *The Great War in England in 1897*. London: Tower Publishing, 1894.

Longmate, Norman. *The Workhouse: A Social History*. London: Pimlico, 2003.

Löwy, Michael. 'Naphta or Settembrini? Lukacs and Romantic Anticapitalism'. *New German Critique* 42 (Autumn 1987): 17–31.

Lucas, John. *The Good That We Do*. London: Greenwich Exchange, 2001.

Mabb, David. 'Hijack: Morris Dialectically.' *William Morris in the Twenty-first Century*. Ed. Phillippa Bennett and Rosie Miles. Oxford: Peter Lang, 2010.

Macaulay, Lord. *Critical and Historical Essays*. London: Longmans, Green, Reader and Dyer, 1869.

———. *The History of England, from the Accession of James II*. Ed. T.F. Henderson. 5 vols. Oxford: Oxford University Press, 1931.

MacCarthy, Fiona. *The Simple Life: C.R. Ashbee in the Cotswolds*. London: Lund Humphries, 1981.

MacDonald, Bradley. 'William Morris and the Vision of Ecosocialism.' *Contemporary Justice Review* 7 (2004): 287–304.

MacFarlane, Robert. *The Old Ways: A Journey on Foot*. London: Penguin Books, 2012. 77.

Mackay, Charles. *Extraordinary Popular Delusions and the Madness of Crowds*. London: National Illustrated Library, 1852.

Mantel, Hilary. 'The Novelist's Arithmetic.' *Wolf Hall*. London: Fourth Estate, 2010. 11–14 of P.S. section.

Marsh, Jan. 'Concerning Love: *News from Nowhere* and Gender.' *William Morris and News from Nowhere: A Vision for Our Time*. Ed. Stephen Coleman and Paddy O'Sullivan. (Bideford: Green Books, 1990), 107–25

———. 'William Morris and Victorian Manliness.' *William Morris, Centenary Essays*. Ed. Peter Faulkner and Peter Preston. Exeter: University of Exeter Press, 1999.

Marx, Karl and Frederick Engels. 'Theses on Feuerbach.' *Collected Works*. Vol 5. London: Lawrence and Wishart, 1976.

Marx, Karl. *Capital.* Trans. Eden and Cedar Paul. 2 vols. London: Everyman's Library, 1957.

Mason, Michael. *The Making of Victorian Sexuality.* Oxford: Oxford University Press, 1994.

———. *The Making of Victorian Sexual Attitudes.* Oxford: Oxford University Press, 1994.

Mayer, Jed. 'A Darker Shade of Green: William Morris, Richard Jefferies, and Posthumanist Ecologies.' *Journal of the William Morris Society* 19.3 (2011): 79–92.

Meisel, Martin. *Realizations: Narrative, Pictorial and Theatrical Arts in the Nineteenth Century.* Princeton: Princeton University Press, 1983.

Mill, John Stuart. *Utilitarianism, Liberty, and Representative Government.* London: Everyman's Library, 1968.

———. *Principles of Political Economy.* Vol. 1. London: Longmans, Green, Reader and Fuer, 1877.

———. *The Subjection of Women.* London: Everyman's Library, 1977.

Miller, D.A. *The Novel and the Police.* Berkeley: University of California Press, 1988.

Mineo, Ady. 'Beyond the Law of the Father: The "New Woman" in *News from Nowhere.*' *William Morris, Centenary Essays.* Ed. Peter Faulkner and Peter Preston. Exeter: University of Exeter Press, 1999.

Morris, William. 'Looking Backward.' *William Morris: Artist, Writer, Socialist.* Ed. May Morris. Vol 2. New York: Russell and Russell, 1966.

———. 'Preface to "The Nature of Gothic".' *William Morris: Artist, Writer, Socialist.* Ed. May Morris. Vol 1. New York: Russell and Russell, 1966.

———. *News from Nowhere. The Collected Works of William Morris.* Vol 16. New York: Russell and Russell, 1966.

———. *The House of the Wolfings. The Collected Works of William Morris.* Vol 14. New York: Russell and Russell, 1966.

Myers, William. *The Teaching of George Eliot.* Leicester: Leicester University Press, 1984.

Newey, Vincent. *The Scriptures of Charles Dickens: Novels of Ideology, Novels of the Self.* Aldershot: Ashgate, 2004.

O'Gorman, Francis and Katherine Turner, eds. *The Victorians and the Eighteenth Century: Reassessing the Tradition.* Aldershot: Ashgate, 2004.

O'Gorman, Francis. '"Suppose It Were Your Own Father of Whom You Spoke": Ruskin's *Unto This Last* (1860).' *Review of English Studies* 51:202 (2000): 230–247.

O'Sullivan, Patrick. 'Morris the Red, Morris the Green – a Partial Review.' *Journal of the William Morris Society* 19.3 (2011): 22–38.

Parrinder, Patrick. *Shadows of the Future: H.G. Wells, Science Fiction and Prophecy.* Liverpool: Liverpool University Press, 1995.

Pedersen, Susan. 'Eleanor Rathbone (1872–1946): The Victorian family under the daughter's eye.' *After the Victorians: Private Conscience and Public Duty in*

Modern Britain. Essays in memory of John Clive. Ed. Susan Pedersen and Peter Mandler. Routledge: London and New York, 1994.

Perkin, J. Russell. *A Reception-History of George Eliot's Fiction.* Ann Arbor: U.M.I. Research Press, 1990.

Pinkney, Tony. 'Versions of Ecotopia in *News from Nowhere.*' *William Morris in the Twenty-first Century.* Ed. Phillippa Bennett and Rosie Miles. Oxford: Peter Lang, 2010.

Poovey, Mary. *Uneven Developments: The Ideological Work of Gender in Mid-Victorian England.* London: Virago Press, 1989.

Ricardo, David. *On the Principles of Political Economy, and Taxation.* Ed. R.M. Hartwell. Harmondsworth: Penguin, 1971.

Ricoeur, Paul. *Memory, History, Forgetting.* Trans. Kathleen Blamey and David Pellauer. Chicago: The University of Chicago Press, 2004.

Ruskin, John. '*Unto This Last.*' *The Works of Ruskin.* Ed. E.T. Cook and Alexander Wedderburn. Vol 17. London: George Allen, 1905.

———. *Love's Meinie. The Works of Ruskin.* Ed. E.T. Cook and Alexander Wedderburn. Vol 25. London: George Allen, 1905.

———. *Fors Clavigera. The Works of Ruskin.* Ed. E.T. Cook and Alexander Wedderburn. Vol 27. London: George Allen, 1905.

Samuel, Raphael. *Theatres of Memory: Past and Present in Contemporary Culture.* Vol 1. London, Verso, 1996.

———. *Theatres of Memory: Island Stories – Unravelling Britain.* Vol 2. London: Verso, 1999.

Sandison, Alan and Robert Dingley, eds. *Histories of the Future: Studies in Fact, Fantasy and Science Fiction.* Basingstoke: Palgrave, 2000.

Seed, David, ed. *Anticipations: Essays on Early Science Fiction and its Precursors.* Liverpool: Liverpool University Press, 1995.

Sennett, Richard. *The Craftsman.* London: Penguin Books, 2008.

Sherburne, James Clark. *John Ruskin or the Ambiguities of Abundance.* Cambridge, MA: Harvard University Press, 1972.

Sinclair, May. *The Life and Death of Harriett Frean.* London: Virago, 1980.

Smith, Peter. 'Attractive Labour and Social Change: William Morris Now,' *William Morris in the Twenty-first Century.* Ed. Phillippa Bennett and Rosie Miles. Oxford: Peter Lang, 2010.

Smollett, Tobias. *The Adventures of Roderick Random.* New York: New American Library, 1964.

Spear, Jeffrey L. *Dreams of an English Eden: Ruskin and His Tradition in Social Criticism.* New York: Columbia University Press, 1984.

Stallybrass, Peter and Allon White. *The Politics and Poetics of Transgression.* London: Methuen, 1986.

Stansky, Peter. *Redesigning the World: William Morris, the 1880s, and the Arts and Crafts.* Princeton: Princeton University Press, 1985.

Tennyson, Alfred, Lord. *The Poems of Tennyson.* Ed. Christopher Ricks. London: Longmans, 1969.

Thompson, E.P. *The Making of the English Working Class*. London: Penguin Books, 1991.

———. *William Morris: Romantic to Revolutionary*. 2nd ed. London: Merlin Press, 1977.

Trollope, Anthony. *An Autobiography*. Ed. Michael Sadleir and Frederick Page. Oxford, Oxford University Press, 1998.

———. *Doctor Thorne*. Ed. David Skilton. Oxford: Oxford University Press, 1980.

———. *Phineas Finn*. Ed. Simon Dentith. Oxford: Oxford University Press, 2011.

———. *Phineas Redux*. Ed. John Bowen. Oxford: Oxford University Press, 2011.

Webbe Dasent, George, ed. *Popular Tales From the Norse: With an Introductory Essay on the Origin and Diffusion of Popular Tales*. Edinburgh: Edmonston and Douglas, 1859.

Welsh, Alexander. *Copyright to Copperfield: the Identity of Dickens*. Cambridge, MA: Harvard University Press, 1987.

Williams, Raymond. 'Socialism and Ecology.' *Resources of Hope: Culture, Democracy, Socialism*. Ed. Robin Gable. London: Verso, 1989. 210–26.

Wills, Sara. *The Greening of William Morris: A Reasonable Share in the Beauty of the Earth*. Beaconsfield: Circa, 2006.

Wood, James. 'Bristling with Diligence.' *London Review of Books*. (8 October 2009): 6–8.

Woolf, Virginia. *Collected Essays*. London: The Hogarth Press, 1966.

Wordsworth, William. *The Prelude: A Parallel Text*. Ed. J.C. Maxwell. London: Penguin Books, 1971.

Websites

http://www.efm.bris.ac.uk/het/carlyle/disclaim.htm /. Accessed 19/01/2012.

http://www.rspb.org.uk/wildlife/birdguide/name/s/swallow/population.aspx/. Accessed 14/06/2012.

http://www.ks.uiuc.edu/Research/cryptochrome/. Accessed 16/06/2012.

Index

Note: An 'n' following a page number indicates a footnote.

For Product Safety Concerns and Information please contact our
EU representative GPSR@taylorandfrancis.com Taylor & Francis
Verlag GmbH, Kaufingerstraße 24, 80331 München, Germany